Fitz

by
Teddy Fennelly

Arderin Publishing Company

Fitz - and the famous flight
- The first east to west transatlantic flight

Published in 1997 by

Arderin Publishing Company
in conjunction with
The Leinster Express,
Dublin Road,
Portlaoise,
County Laois,
Republic of Ireland

ISBN 0 86335 023 2

A catalogue record of this book is available from the British Library.

Designed and printed by
The Imperial Print and Design Co. Ltd.

This work is dedicated to my wife, Carmel, and all my family who have been so patient and supportive as always.

CONTENTS

List of Illustrations

Photographs are from the Col. James C. Fitzmaurice collection courtesy of Mrs. Pat Selwyn Jones unless otherwise credited.

Page

Page

Introduction

For thousands of years mankind looked up into the skies and contemplated the wonders of flying. The mastery of aeronautics was the reserve of one species of life alone - the birds. The mythical saga of Icarus' tryst with the sun illustrates that man has been trying to emulate the distinctive characteristics of our feathered friends since time immemorial.

Controlled flight in a heavier-than-air appliance was finally achieved in the early years of the 20th century. The science of flying has developed rapidly ever since the brothers, Wilbur and Orville Wright, managed to keep their little machine airborne for all of twelve seconds at Kitty Hawk, North Carolina, on 17 December 1903.

Less than six years later Frenchman, Louis Blériot, flew the English Channel. He covered the twenty miles in just under forty minutes. Europe was now only a matter of minutes from England. This clearly reflects the rapid development of the aeroplane.

As well as land-based planes two other type of aircraft developed side by side, the airship and the seaplane. Both proved popular for a time but they had their limitations and the greater versatility of the land-based plane ensured that it was the version that was to make the most dramatic strides forward into the mid-century and beyond. World War 1 speeded up the development and the planes in use at the end of hostilities in 1918 were much faster, easier handled and more reliable than the models that had been available in 1914.

Eyes were now turning further afield to such places as India, South Africa and Australia for new challenges in flying. But the biggest test of all was America. Could the two most economically advanced continents separated by a wide and turbulent ocean be bridged by air? The answer came quickly. Two British airmen made the first nonstop crossing of the North Atlantic in June 1919, less than sixteen years after the Wright brothers' brief but barrier breaking heavier-than-air flight.   Captain John Alcock and Lieutenant Arthur Whitten-Brown flew their Vickers Vimy bomber from west to east before crash-landing in a bog near the town of Clifden on the west coast of Ireland.

The Atlantic had been crossed - but until it was flown in both directions it had not yet been conquered. Flying the ocean west to east has huge advantages over doing it the other way round. The most obvious advantage are the prevailing winds which back flights from the west - but there are others as well which are examined in this book.

The race to be the first to fly the Atlantic in the more difficult direction was to capture the imagination of aviators, aircraft manufacturers and the wider public alike.   It was seen as the most intimidating barrier to be overcome and the most prestigious prize to be won. Considerable national pride was at stake. Britain, France and Germany were the main contenders with the US also taking more than a passing interest in the race to be first. But the rate of attrition was high and many aviators and their aircraft were lost in the attempt to lay down a significant new marker in aviation development.

By the spring of 1928 the public outcry was so great at mounting failures and loss of life that it forced officialdom in many countries to discourage any further transatlantic attempts. The east-west flight was considered so dangerous it prompted one leading New York newspaper to tell its readers that American flyers, including their most famous aviator of all, Charles Lindbergh, had refused to even contemplate such an attempt. "From the first they recognised its peril. Of late they have called it impossible", it reported.

It was in pursuance of this impossible dream that the lives of two Germans and an Irishman converged. All three men had been involved in abortive attempts in the autumn of 1927. Captain Hermann Koehl and Baron Von Huenefeld in the aircraft *Bremen* had taken off from Germany and Irish Army Air Corp chief, Commandant James Fitzmaurice, known by friend and foe alike as Fitz, along with the English aviator, Capt. R.H. McIntosh, had used Baldonnel aerodrome near Dublin as their takeoff base in the *Princess Xenia*. Both attempts had been forced back by bad weather experienced off the Irish coast. The two Germans and the Irishman were downhearted at the failure but they were determined to have another go at the first opportunity.

Koehl, a decorated WW1 bomber pilot and the Baron, a Prussian poet and aristocrat, worked on the Atlantic project with aircraft manufacturing genius, Professor Hugo Junkers, at his plant in Dessau all through the winter of 1927/'28. Fitzmaurice meanwhile concentrated his efforts on an all-Irish attempt from his base at Baldonnel. Koehl and the Baron were in a predicament because the German government had banned any further attempts from their country. Fitzmaurice had problems too. He could not get sufficient financial backing for his plan. Circumstances brought both ventures together and a joint German-Irish bid was launched. In the early hours of 12 April 1928 the three pioneers took off from Baldonnel in the *Bremen* - destination New York. It was a flight into history.

Fitzmaurice's key role in the flight of the *Bremen* is an absorbing story but no more so than that of his life and times.   Apart from his famous transatlantic escapade, he played a part in and was first-hand witness to some of the major events of the twentieth century.

As a schoolboy he helped the Aldritts, a family of automobile engineers in the Irish midland town of Maryborough (now Portlaoise), build the first aeroplane in what is now the Republic of Ireland.   The flimsy little contraption rose briefly before crashing and ending up in an ignominious pile.   But the experience evoked in the young man a fascination for flying and aeroplanes.

Fitzmaurice grew up with a passionate love for his own country which was still under British rule and longed for its independence but by a strange twist of fate at the outbreak of the Great War he, like so many of his compatriots, joined the British Army during World War 1.

The young Irishman saw action in the trenches in the bloodiest battle in history, the Battle of the Somme.   His bravery and leadership qualities became apparent during these months of death and desolation at the front and he received a commission in acknowledgement.   When the opportunity came to join the Royal Flying Corps, the forerunner to the RAF, he welcomed it with open arms.   He had visions of becoming a bomber pilot but this was not to be.   He was posted to a unit at the front on 11 November 1918, Armistice Day, and so just missed out on aerial combat.

After the war Fitzmaurice became involved in experimental air mail deliveries but got off to a bad start by losing his way on his first flight from Folkestone to Cologne.   He found himself confined by the Germans for three weeks and in the middle of an international incident.   Later he was selected as second pilot on the first ever experimental night air mail flight in Europe.   During this period he gained valuable flying experience in various makes of aircraft and in all kinds of weather conditions.

Fitzmaurice was demobbed but in 1921 he returned to the

RAF again on a Short Service Commission. He took part in the first RAF Pageant at Hendon Aerodrome in July of that year. He resigned from the force and in 1922 returned to an Ireland in turmoil. The founding of the Irish Free State some months previously had partitioned the island and led to civil war in the south. He sided with the elected government and was one of the first pilots commissioned in the new Irish Army Air Corps. He left an account of some of his experiences during these dark days in Irish history. He described the Ireland he had returned to as "God's own country populated by the devil's own people". It was a country full of contradictions, confusion and intrigue.

As a former British Army officer he became the target of a vicious campaign to finger him as a hated Black and Tan conspirator but the accusations were groundless and he emerged with his reputation and good name intact to become Officer-in-Command of the Corps.

He was a man forever seeking a new adventure and at Baldonnel he became besotted with the notion of being the first to fly the Atlantic from east to west. He failed at his first attempt but lived to try another day. Fate played its part in his teaming up with the two Germans, whose countrymen he had fought against in the war. The names of Fitzmaurice, Koehl and Von Huenefeld will be forever linked with the famous flight of the *Bremen*. So too will the name of celebrated US pioneer airman, Floyd Bennett, who died in a bid to rescue the aviators from the remote snowy wilderness of Greenly Island where the plane landed.

The story of the flight of the *Bremen* captured the public's imagination on both sides of the Atlantic. A nonstop transatlantic east-west flight had been considered an impossible dream, even by the experts. The newspaper coverage reflected the immensity of the achievement. The story, for instance, was headlined in the *New York Times* on nineteen days out of twenty one. The scenes of jubilation and adulation in New York that greeted the heroes were unprecedented, even surpassing the welcome given to their

own American transatlantic hero, Charles Lindbergh, the year
before.   A special bill was rushed through Congress to allow US
President, Calvin Coolidge, present the airmen with the
Distinguished Flying Cross.   They were the first foreigners to receive
the honour.   After a triumphant tour of US cities the airmen
returned to a marvellous welcome in Europe, although the British
response was somewhat frosty.

On his return to Ireland Fitzmaurice was made a Freeman of
the City of Dublin, where he had been born in 1898.   A month
later he helped found the Irish Aero Club and became its first
chairman.   He harboured plans for making his country a key
player in the exciting new world of civil aviation which he knew
was just around the corner.   But when his own people showed
little enthusiasm for his ideas he quit the country and went to
seek his fortune in America.   This was a move he lived to regret in
later life.

Good luck had always been on his side at important moments
in his life to date but that was all to change.   He was now famous
and strove earnestly to gain the fortune that he felt should have
gone along with it.   But time after time just as he was about to
capitalise on a major deal that would secure his future, the chance
inevitably slipped from his grasp.   He was, for instance, on the
point of clinching a lucrative contract in New York on the day the
markets collapsed on Wall Street in 1929.

Fitzmaurice went to Germany to seek out opportunities there.
His visit coincided with the emergence of the Nazis to power in
the early 1930s.   He was entertained to afternoon tea by Hitler
and witnessed the razing of the Reichstag building in an arson
attack.   There was no fortune there for him.

In 1934 his entry was a hot favourite to win the biggest air race
in history, from England to Australia, only to be disqualified on a
technicality hours before the start of the event.   His luck was on
a downward spiral and as the years slipped by so did his
opportunities.   In the meantime his marriage had broken up.   On

the approach of WW2 the world was preoccupied with other matters and Fitzmaurice faded into the background.

With the Irish Government failing to reward him for his achievements he spent most of his later years in England where he lived a rather frugal existence. In 1953 requests to mark the silver jubilee of the *Bremen* flight by issuing a special stamp were turned down. A government official explained that "it would be out of place and would be regarded as overemphasizing Irish participation in what was essentially a German undertaking". Fitzmaurice was recognised internationally as a world famous aviator and was the father of civil aviation in Ireland but officialdom in his own country dared not breathe his name. He lived out his final years in Dublin in modest circumstances, in failing health and almost blind.

Although Ireland had turned its back on him during life, when he died in 1965 it made him a hero again. He was given a State Funeral with full military honours - a distinction reserved only for those deemed to have given extraordinary service to the State. This simply served to validate Fitz's embittered view of the country of his origin. "If you have the misfortune to do anything useful for Ireland they do everything possible to destroy you. Then when you are dead they dig you up and laud your achievements as a bolster to their own mediocrity."

The first time I heard of Col. James Fitzmaurice was at home in the 1950s. My late father mentioned a few times that he remembered him from his schooldays at St. Mary's Christian Brothers School in Portlaoise in the early years of the century and spoke admiringly of him making the first east-west transatlantic flight with two Germans.

I never heard or thought much about the man subsequently until in May 1995, when as editor of the *Leinster Express*, I received a letter from Michael Colley with a Dublin address informing me that a famous Irish aviator who had spent his youth in Portlaoise, where the newspaper is based, had in his view not received the recognition he deserved.

He was referring to Col. Fitzmaurice and briefly outlined his achievements, which impressed me greatly. He wished to see an article published but on doing a little research into the story I realised that it warranted more, much more, than a column or two in a newspaper.

From the early stages of my research I realised that Fitzmaurice had, rightly or wrongly, achieved for himself a reputation as a philanderer and a gambler. What I discovered was that reality did not quite measure up to the myth. Like the rest of us he had his human failings. He loved the limelight and the good life and at times displayed an air of affectation which many people disliked. But in terms of ability and achievement I soon realised that the man was seriously underrated. As an aviator, as a soldier, as an innovator and as a thinker he was a man apart. He was, as Mr. Colley had pointed out to me in his initial letter, "one of the most distinguished citizens of this century".

Fitz, indeed, was a remarkable man and his story is one worth telling.

First East to West Atlantic Flyers

A Soldier, not of Fortune, but of some
Idea laboured by philosophers:
A soldier always, though there's monk in him.
And poet also: watch how he salutes
The anthem, or the ensign, or the line
 Of marching men: his hand upraised, his eyes
Salute a drill, salute a chivalry:
Frederick of Prussia, Frederick Barbaross!

Something that's like the fabulous content
In whales or hippopotami is in him
This small-eyed man of ample girth who stands
Square, a steersman!   Vision must become
Readiness, wakefulness, and unfailing craft
To burst through longitudes, to beat the winds,
And fog and squalls make light of!   This is he
Who fronts a course the arc-Atlantic wide.

Jaunty and gamey, like a lad that's in
A ballad that they sing in Kerry fairs,
One joins himself unto the two are here,
And he is of the breed of those who were
Soldiers of Fortune born, who were wont
To put all skill and spirit in a charge
The men who followed where the Wild Geese went;
Fortune still counts, and with them she will be!

-Padraic Colum

Prologue

Revisiting Portlaoise in 1951 was for him a nostalgic trip down memory lane. It was here he was nurtured, it was here he went to school. The world outside had changed utterly since he was last here but the town in the grey postwar years of rural Ireland was much the same as he recalled it almost forty years before.

Some of the older townspeople who remembered him and his feats were glad to press the flesh of the once famous, but now almost forgotten, aviator. Few others he met recognised the man or knew anything about what he had achieved. The hero had come home but there was no hero's welcome to greet him!

He stood tall and straight, retaining the upright bearing of an old soldier yet looking considerably more than his 53 years. He seemed an affable man, deep-thinking and quietly spoken. Outwardly he oozed an air of self-confidence and affluence but on closer examination one could perceptibly detect that this was merely a contrivance to hide his underlying disillusionment and the fact that he had fallen on bad times.

He retraced his steps to the home of his childhood, one of the prison cottages on the Dublin side of the town, which rekindled happy memories of family and growing up.   The assortment of shops and houses on the narrow main street were familiar even if the faces were different.   He reminisced of dedicated tutors and cherished soulmates as he passed his old school at Tower Hill where he had been a reluctant scholar.   He took a tender look at the ancient ruined tower opposite, which gave the street its name and around which he had played so often as a boy.

Just up the road was Aldritts' garage.   This was his "Aladdin's Cave" of bygone years and the prime reason for his visit.   Here he met his dear old friend and mentor, Louis Aldritt, and with misty eyes gazed at the shell of the little aeroplane he had once helped to build.   It was here in this humble haven of mechanical miscellany that his interest in aviation had been sparked.   It was here where it all began.

Chapter 1

The Early Years

M ichael Fitzmaurice and his wife, Mary Agnes, (formerly Riordan) both hailed from solid farming stock in County Limerick. They were an honest hard-working Catholic couple devoted to their religious duties, their country and their family.

Michael was a prison warder based at Ireland's biggest jail, Mountjoy. The family lived at No. 35 Mountjoy Cottages, on Dublin's North Circular Road, one of a row of houses attached to the prison which were occupied by employees in the service and their families. No. 35 was a modest two-storey, two-bedroom abode just like the others in that neat row of late Victorian artisan dwellings.

There were three boys in the Fitzmaurice family, Louis, James Christopher and Patrick Leo and one girl, May. James Christopher was born on 6 January, 1898, one of the most important holy days in the Christian calendar. It is the feast of the Epiphany in the Roman Catholic Church and celebrates the Three Wise Men from the east paying homage to the infant Jesus. In the Orthodox (Eastern) Church it is their Christmas Day, celebrating the birth of Christ, the Saviour.

Michael and Mary Agnes were devout believers but they hardly expected the arrival of a messiah, a saviour of the world, on that cold January late nineteenth century morning. Like most God-fearing parents of the day they would have been more concerned about their new arrival's health and welfare and most likely hoped that he would follow in his father's footsteps by acquiring for himself in time a steady job and live a reasonably happy, comfortable and respectable life.

James Christopher was not, however, one to conform to such mundane expectations. From his earliest days he showed signs of an individualism and an adventurous spirit that in later years were to land him in many amazing and often perilous situations. These traits helped mould him into an internationally acclaimed aviation pioneer who was to play a leading role in one of the greatest achievements in human endeavour of the twentieth century.

He recognised from an early stage that he was not simply one of the crowd. "From infancy I had always been regarded as a somewhat strange sort of bird swayed mostly by impulse," he wrote in later years.

James Christopher spent his first four years in Dublin but on his father's transfer from Mountjoy to Maryborough (now Portlaoise) Prison on 23 May, 1902, it was the misty Irish midlands, fifty miles from the Irish capital, that was to be his home throughout his formative years. The family lived in a prison house on the Dublin Road which, like its Mountjoy counterpart, was one of a row and now also demolished.

He was outgoing, good-humoured and well-liked by neighbours and schoolmates but he often found himself in hot water with his teachers and his parents because of his inclination for boyish pranks.

He never claimed to be exceptional at school. "As far as I can remember I was always the last boy in the last desk of each class I passed through and just managed to scramble through the various exams."

Nor was he different from so many other students in fearing the worst in his end of term reports.   These school reports invariably disappointed his parents. "They did not seem to believe that I had sufficient pride to feel hurt at the marks that I received but added to my sense of ignominy with a stern lecture."

Fitzmaurice remembered his early years in Portlaoise as quite an ordinary upbringing for the time.   "Here I lived and received what little education I can boast of at the Christian Brothers' School until I reached the age of 16.   These were peaceful days with wide cool green expanses of grass in the school yard, woods where we went bird-nesting, and friendly taskmasters who exhorted us to study hard are but a fragment of memories from my boyhood days".

But he often strayed off the straight and narrow and at such times the "friendly" taskmasters were not quite so friendly.   He remembered "breaking out of bounds to visit the forbidden sweet shops and practising other boyhood mischief" which brought the inevitable school punishment.   He took it all in his stride.   "These whippings were only passing summer storms that failed to divert my path from that of the average schoolboy of those days."   (It should be remembered that corporal punishment was commonplace in Irish schools until it was outlawed in the 1970s. Fitz's reference to beatings for minor indiscretions which he dismissed so lightly indicate the degree of acceptability of corporal punishment for misbehaviour that prevailed in his time.)

The Christian Brothers were noted for their dedication in imparting a good standard of education to the boys in their charge. They strove earnestly to fit out their students properly for the challenges ahead and if sometimes their disciplinary code was severe this was largely attributable to their zeal for their work and in its own way reflected, and was part of the boys' preparation for, the rigours of life in the Ireland and the world outside of the period.

Fitzmaurice may not have realised it at the time but, like so many other products of the Christian Brothers' system, his early educational grounding in their care combined with his natural talent and craving for new experiences and discovery, was to equip him admirably for the great adventures that lay ahead.   In later life he was profuse in his praise for the part the Brothers had played in his upbringing. "Thanks to them I entered the battle (of life) well equipped with a sound secondary education, a tough stubbornness and a grim determination to succeed that enabled me to surmount the numerous obstacles which, in the course of time, were to beset my onward path".

Fitz, some years later as a young officer in the British Army, listened with feelings of wonder and amazement to the stories "of my English contemporaries concerning the magnificence of the educational institutions to which they had access".

"Their great public schools were always of outstanding splendour as examples of medieval architecture...   They were referred to as the *alma mater* and the *venerable old pile*. They all seem to have been built in a square called the *quad* and were full of *clock towers, pinnacles* and *spires*. The fathers of these boys were invariably known as the *pater* and big boys called *prefects* were terrible autocrats to the smaller fry...   There was always a wonderful place called the *tuck-shop*, and there were *forms, terms* and God knows what!   In addition all of these seats of learning were noted for their prowess in the realms of sports and games and always provided a *games-master*."

There was no such grandeur in Fitz's schooldays. "My *alma mater* could not boast of any of the splendours of the English public schools. It was a simple two-storied building, the ground floor of which housed the small boys in the elementary classes, the upper floors being utilised for the secondary education of the older boys, that is to say those whose parents could afford to maintain them at home during that period.

"The playing fields, like the building itself, were extremely modest consisting of only one handball alley in the rear, mainly used for the consumption of the midday meal brought by the pupils, which in many cases amounted to nothing more than a couple of slabs of dry bread."

Though the school, St. Mary's, like all Christian Brothers' schools,

Fitzmaurice family group - pictured at the wedding of the aviator's brother, Louis, to Lil Anderson in 1926. Back row: Michael Fitzmaurice (father), Fr. Michael Quinlan, S.J., Tom Ellis (father of Brendan Ellis - see chapters 11 and 24), Patrick Leo Fitzmaurice (brother), Parish Priest of Star of the Sea. Seated: Mrs. Fitzmaurice (mother), Peg Anderson, Louis Fitzmaurice, Lil Anderson, Mrs. Anderson. Front: Violet Fitzmaurice (wife), Pat Fitzmaurice (daughter), Rose Anderson, May Fitzmaurice (sister).

had a strong Roman Catholic ethos, it also catered for Protestant boys. "Their presence amongst us was an ideal tonic in a country where religious passions were, even in those days, wont to run high. It developed in all of us at an early age a strong sense of religious tolerance and general good manners."

There was no distinctive dress, not even school ties. "In fact we wore no ties at all; and the clothing of a great number of the boys, invariably passed down from older brothers, was badly worn though neatly patched. The majority had shoes and stockings, though many of the poorer boys were completely devoid of such luxuries - and quite a few walked as much as two miles or more to school each day in all kinds of weather conditions. In addition to being poorly clad, and in cases suffering from malnutrition, they took their share of the harsh punishments which were dished out to one and all without fear or favour.

"School fees comprised of the meagre sum the pupils' parents could afford, rarely more than 2d (1p) a week with the balance needed to run the school donated by townspeople in an annual whip-around."

Fitz admitted to feelings of awe from all the boasting of English officers of high achievement and architectural splendour in the English schools. But he was never overawed. Far from it. He admired the many fine traits of the typical officer but was not impressed at all with their brainpower, wit or cleverness. "I was bewildered by their appalling ignorance, extraordinary limited intellectual powers and almost complete lack of imagination." Instead of coming from a deprived educational background Fitz was firmly of the opinion that the Christian Brothers had given him and his compatriots a head start in life.

He felt proud of the products of St. Mary's. "They had the stuff of greatness in them. The driving urge that led to their successful achievements owed its impetus to the desire to defeat the poverty stricken conditions of life into which they were born.... How different they are from the mollycoddled products of the schools provided by the English Welfare State!".

One teacher more than any other stood out in Fitz's memory - a Brother Egan. "He was a brilliant and tireless master who put everything he had got in height, weight and strength into wielding that cruel instrument called the leather, which he carried around in the pocket of his soutane. A double six - six on each hand - on a cold winter's day rendered one completely *hors de combat* so far as the art of penmanship was concerned and brought to an end all efforts at concentration in my embittered mind.... I acquired a sound secondary education, thanks in the main, to the dogged perseverance and strong right arm of Brother Egan, who was always convinced that I would, in the ultimate course of time, come to some bad and sticky end."

In an off-the-cuff anecdote to the Brother Egan saga in his memoirs Fitz, with typical wry wit, noted that it was comforting to know that even such men are not gifted with the supernatural faculty to dip into the future. Unlike his mother! "She was psychic and possessed the most extraordinary telepathic powers that I was later to discover whenever trouble came my way during her lifetime ... (Her prediction) that the opposite sex would have a most profound influence on my life proved to be only too true."

Happily all his teachers were not as heavy-handed at Brother Egan. Such as "Hoggy" Ryan - "a grand classical scholar, he was also one of life's classical failures". In class he would constantly chew tea leaves which he carried loose in his pocket for the purpose, the boys assumed, of killing the stale fumes of whiskey emanating from his breath. "Full of wit he was a gifted teacher possessing the knack of imparting knowledge without the use of punishment... We learned a lot from 'Hoggy' that was most definitely not included in the school curriculum. We always looked forward with pleasurable delights to the periods devoted to lessons under his care."

Fitz was indeed more at ease with ex-curricular activities and fondly reminisced on his idyllic days in the Irish midlands occupied by bird-nesting, robbing orchards and poaching, pursuits frowned upon by the more righteous members of the community. One bright star in his young life was old Tom, the poacher "who imparted to us most of the tricks of his illegal trade". This included the art of landing a fine freshwater trout by delicately tickling its underbelly. Old Tom was not an admirer of his young charge's efforts at mastering the art.

"You'll never have hands for a horse or a woman", he would say if Fitz let a fish slip away.

Old Tom's tutelage was to come in very useful to Fitz in later years. "We not only learned how to poach a pheasant, but what was more important, how to move through the woods at night without attracting the attention of the gamekeepers who seemed to be forever on guard. Later in the Great War old Tom's lessons in these matters, coupled with the detailed plans we drew up and put into operation in our raids on other people's orchards, proved to be my *ab initio* training in infantry tactics. Had we been caught whilst engaged in those nefarious activities dire penalties would have been inflicted upon us. So the keynote of our operations was never to make a mistake. In the numerous raids I carried out on the enemy trenches while serving for the infantry in World War 1 these lessons stood me in very good stead, preserving my life, avoiding being badly wounded, or at the very least, being made prisoner of war."

Two of Fitz's closest boyhood friends were Jerry Ryan and Willie Egan, next door neighbours on the Dublin Road and of the same age group. Ryan, as a Professor in St. Gerard's College, in Castlebar, Co. Mayo, wrote afterwards in a book published to commemorate the centenary of the founding of Portlaoise CBS that all three were "inseparable companions - almost like the Three Musketeers". (Coincidentally the book written by Fitzmaurice and his German companions, Koehl and Huenefeld, on the record-breaking flight of the *Bremen* monoplane in 1928 which was published shortly after the flight was titled "*The Three Musketeers of the Air*").

Ryan recalled his friendship for Fitz and told of some of their boyhood antics. "How many hours we spent, with other companions, in the old ball alley after school - 'butting' balls and learning to make them curve around the corner when we 'served' them. Many a trip we had to make into Monsignor Murphy's grounds - to his annoyance - after lost balls! What exciting games of 'Prisoner's Base' we played and how Bro. Lynch in the earlier classes had us instilled with the spirit of Greeks and Romans.

"Jim Fitzmaurice was always excellent at games and of an adventurous spirit. He was also good at his lessons but not too keen on them. What a fright we got and how we sympathised with him when he broke his arm in a fall from a high tree in what was then called 'Kearney's Field' on the Dublin Road.... I still recollect the smell of ether pervading his sickroom on visiting him after his arm was set. Little did we know that he would one day be world-famous!"

Fitz himself later recalled that tree-fall incident which left him with a broken arm and a lot of answering to do. One of his greatest hobbies in those days was collecting wild birds' eggs. It developed in him a keen interest in ornithology, an interest that he retained throughout his life. He often boasted that he had a collection of wild birds' eggs which was comparable with the finest in the British Isles. The accident happened on a "bird-nesting" trip.

"When I was about ten years old, in company with a group of other small boys, I located a goldfinch's nest in what appeared to be an accessible position on the outside end of a high-up branch of a very tall fir tree. In my attempt to reach the nest it almost brought my life to a very early termination. The branch on which it was located was about sixty feet from the ground. Having 'shinned' up the rough tree trunk I continued climbing until I reached a branch immediately beneath the one on which the nest was located. Suddenly the twigs to which I was hanging broke with the result that I crashed headlong to the ground. I should have been smashed to pulp but fortunately the lower branches through which I fell broke my fall so that I escaped with a compound fracture of the left arm."

Fitz, as was his manner, tried to make the best out of a bad situation. Bound up in splints and bandages he looked every inch the wounded hero to schoolmates and young girlfriends alike. Meeting one he believed was a female admirer he made light of his injuries in the hope of creating a good impression.

"What's the matter, Jim?", his young ladyfriend enquired.

"Oh, just a broken arm", Fitz nonchalantly replied.

"How did it happen?", she asked.

"Climbing trees", Fitz coolly responded expecting an overwhelming show of sympathy. He was surprised to be faced by a very irate young lady instead.

"You were robbing little birds' nests", she shrieked. "You little beast! I wish you had broken your neck."

Fitz was certainly no hero in that young lady's estimations and he admitted afterwards that the modest encounter gave him food for thought on how best to impress a member of the opposite sex!

Chapter 2

Aladdin's Cave

The ruined tower opposite the boys' school is part of the outer wall of the old Fort of Maryborough, which dates back to the 16th century Plantation of Laois and Offaly in the reign of Philip and Mary.   During that period the counties were renamed Queen's and King's with Maryborough (named after Queen Mary) and Philipstown (now Daingean, named after King Philip) incorporated as the administrative centres of the respective territories.   This was the first of the English Plantations of Ireland and was designed to crush the local Irish chiefs, the O'Moores of Laois and the O'Connors of Offaly, and to resettle their lands with English planters.   The ancient tower had been witness to the bloody demise of the old order and the establishment and maintenance of English rule in Ireland through the course of almost four hundred years.

If reminders of the town's beginnings and of many centuries of Irish history lay literally within a stone's throw of the classrooms where the young Fitzmaurice sat, so too lay the trappings of another kind that was to revolutionise the world of the twentieth century - the conquest of the air.   Just a few steps up the road was Aldritts' Garage run by a family of renowned motor engineers, brothers, Louis, Frank and Joe and their father, Frank snr.   The Aldritts not only repaired and serviced motor cars but they designed and built automobiles as well.   They also used their considerable technical and mechanical expertise to build an aeroplane, the first to be constructed in what is now the Republic of Ireland.

In his writings Fitzmaurice tells of how, quite accidentally, he became involved in that operation.   "Wilbur and Orville Wright had started something that was to affect my whole life and bring to me a fair degree of fun, fame and fortune.   News of the fame that came to Wilbur and Orville during their flying demonstrations at Pau (France) in 1909 drifted into our somnolent little town of 3,000 souls in rural Ireland.   I was then a precocious lad of eleven years whose main amusement, when not engaged in such frowned upon practices as poaching trout and robbing orchards, was watching the horseless carriages chugging and snortling along the rocky road to Dublin in a blinding cloud of limestone dust. This traffic brought to our tiny town of Maryborough a new industry - a motor garage - presided over by that kindly soul, Mr. Louis Aldritt."

One day by chance, as he dawdled along Tower Hill and up by the school, Fitz tripped in a doorway and fell flat on his face into "Mr. Aldritt's humble little garage".   The embarrassed schoolboy could feel many eyes staring in his direction.

"Well, well, who have we here?", came a gentle voice from underneath a vehicle that was being serviced by someone he could not fully see?   "Come to join the trade, I suppose?   Well you're a bit on the young side, but we'll see what we can do with you."   It was Louis and as he spoke he ambled over to the doorway and helped the hapless intruder to his feet.

Fitz thanked Mr. Aldritt profusely as he shyly retreated to his allotted corner.   His inquisitive mind soon began taking stock of all around him. He was enthralled with what he saw.

"To my youthful mind this workshop was more wonderful than Aladdin's cave.   From then onwards I spent my every idle hour there and pottered about endeavouring to help, although in actual fact I was probably just a little nuisance getting in everybody's way."

He goes on to tell of the building of the aeroplane and of his youthful enthusiasm in the unusual and wonderful project .

"My friend and mentor soon became smitten with the flying bug and set to work on the construction of a flying machine. Young as I was I became one of his keenest disciples when everyone else believed he was just plain nuts.

"This wonderful creation slowly took shape and soon my extremely limited vocabulary became considerably enhanced by such high sounding technical words as longerons, fuselage, ailerons and other such terminology.   I felt exceedingly highbrow and more than elated to be allowed to consort with such grand company.   It was a labour of love and was finally completed. With great ceremony it was wheeled to the largest meadow in the vicinity.   The little motor was started up as it stood poised, head into wind, for that impatiently awaited moment - the takeoff.

"Never before had the inhabitants of our small town reached such a feverish pitch of excitement. Slowly gathering momentum the little machine hurtled across the meadow but shortly after it became airborne it nosed over and crashed ignominiously becoming almost a complete write-off. Months of precious work had, in a fraction of a second, been reduced to naught. A tangled mass of wood, wire and fabric lay bleeding on the greensward as the petrol and oil seeped slowly into the soil.   It was a sadly dramatic sight for all of us. I almost cried."

Fitz tells of the reaction of bemused onlookers.   " 'Glory to God', they exclaimed.   'Twas flying in the face of Providence... Sure if God meant us to fly we'd have been born with feathers and wings.   'Twas nothing more than brazen, blasphemous

The workshop at Aldritts' Garage. This photograph dates from the 1920's period. The shell of the old aeroplane Fitz helped to build can be seen perched on the rafters above the workshop floor.

impudence it was.' " Another source confirms the hostile reaction from locals, especially the parish priest (Catholic) and rector (Church of Ireland) who were of the one opinion on the fiasco. They visited the garage and told the Aldritts that "they should be ashamed of themselves, because it was unnatural for man to fly".

The aircraft, a monoplane similar to that used by the famous early pioneer aviator, Louis Bleriot, was powered by a three cylinder in-line water-cooled engine, cast in Dublin by Tonge and Taggart and with a forged crank from R. & E. H. Hall of Salford, fitted with a Bosch magneto.

Donie and Frank Aldritt are nephews of Louis. Donie was told by his father, Joe, that although the machine had developed enough power to lift off the ground the contraption's weight, with its water-cooled engine, was too heavy and the undercarriage was insufficiently robust to contain the impact of the rapid fall. His uncle Frank was pilot in the abortive attempt to become airborne. Donie also revealed that the bamboo shoots used in the construction of the wings were grown on the extensive Coote family demesne in Ballyfin, six miles from Portlaoise. Carpenter on the project was a highly skilful local artisan, Johnny Conroy, father of a family of reputable tradesmen.

Donie's brother, Frank, recalled his grandmother, Frank snr's wife, telling him stories of the machine lifting into the air. She got such a fright that she immediately demanded that her husband stop the experiments before he killed himself and perhaps other members of the family as well. Old Mr. Aldritt acceded to her request and his aircraft was moved into the workshop where it lay for many years.

Fitz revisited the scene of his boyhood's Aladdin's cave many times in later years. In his writings he recalls what he saw and the nostalgia he felt on one such visit made in 1951.

"It had changed but little over this half century, for such is the tempo of life in rural Ireland. To my amazement, I saw hanging from the old rafters the bare wings and fuselage of that ancient aeroplane that had first attracted me, like iron filings to a magnet, to the baby world of aviation then stirring feebly in its swaddling clothes. The main spars of the wings were old bamboo curtain poles of the Victorian - Edwardian days, but I was amazed at the perfect construction of the compression ribs in the making of which I had assisted. In a corner reclined the three cylinder water-cooled engine that had been built with such loving care by the hand of my dear old friend of the days of long ago. I was emotionally moved by a deep feeling of nostalgia for the days that are gone as the kaleidoscopic cinema of the intervening years unfolded itself before my somewhat tear-dimmed eyes."

If the crash landing of their flying machine was the end of the aviation pioneering experience for the Aldritts it was to be the catalyst which shaped the exciting future in flying for their young helper.

Seeing that flimsy home made machine rise from the ground - be it ever for so short a time and despite its inglorious ending - aroused the young man's interest in flying, an interest that grew into a passion as the years rolled on. Fitz in his memoirs recalled the moment the spark caught fire. "In those days the greatest ambition of all small boys was to become a railroad engine driver. I had, however, watched this crude contraption take shape and reach its tragic end, but I had actually seen it airborne and my boyish enthusiasm became inflamed. From that moment I decided that this new art of flying, **if it ever came to anything**, would be one of my foremost interests in life, come what might. Little did I dream of the tortuous, uphill path that lay in the achievement of that ambition, or of the part I was destined to play in the chain of aeronautical events that was to lead up to today's distance shattering, globe encircling commercial air operations, the greatest boon and blessing in man's peaceful activities. Nor could I, or anyone else, foresee the dreadful havoc that this same science, allied with others then undreamed of, was to bring to man's very doorstep to his detriment and degradation and almost complete undoing."

Fitz's school years in Portlaoise were happy ones for the most part. But prior to his sixteenth birthday his parents decided that his future lay in the world of business and suddenly his lifestyle took a turn for the worse. He was sent to a private college in Waterford, a port city on the south coast and about seventy miles from his home, to undergo a course in business training. The idea of spending his life behind a counter or with his head stuck into a ledger did not fit in at all with the young man's volatile temperament and his longing for adventure.

His time there was one of turmoil. He rebelled against the system and against his parents plans for his future. He was constantly in trouble with the college authorities. Eventually after a particularly risky prank that backfired he was sent packing in disgrace as an incorrigible.

Fitz later recalled his brief interlude at the college and the incident that brought matters to a head. "The nature of this business training followed very much on the lines of my earlier academic training. I slept in a large dormitory with a number of other boys about my own age and at nine o'clock every night we received a signal for lights out. During the day we usually hatched some diabolical plot for mischief and immediately the signal for lights out was given we would proceed to execute our plan. The particular scheme which foreshortened my career in business studies was made up of a plan to attack a neighbouring dormitory. My Napoleonic prowess for strategy placed the members of my dormitory under my leadership for the attack which was to take place at midnight. One mistake, however, was made in that we overlooked the fact that the dear old housekeeper slept in the room directly underneath the dormitory which we were attacking. As the 'zero' hour arrived we crept silently down the long hall. The ghostly moonlight, shining through the window, was reflected from the shimmering nightshirts of the more timorous members of our raiding party. Stealthily we opened the door, massed for the attack, and launched ourselves upon the beds of our unsuspecting victims. The battle was at its height when our scouts observed that the house authorities were coming up the stairs to investigate the situation. Word was passed along and a general scramble started towards our room. Strategic as had been our advance, I must admit that our retreat was rather poorly planned.

"Smothered in a tangle of bedclothes and rolling grotesquely about the floor, I learned that my lads had given way to superior forces when I catapulted directly into the stomach of one of the portly house authorities. The following morning a very severe manager informed me that the ceiling had fallen upon the housekeeper and had scared her out of her wits. He also informed me that my continued presence in the house was not conducive to the maintenance of the best possible standard of discipline among other students. A railway ticket was handed to me, my bags were packed, and I commenced the most miserable railway journey of my whole life.

"My arrival at home coincided with the receipt by my parents of a long letter from the school giving details of my disgraceful conduct. A very serious lecture was delivered and after negotiations between my parents and the officials of the business school which lasted several days, I was finally allowed to return to continue my studies."

It was now 1914 and catastrophic events on the European stage were soon to override his parents plans for a career in the mundane world of business. Fitz's teenage life was about to take another turn.

Chapter 3

The Redmond Volunteers

The uneasy relationships between neighbours, England and Ireland, and between the Catholic and Protestant traditions on the island of Ireland, have dominated the course of Irish history over the past seven hundred years. It is a turbulent and bitter history with the Catholic nationalist tradition invariably seeing themselves in the role of an oppressed majority.

Fitzmaurice came from stoutly Irish Catholic stock. His parents were conservative in terms of religious observance and in their social behaviour. As an employee of the prison service his father was in the pay of the Crown. Respecting the law and authority was something stressed in their upbringing as well as something expected from Fitzmaurice the elder's station in life.

But like the vast majority of Irish Catholics, especially those from a rural background, Michael and Mary Fitzmaurice were also ardent Nationalists and yearned for the day when their dream of an independent Ireland became a reality. They knew their history and James proudly boasted that his family could trace the Norman lineage from which the Fitzmaurices were descended.

The parents spoke to their children of the richness of the Irish past, steeped in the mists of antiquity and advanced in enlightenment. The children relished hearing stories at home and at school of legendary Irish heroes of long ago and of the great Irish saints and scholars and the famous seats of learning, such as Glendalough and Clonmacnoise. They also heard of the courage and durability of the Irish race through centuries of discrimination and persecution.

The free spirit of the native Irish Catholic had survived the religious persecutions of King Henry V111, the brutal destruction of the old clan system in Elizabethan times, the reign of terror of Oliver Cromwell in the mid-17th century, the denial of even the most basic of human rights for most of England's rule, especially during the Penal Days, and the inevitable ruthless establishment backlash to any and every Irish whimper of dissent.   Such was the stuff of history on which the young Fitzmaurices were fed.

The Great Famine was the biggest disaster of all to befall the native Irish. It did not happen in the dim and distant past but in the mid-19th century, a mere generation or two before Fitz's arrival. This was not a persecution by the gun, sword, lash or gibbet but was caused by the failure of the humble potato crop, the staple diet of the impoverished masses. Over one million people died of starvation and related diseases in a grim five year period and as many again fled the desolated land for foreign shores, mainly America bound. This was a tragedy of apocalyptic magnitude, the blame for which for the most part was attributable to the incompetence of the Westminster response. The spirit of the Irish was all but broken.

But from the depths of despair emerged a new generation to take up the torch of independence and freedom. Organisations such as the Land League, the Gaelic League and the Gaelic Athletic Association inspired a Celtic revival in the arts, culture and sporting pursuits and by the turn of the century there was a new found confidence in being Irish and in all things Irish. This time the pursuit of independence was directed mainly through dialogue and political means. This was the era and the Ireland into which James Christopher Fitzmaurice was born two years prior to the turn of the century.

The early years of the 20th century were promising times for the Irish nationalists and the young Fitz, like the vast majority of his tradition, could at last see signs of a new Ireland emerging. The growing demand for self-determination for the country was slowly gaining currency at Westminster and after several attempts over a generation a new Home Rule Bill finally passed through the House of Commons in 1912. Although rejected by the House of Lords, the Bill passed into law in 1914, because the Lords right to veto legislation had been lately curtailed. All that was now required for enactment was the formality of the Royal Assent. The outbreak of the First World War in August 1914 caused the implementation of the Government of Ireland Act to be postponed until the conflict was over - but by 1918 much had changed.

If Fitzmaurice grew up with an undiluted Catholic and nationalistic view there was a very different interpretation of history and of politics taken by the Protestant unionist tradition on the island. Much of the province of Ulster had (and still has) a Protestant majority, mainly Presbyterian. They had fared substantially better than the Catholics during the 19th century and saw their future in a British context rather than an Irish one.

The Catholic Church had become a very powerful institution in Ireland since the days of religious emancipation won by Daniel O'Connell in 1829. The unionists were fearful of the emergence of a new nationalist state run by the Catholic bishops. The prospect of being forced into a new situation dictated to by the Catholic Church, as they saw it, was more than they could take. Home Rule was "Rome Rule" as far as they were concerned and this was something too awful for them to contemplate.

It was hardly surprising, therefore, that the introduction of Home Rule to Ireland was fiercely resisted by the Ulster unionists. Lord Randolph Churchill, father of Sir Winston, had sounded the rallying cry "Ulster will fight; Ulster will be right". The first bill introduced by Liberal Prime Minister, William Ewart Gladstone, in 1886 had been greeted by the worst riots ever seen up to that time in Belfast. A quarter of a century later Sir Edward Carson, an eminent barrister and MP for Dublin University, took up the flag. He became leader in 1910 and united the loyalist front in resistance, by use of force if necessary, to a nationalist political takeover of the country. The Ulster Volunteer Force was formed in 1913 and by the next year it had become a well armed and well drilled fighting force.

The formation of an armed volunteer force in Ulster led to the setting up of a rival nationalist militia, the Irish National Volunteers, under the leadership of John Redmond, in November 1913. The decision of the young James Fitzmaurice to terminate his uneasy relationship with the business school in Waterford was hastened by the more exciting events taking place on the island - and a little later by events happening further afield. Now in his mid-teens and nurtured on a diet of Irish nationalism he was fully prepared to do his bit for his native country. If that meant fighting for his country then so be it. He instantly responded to Redmond's call to arms and became an Irish Volunteer at the tender age of 16.

"I joined up with the burning enthusiasm of the son of an Irish nationalist father and had romantic visions of playing an important part in my country's cause as that played by my famous forebear and namesake, Sir James Fitzmaurice, in the Elizabethan Irish Wars".

The belligerent response by the unionists to the constitutional progress of Home Rule was an early and salutary lesson for the young Fitz of the constant and close relationship between politics and violence in the Irish context. His knowledge of Irish history allied to what he observed happening in the country at the time led him to the conclusion that "the strength of a nation in the last resort lies in the number of armed men rather than in the number and vehemence of the politicians, and that oratorical power and manpower were not synonymous terms". Sentiments such as these hastened the revolution that was not far off. Because his life took a different path, it was a revolution in which he was to play no part.

John Redmond

Fitz, now employed as a trainee salesman at Hearnes' drapery store in Waterford, spent all his spare time in the evenings and at the weekends drilling and field training. The volunteers had uniforms and carried wooden rifles in the open for drill purposes. But he and his comrades trained in target practice with a service rifle fitted with a Morris tube in a miniature rifle range and he was the "proud possessor of a service rifle of Boer War vintage".

To Fitz's young mind the political controversy on Home Rule had dragged on endlessly. The fervour with which nationalists had rallied around Redmond's Volunteers in the early months began to fade as time passed without an end to the controversy in sight. Fitz was a typical young enthusiast prepared to take on all comers, including the unionists if need be, to secure the concessions already agreed, but being stalled, by the British Government. Lack of "real action", as he termed it, led to a drop in morale in the force.

He was full of admiration for the drill instructors, mostly ex-British Army NCOs. But he bitterly resented the role played by the officers. These were "an inept lot of shopkeepers and suchlike, masquerading under the delusion that officers were produced by the tailors who made their uniforms. From a military point of view they were a pathetic lot of cretins who neither looked like, nor behaved like, soldiers."

Fitz obviously longed to be a "real" soldier. His opportunity was soon to come. But not in the uniform or in the cause he had anticipated.

Europe was in turmoil. British Foreign Secretary, Sir Edward Grey, told the House of Commons, "the lights of Europe are going out". On 4 August, 1914, the Liberal Prime Minister, Herbert Asquith, declared war on Germany. This was the start of the war to end all wars. "The bolt from the blue had fallen," is how Fitz later described the news of the outbreak of war. "The curtains were being rung down on the golden age. The good old days had come to an end."

It was a watershed in Fitz's life as it was in the history of mankind. Fitz, the boy, was soon to become Fitz, the man.

John Redmond made what proved to be a fatal blunder when he offered his Volunteer force to defend the country side by side with the Ulster Volunteers at Parliament in Westminster in September 1914 without seeking guarantees for the enactment of Home Rule. Fitz was an admirer of Redmond but, like so many in the nationalist camp, felt very letdown by the leader's lack of circumspection.

"Redmond, a man of great intelligence, gentle manners, sublime dignity and overpowering charm, lacked the shrewdness required in political negotiations with such proven masters of the art of chicanery as the English political leaders. The outbreak of war transformed him overnight into a courted and necessary ally whose support had to be won and kept by the British Government no matter what the price demanded. He was no longer the unwelcome suppliant begging for the passage of his Home Rule Bill at the hands of a reluctant Government. Although the same Government was breathing pious platitudes about the right of small nations, he offered his small nation without any guarantees or security."

Redmond's House of Commons blunder in 1914 led to a split

in the Volunteer movement. Sinn Fein was born and sworn to the ideal of an Irish Republic. Had Fitz joined the anti-Redmondites he would very likely have become one of the activists in the 1916 Rising and played a part in the War of Independence that followed. This revolution resulted in the Anglo-Irish Treaty of 1922 which led to the foundation of the Irish Free State, consisting of twenty-six counties, and a new statelet of Northern Ireland, under British rule, consisting of six counties.

Despite his failing to deliver Home Rule Redmond from Fitz's perspective still remained leader of the Irish people and to him the Irish owed their loyalty.

The National Volunteers got caught up in the war frenzy and Fitz was filled with the sense of "thrilling adventure" that was such a mark of his character, carrying out various duties on a voluntary basis for the local British Military Commanders. The British Government proceeded, however, to ignore the Volunteers and instead of organising them into distinctive Irish Divisions they carried out a recruiting campaign for the British Army. The gloss soon wore off the role of the Volunteers and he, like so many of his mates, went off to join Irish Regiments of their own choice.

Fitz was fascinated by the paradox of Irishmen fighting England's war. "The Irish were going to war in a cause propounded by their centuries old enemy. They were going to fight for the independence of small nations. Had they not 'won everybody's battles but their own?'". He saw it all as "amazingly bewitching".

Chapter 4

In the Army

The war was still in its first year and Fitz was becoming more disillusioned with the lack of activity and direction of the Volunteers. He was 17 years old, under the recruiting age, but with a burning ambition to become a soldier and see some real action. Without his parents knowledge he and some friends enlisted in the Cadet Company of the 7th Battalion of the Leinsters. The minimum age for active service was 19 but he bluffed his age and his veracity in the matter, as with so many other young recruits, was not questioned.

A commission lay at the end of a successful training period for the young cadets but this was not to be for the young Fitz for as soon as his parents discovered what he had done they approached the commanding officer and producing his birth certificate they obtained his release from the regiment. This was a humiliating experience for a young man intent on active military service. It made him more determined than ever to become a soldier and come hell or high water nothing would get in the way of his ambition.

Over the course of the following three months he chanced to

meet on occasions an army sergeant dressed in the war regalia of the 17th Lancers, known as the "Death or Glory Boys". Fitz was most impressed with what he saw and what he heard. "His military bearing and exceedingly smart uniform completely captured my imagination. He epitomised everything that a crack cavalry regiment of the line stood for. He reflected the glamour of that famous epic of British military history, the 'Charge of the Light Brigade' at Balaclava in the Crimean War, in which the regiment participated and won such signal honours. I decided this was to be my regiment."

Within a few days he was back in the army but now there was no easy commission. He was to learn the soldiers' trade the hard way.

"In reporting for duty, I arrived at Kildare railway station at night in a dreadful downpour of rain accompanied by a bitterly cold northwesterly wind. My transport to Barracks was a rough manure cart drawn by a mischievous looking mule. On arrival I was posted to No. 2 Troop "A" Squadron and wended my way to the barrack room over the stables where I was introduced to the Corporal-in-Charge, one Bill Beaumont. I went to bed in my rough soldier's cot. But I did not sleep!"

The young recruit found it difficult to relax in these new and strange surroundings. The sleeping quarters were adjacent to the stables where the horses were tethered to an iron manger by a leather halter attached to a metal chain passing through a hole in the front edge on the manger and secured by a wooden ball at its end. The constant clanking of chains throughout the night were like devilish sounds to the uninitiated and after a restless first night on the Curragh with little sleep Fitz arose to the sound of reveille.

"The lights were switched on and a large dixy-can of unsweetened boiling hot chocolate was dumped in the middle of the barrack-room floor by a cookhouse orderly. One rose painfully, grabbed an enamel mug and, having filled it, returned to the seclusion of his virgin couch, sipped the chocolate gently whilst ruminating on the possible happenings of the day ahead."

There was little time for ruminating, however, because after reveille at 5am the soldier had to don fatigue dress, make up his bed, sweep under and around it and be on parade for roll-call at 5.15.

Fitz's first hours as a soldier were spent in watching intently at the way the various troopers tackled their different chores. This consisted of cleaning out the stalls, providing fresh dry peat bedding and rubbing down their mounts with dandy-brushes and currycombs. The activity all around him had him almost hypnotised but his trance was soon broken by the booming sound of an irate NCO directly behind him.

"What the ... do you think you're ... doing?" It was his erstwhile charming friend, Sergeant Mullaney. Gone was the gentle urbanity which had characterised previous meetings. Fitz was dumbstruck and lost for words.

"I don't know what I should be doing," he muttered.

"Don't know what to do .....**WHAT**? Who the ... hell do you ... think you're talking to?" bellowed the outraged sergeant.

The emphasis on the questioning "what" gave Fitz the clue to the error of his initial reply.

"I don't know what I should be doing, **SIR**", he replied much more distinctively than before.

That response soothed the savage breast a little and the sergeant proceeded to give him his instructions in a more subdued tone. "Then get hold of that flamin' broom and sweep up the stable", Sergeant Mullaney ordered. Fitz jumped to it. He was in the army now and was on parade.

Fitz was a quick learner. He was helped along the way by a wily old codger, who was nicknamed "Old King Cole". He was soon to discover that this veteran of many years and few battles was a considerable personage in the regiment.

" 'Old King Cole' belonged to that peculiar band of long-serving troopers with not less than twenty years service each, without one good conduct stripe between them. They were rarely around during the actual working day but always turned up for meals and on pay days and were to be seen in the canteen and barrackrooms at night. They were completely wrapped up in a strange aura of mystery. They knew every trick of the trade and acted as mentors to the new recruits until the young soldier succeeded in fighting his way out of their greedy clutches. They taught the rookie how to make up his cot correctly, how to fold spare uniforms in the racks overhead, how to clean arms, saddlery and equipment, how to roll a greatcoat for attachment to the front pommel of a saddle and the other one hundred and one things that came the way of a trooper in the course of his duties. For all these items of instruction they extracted a small fee by the simple expediency of refusing to pass one's equipment and arms for the following day's parade until it was paid."

Fitz was taken to the Quartermaster's stores and was issued with a lance, sword, rifle and bayonet, bandoleer, red and white pennant, white head rope, set of saddlery and all the other accessories of a trooper's equipment. He was then introduced to his allotted mount, a lovely black mare named Emma.

"She immediately nuzzled up to me. We became the staunchest of friends from the very first moment as she quickly found the lump of sugar I carried in my tunic pocket for her. As she looked at me with those ever so soulful, velvety black eyes she seemed to convey nothing but the deepest feelings of sorrow and compassion for me, her new lady's maid, for that was what I now was - and all for one and tuppence a day."

Life as a trainee trooper was not a bed of roses nor had Fitz expected it to be. The days were long, the work was hard and life was tough. He soon discovered that being a trooper in a crack cavalry regiment was not always the glamorous life it appeared from the outside. In his very first assignment he was detailed to join a fatigue party engaged in loading manure into a horse's cart with a heavy pitchfork. There were many such unpleasant duties but they were part and parcel of a day's work and Fitz did not complain. He was young, enthusiastic, with a love for horses from his schooldays and he had achieved his ambition of becoming a soldier.

He quickly settled into his new environment but there were some shocks in store. He tells in his writings of one such incident that sent quivers down his spine.

"One morning as I returned with my ride from the Riding School a trooper's mount became restive as we entered the corner of the metalled Barrack Square. It finally reared and then bucked, unseating the trooper with whom I had become very friendly. As he was thrown, his left foot became jammed in the stirrup and the horse galloped away to the stables, dragging him in its wake. His brains were smashed to pulp on the hard surface over which he was dragged. Breakfast was a melancholy affair that morning."

Fitz became friends with many interesting characters in "that most peculiar assortment of wartime cavalrymen". One such acquaintance was Trooper Rutherford, a young Yorkshire barrister. Although he was considerably older than himself, Fitz liked him from the start and they got on well together.

"He was tall, freckled, blue-eyed and good looking in a rugged sort of way. He was given to honest thinking and speaking and it was this honesty that appealed to me from the beginning. I liked the way his mind worked. It had the analytical keenness of a trained lawyer. He had a capacity for seeing ahead - looking around tricky corners. Under his tutelage I got down to a serious study of the soldier's bible, the Manual of Military Law and King's Regulations, which was to stand me in good stead during the whole of my military career."

The peculiar assortment also brought trouble in a cavalryman's uniform. It came in the form of a "hard-bitten, tough, East London, Jewish Cockney who had all the appearance of a prizefighter". This was not the sort of character that the young Fitz, relatively tender in age, upbringing and physique, would seek out for a fight. But when the chips were down he never backed away from a challenge, even if the odds were stacked against him. The confrontation with the rough-hewn Cockney came one morning at "stables". The order of jobs during "stables", which was sounded by about fifty boy soldiers on silver trumpets from the barrack square, was to water horses, groom, pass grooming inspection, then feed and file away for the midday meal. In watering, the horses were led to the troughs in single file and lined up at each side, each trooper holding the halter rope while standing at the horse's head. The Troop Sergeant supervised from the end of the trough.

Fitz relates what happened on that bitterly cold morning. "My Emma, having had a good swig of water, raised her head high into the air and in so doing a stream of water dribbled from her mouth flowing down the neck of the open shirt of my neighbouring trooper. Brutally he hauled off with his fist striking Emma on the muzzle. Had he struck me all would have been well. Striking Emma was an entirely different matter. She and some other horses in the immediate vicinity reared up, broke away and careered across the barrack square."

Fitz's temper snapped. He lashed out a hard and well directed punch to the trooper's jaw. Within seconds both were in a clinch and on the ground. The Troop Sergeant immediately intervened and soon had the brawl under control. He ordered four men to "fall in" and the two adversaries were marched off to the guard room and lodged in cells charged with fighting on parade. The following morning the Squadron Commander referred the case for investigation to the Commanding Officer, Colonel Portal, D.S.O. This was serious stuff for a young recruit. Fitz gave his version of the incident and called evidence to prove his case. After a severe admonition by the Colonel the charge against him was dismissed on the grounds of extreme provocation. His adversary had, however, an additional charge preferred against him of ill-treating an animal the property of His Majesty's Government for which he was sentenced to a period of detention in the "glasshouse", as the Military Prison was known.

The "glasshouse" was not a holiday camp. The regime was tough and the punishment dished out was severe. In the evenings Cockney would be feeling more than a little aggrieved and as the days passed ever so slowly and painfully by his indignation grew within him for the young Irishman. He passed out threatening messages daily and these were carefully passed on to his fearful adversary. If the days passed slowly in the "glasshouse" they were fleeting swiftly by for Fitz, who was growing more filled with apprehension as the release day drew near. Not even his good friend, Rutherford, could lend him any consolation. His fears were so heightened he seriously contemplated desertion many times but this was not a real option because the consequences of such an action were too serious to bear consideration.

The hour of reckoning finally arrived. The day broke dark and threatening. Fitz was filled with the most awful forebodings. Releases took place at 6pm when an escort arrived to accompany the delinquent back to his unit. The barrack room was full of troopers by 6.20pm, looking forward to a good fight. He whiled the seconds away nervously cleaning his arms and equipment for the next day's parade. The scene was set for the great confrontation.

Shortly after 6.30pm the latch on the barrack room door clicked, the door opened - and trouble stalked in. To Fitz's eyes he looked fit and well and most fearsome in his "glasshouse" styled close-cropped haircut. Cockney did not delay in getting down to the business of the evening. After dumping his rifle and kit on his bunk he duly removed his tunic, rolled up his sleeves and smartly proceeded in the direction of his trembling adversary.

There are no rules in barrack-room fights and nobody interferes. Cockney skipped the preliminaries. A mighty clout on the side of the jaw knocked the fragile young Irishman off his bed and sent him crashing into a neighbouring bunk. Fitz knew there was no way out. He could put up some resistance and retain his honour at the expense of a bruised body or simply throw in the towel, take what was coming to him and end up with a bruised body and humiliated as well. He reminded himself that he was Irish and his belief in the indomitable character of his race. That belief was now being put to the test. His response was swift.

"I bounced to my feet and went straight at him only to receive another very sharp jolt on the jaw which put me back on the floor. This time I was on my feet more quickly. He was expecting me to walk straight into him and receive another lovely smash in the face. I jumped on a cot and launched myself on him. He was caught off balance and went down smack on the floor with all my catapulted weight on top of him. Still the struggle proceeded on the floor ... and I felt I had some slight advantage in that position. Somehow he managed to get to his feet. I immediately followed suit."

The fight continued in intensity with Fitz's determination and inventiveness compensating for his lack of size, strength and experience. He soaked up a lot of punishment but felt that Cockney had been shaken from his first fall on the floor and looked more vulnerable now. Having withstood another fierce assault Fitz responded with a second leaped attack from a bunk and connected sweetly on the jaw of his rival. This sent Cockney reeling and he finished up with his backside striking the bottom of the lance-rack. The impact caused the lances to topple out of their clips and fall on top of him in glorious confusion. Fitz stood close to the stove in the middle of the barrack room awaiting the trooper's next move. Cockney rose gasping for breath, grasped one of the lances at his feet and javelin-like hurled it straight at his rival. This proved a fatal error on his part. Fitz ducked instinctively and the lance flashed past narrowly missing one of the onlooking troopers sitting on a bunk nearby. Within a split second all present jumped to their feet and surrounded the Londoner. He was grabbed roughly and frogmarched down the iron staircase where he was thrown into the water trough, removed and rolled in the manure heap dripping wet - a procedure that was repeated three times before being unceremoniously dumped, with kit and arms beside him, and told to get a transfer to another squadron.

Although left licking his wounds Fitz had survived his biggest army test to date. He thought it strange that though the scars of battle were obvious to one and all, nobody asked how he got them, nor was there any mention of his "friend" who disappeared. "I found I was being treated with a greater degree of consideration. I was on my way to becoming a good cavalry soldier."

Fitz liked the life of soldier. Horsemanship presented him with little difficulty but he had to spend many difficult hours on the barrack square and in the riding school before mastering the art of handling the lance, sword and rifle. His efforts did not go unrewarded because he became the leading file of his ride in the equitation school and soon after passing out as a trained soldier he was promoted "to the dizzy altitude of acting unpaid lance corporal". He was indeed proud and happy. "That single stripe in my tunic seemed to exude all the concentrated rays of the sun's light."

His period of probation was three months before being duly confirmed in the rank. That stripe was important to him for many reasons, not least the money, for now he got an increase of 3d (less than 2p) bringing his pay to the princely sum of 1s 5d (7p) per day.

One day while engaged in breaking and training young troop horses in the remount Fitz suffered a nasty fall which necessitated hospital treatment. On his discharge from the hospital his medical officer ordered a period of light duty for him and he found himself posted as a noncommissioned officer in charge of waiters in the Sergeant's Mess. This effectively made him "head waiter" which was certainly not to the young soldier's fancy - but orders were orders. It was not long before he was again posted for duty and at the next overseas listing, although still short of his eighteenth birthday, he found his name listed for service in France.   In due course the draft marched out of camp en route to the continent to the strains of "Come Back to Erin".

Chapter 5

The Battle of the Somme

B y the opening months of 1916 the Great War had developed into a grim and stagnant trench battle and the cavalry units had largely become redundant.   The heavy regime of training that the troopers had gone through on the Curragh was of little use on the Western Front as the opposing armies, using similar tactics, dug in within earshot of each other and with only a few hundred yards of No Man's Land often separating the front lines.

Fitz's draft were shipped to Le Havre from where they were posted to the Infantry Base Depot at the huge encampment at Etampes.   On arrival they were split up into various infantry regiments. In the early stages of the war Irish enlistments were usually detailed to Irish regiments but as time passed by drafts intended for Irish regiments were mostly diverted to other units whose shortage of manpower was critical.   The need for replacements became so great at the front due to heavy casualties that often half-trained soldiers found themselves on active duty. In any event Fitz did not appear to be unduly upset when he was posted to an English unit, the 7th Battalion of the Queen's Royal (West Surrey) Regiment, the Second Regiment of Foot and one with a proud reputation in the field. The battalion, which formed part of the 55th Brigade in the British 18th Division, consisted mainly of South London Cockneys, whose sardonic wit and grim humour was very much to the young Irishman's liking. The 7th Queen's War Diary shows that the unit (total all ranks 971) was shipped from Folkestone to Boulogne on 27 July, 1915. Within two weeks its men were at the front and by the time of Fitzmaurice's arrival ten months later they had seen almost continuous action in the front line and had suffered considerable casualties. The West Surreys were by now a battle-hardened lot, "sterling characters" and "undoubtedly the finest infantry soldiers in the British Army" in Fitz's estimation. He benefited greatly in experience from these "gallant old-timers".

By now plans were well advanced for the biggest assault of the entire war and one of the bloodiest battles in the history of warfare, the First Battle of the Somme. The 7th Queen's was earmarked to play a key role. The fine training routine completed by the 7th Lancers on the Plains of Kildare in Ireland was a poor preparation for active front line duty on the banks of the Somme in the summer of 1916. This was very much a culture shock for Fitz and his trooper comrades. His smart cavalry attire was replaced by ill-fitting and shabby infantry uniform. "This peculiar abomination of webbing straps, cross straps, ammunition pouches, haversack, pack, entrenching tool and God knows what was dished out to us in bits and pieces ... It was a most curious assortment of junk. We had drunk the cup of bitterness to the dregs."

Morale among the troopers was at rock bottom as they marched back to their bell-tents in a state of complete abjection. Now they were to go through an intensive course in the rudiments of infantry drill and in the art of being a foot soldier. If this was a painful time for the troopers it was soul destroying for the war toughened NCOs, to whom fell the task of training them. The language in use passed for the King's English but it bore little relationship to the textbook variety or that spoken in everyday life. Fitz eloquently described the infantry Sergeant-Major of the period as a despot of a very high order. "He was possessed of a caustic wit which could be soul-searching for the sensitive. As a vendor of cheap obscene invective he was supreme. At the same time he was, in the majority of cases, a good soldier and an excellent leader. In the heat of action he was capable of developing a most benevolent attitude towards the young soldier enduring his baptism of fire."

The happiest moment for the Sergeant-Major in charge of the retraining process of Fitz's group during the troopers three week period at Etampes was when he marched the lot to the railway siding to catch a train en route to where their battalion was located up the line. But something went amiss with the Railway Transport Officer's arrangements and the group had to be marched back to camp again, much to the chagrin of the frustrated NCO. This happened twice more before at last a train did arrive and less than fond farewells were exchanged as the newest consignment of gun fodder headed for the front. "Good luck to y'all, ye grimy lot of bastards", bellowed the Sergeant-Major as the train slowly gathered up speed before disappearing into the distance.

The 7th Queen's was on a training break from the line when joined by the troopers. Fitz found the first reveille parade with his new battalion "chillingly" impressive. "We were formed up on three sides of a square when the Adjutant, accompanied by the Regimental Sergeant-Major, carrying a hurricane lantern, arrived on parade in the first faint light of dawn. Roll-call had already been taken and the various companies had been reported present and correct or otherwise. We were 'stood at ease' whilst the Adjutant read the Battalion and Corps Orders for the day. These orders were much the same as those to which we were accustomed at home. We new arrivals were, however, given serious food for thought when he came to the section of Corps Routine Orders under the heading of 'Punishments'. It brought us sharply face to face with the stark realities of war."

The stark realities Fitz referred to in his memoirs were mainly the outcome of trials by Field General Court Martial and contained an enormous number of sentences of death before a firing squad for failure to live up to the exacting standards of active service in the field. These offences included cowardice in the face of the enemy, deserting the line and self-inflicted wounds for the purpose of evading active service. The executions were usually carried out at dawn. This was a shock to the system for a young volunteer who was prepared to fight to preserve the democratic order but had not yet experienced life under fire. Fitz prayed that he possessed "this peculiar to define thing called courage" and he presumed, somewhat tongue-in-cheek, that "the top-brass who presided over those summary trials had a superabundance of this noble virtue". One way or the other he was determined not to be introduced to a firing squad at such an unearthly hour and trusted he would not be found wanting.

The Regimental Sergeant-Major was known as "Choaky Bill". As there was always a strong antipathy amongst infantrymen for the cavalry, "Choaky Bill" pulled out all the stops for his new arrivals. "Queen Mary's Horse! Wot a 'horrible lot o' bastards! England's last f.... hope. Thank God we've got a ruddy Naivy! Never in **ALL ME LIFE** have I seen such a lousy lot. An' they calls ya soldiers! Why I've **SPAT OUT** better soldiers than you perishin' lot. **MEGAUD!** What have I done to deserve this? But let me tell you somethin'. I'll make soldiers out of you scummy lot if it's the last ruddy thing I do. **SEE!**"

So it went on and on and on. But the sensitivities of the troopers had long since disappeared - and nobody took the least notice. Very soon they were to get down to the main business of making and waging war.

Fitz's first mission was to transport food and equipment from the areas behind the front line to the foremost lines of battle. The land over which he had to travel had been the scene of a battle a few days previously and was heavily cratered by shellfire. Dead soldiers law strewn about everywhere.   Dead Germans, dead French and dead British soldiers. It was as if he had fallen headlong into hell.   "Never before had I seen a dead person.   My whole being and soul was filled with dread and disgust."

Fitz was soon despatched to the trenches and he hated every minute of it.   He admitted later that he was "always terrified and had to hold myself together with some effort so that I didn't lose control of myself and rush out of the trenches ... it is said that a person can get accustomed to anything.   My experience during those shocking days in the trenches altered my opinion".

From the early months of 1916 the British troops in France consisting of the few remaining regulars from the original British Expeditionary Force and the new enthusiastic recruits to Kitchener's Army had been anticipating the "Big Push" which they hoped would bring the fighting to a hasty end as had been widely predicted when war was declared in 1914.   Preparations were at an advanced state by mid-June.   The battleground was to be along a 20 mile (32km) front on both sides of the River Somme from Gommecourt in the north to near Chilly in the south.   The object of the gigantic offensive at the Somme was to divert the Germans, who were putting fierce pressure on the French positions at Verdun.   The aim was to break or shift the almost unassailable German lines protected by trenches, parapets, barbed wire and redoubts and bristling with enormous array of artillery.   The formations drawn up had the British Third Army (Allenby), the Fifth (Gough), the Fourth (Rawlinson) and the French Sixth Army (Fayolle) facing the formidable defences of Bavaria's First Army under Prince Rupprecht.

The offensive was preceded by a long and intensive bombardment which was intended to destroy the German trenches and defensive systems.   But the enemy dugouts were deeper than anticipated and often up to forty feet (12m) below ground. The bombardment was largely ineffective and, in fact, created some unexpected problems for the Allies because the huge number of craters left as a result proved an obstruction for the soldiers advancing towards enemy lines.

At precisely 7.30 on the morning of 1st of July the offensive began just north of the River Somme with the soldiers of the Fourth Army, under the command of General Sir Henry Rawlinson, ordered to go over the top and proceed across No Man's Land at a steady pace. Meanwhile the French Sixth Army were attacking German defences mainly south of the river. The mostly untried young British soldiers, carrying up to half the weight of an average man in equipment, struggled out of their trenches and stumbled cumbersomely across the battle scarred No Man's Land. Speed and surprise were their only chance of success but they were favoured with neither. The once beautiful and peaceful French countryside on a fine summer morning was soon turned into a kaleidoscopic theatre of death and horror. Faced directly by German guns the brave men of the Fourth Army went sent like sheep to their slaughter. They had little or no chance of survival. It was a holocaust and brave young men fell dead and dying in their thousands, some before they had even passed their own wire defences, in what proved to be a suicidal effort and the bloodiest day in the history of the British Army. It is estimated that the British had lost over 30,000 men in the first hour of the attack. Rawlinson kept sending his troops forward. By noon he had sent 100,000 into the fray. Meanwhile the French had made good headway while to the north other British units were reporting limited progress. At the end of that dreadful day the German line was partially broken but at a terrible cost of 60,000 British casualties (including 19,000 dead). That was the grim first day of a battle that was to continue with the utmost ferocity over the following months.

In "A Short History of the 55th Infantry Brigade in the War of 1914-18" printed (for private circulation only) shortly after the end of the war, there is an account of the part played by the Brigade, to which the 7th Queens were attached, on that first fateful day of the Somme offensive.

"The Brigade held the line in front of Carnoy, the objective being a trench line about 200 yards north of the Montauban-Fricourt road; included in the objective was part of the village itself. During the preceding week an immense amount of work was done in the formation of food and ammunition dumps, digging of 'jumping off' lines, etc."

The report next tells of the order of battle: "7th Queen's on left, 8th E. Surrey Regt. on right, 7th Buffs in support with the task of clearing the Carnoy craters, 7th R.W. Kent Regt. in reserve. The enemy artillery was fairly quiet during the night, although it increased considerably in the morning. The morning of July 1st dawned very fine but misty. At 7am our barrage became intense and remained so till 7.22 am when the artillery ceased to lengthen range; at the same time all guns of the Trench Mortar Battery opened an intense bombardment for eight minutes, when the whole Brigade went forward to the assault.

"At 7.28 am the Royal Engineers had blown two Russian saps right across 'No Man's land', and these proved of great value in enabling men to move forward under cover. Everything went according to plan. The 6th Bavarian Regt. held the Carnoy craters to the last; it took six hours before the last machine gun was silenced, and snipers continued to fire all day.

"On the rest of the front, held by the 62nd Rhineland Regt., a stout resistance was put up in the first three lines of trenches, but after that the Germans became demoralised and ran. The final objective was gained in four and a half hours, and brilliant work was done by all units concerned.

"The 7th R.W. Kent Regt. took over the line on the following morning and held it under heavy fire for four days, after which the Brigade was relieved. All units suffered heavy casualties (about 60 per cent)," according to the contemporary account.

Each Division were set a number of key objectives. Sometimes it was a fortified village which had to be taken. Sometimes the trenches which linked up the various strongly defended villages, carrying the threat to the garrisons of being surrounded and isolated, were the target. These were all demanding and dangerous assignments. But in Fitz's opinion the most difficult of these objectives were the woods dotted all over the French countryside and strongly defended by the enemy infantry and machine-gunners. These woods like the fortified villages were littered with, and linked by, a complex system of trenches and communication alleys which made their capture a most difficult undertaking. The principle followed was that the objective, whatever it was, was always completed, if not at the first then on the second, third, or subsequent attempts. It was also the aim that when a yard of ground was taken by the Allies it was permanently held. Fresh divisions, after a short rest, were thrown in to relieve exhausted units and this was an endless process.

Fitz's unit's first experience of this type of fighting was at Trones Wood, which was on the new front line. A number of attempts had been made in the second week of July by "the gallant Lancashire men of the Thirteenth Division" but their efforts were repulsed with heavy casualties and the 18th Division (of which Fitz's unit was part) was sent in on 13 July to relieve them. The Thirteenth had stubbornly held on to one corner of the wood and this was used as the launching pad for the final successful assault. Their orders were curt and to the point. The wood had to be in British hands within a day at all costs as a general attack on the main German lines was planned for 14 July and failure to achieve their objective in the time specified put the whole plan at risk.

The German defence was exceedingly strong consisting of three fiercely held redoubts, one on the central east edge, one in the south centre and one in the west central edge. These, combined with a complicated system of trenches dotted throughout the wood, had helped the Germans in repulsing all previous attacks. Troops who had succeeded in working their way around and in between the German redoubts found themselves confronted by the enemy securely entrenched.

Fitz takes up the story. "Our Brigade opened the attack on the south end of the wood and were subjected to a very heavy artillery barrage which inflicted very heavy casualties before we had reached the edge of the objective. My battalion, the 7th Queens, attempted to enter the wood on the northwest where the Longueval Alley ran up from Bernafay Wood on the left. Only a scattered handful of us managed to gain the top of the wood where we held on for some hours in the face of the heavy barrage and the withering machine-gun fire from two strong German entrenchments. Our sister battalion, the 7th West Kents, succeeded in working their way from the south and past the central and eastern German strong points when they lost touch with each other owing to the deepening gloom of the evening. They formed themselves into two or three separate groups completely surrounded by the enemy.

"The 54th Brigade was thrown in and went forward about midnight. The 6th Northamptons and the 12th Middlesex led the assault in the pitch darkness stumbling continually over fallen trees and dead men who were littered all over the wood. Shortly before dawn the Northamptons captured the south central German strong point and then pressed forward. In the morning the wood was full of scattered groups of British infantry and the situation was terribly confused. Order was soon restored and the remaining strong points on the west and eastern sides of the wood were soon captured. Numbers of the defeated enemy began streaming out of the eastern side of the wood making for Guillemont. They were subjected to extremely heavy machine-gun fire and sustained very heavy losses. The whole wood was soon swept clear of the enemy though it was still under very heavy enemy artillery fire. The objective was taken in less than the time specified and the entire right flank of the army was completely held and covered for the important operation timed for the 14th. We were successfully relieved in the morning by the advance of the 54th Brigade.

"We had been initiated into that dreadful form of wood fighting. All those who took part in such engagements and survived will agree that this type of fighting proved more awesome to the mind and more exhausting to the body than any other form of engagement," Fitz contended.

The battle raged on and the War Diary of the 7th Queens shows their time divided between duty in the trenches and periods of training. Fitz's hatred for the trenches was at its most intense at night-time and he found it difficult to pass "these barren empty hours". He found that one way out of his dilemma was to volunteer for patrol duty into No Man's Land. He was a specialist in throwing hand grenades and was happier with the mobility and adventure attached to such missions. He became noted for his daring and courage in these commando type operations and his acts of bravery did not go unnoticed by officers in the battalion. No one suspected that his bravado emanated from his deep underlying fears of the trenches. "I never had the courage to admit that the only reason I went on these nerve-wrecking expeditions was because I dreaded staying in the trenches", he later admitted.

The training during August related to vital assignments coming up in September. These were the taking of the almost impregnable fortresses at Thiepval village and Pozieres ridge and the dreaded Schwaben Redoubt. Their capture would give a dominating fire-command over all the German positions to the north of the River Ancre. At least 400 guns were mounted over this relatively small sector of front and the enemy were firmly dug in along a most complicated defensive system. Thiepval and Schwaben had been the scene of horrific bloodshed in the early days of the Battle of the Somme. The 36th Division, comprised almost totally of Ulster Unionists, attacked uphill against these heavily fortified positions on the opening day of the Battle and suffered dreadful losses. They died in their thousands as they attempted to break the

German line. What little gains were made were soon negated by German counter-attacks. Now, almost three months later, these key strategic positions were still in German control.

The Eighteenth and the Eleventh Divisions, part of Gough's Fifth Army, were chosen for the attack on Thiepval which was timed for 12.35 on the afternoon of 26 September. Fitz's Brigade, the 55th, was held in reserve for the assault on Schwaben Redoubt after the capture of Thiepval village. They watched as the 53rd and 54th Brigades moved forward under a covering barrage across "No Man's Land" which had an average depth of 250 yards (230m).

Fitz later recalled the scene. "Carrying their rifles at the 'High Port' they rolled over Joseph Trench, the advanced German position, which was taken by surprise; but before they reached it large numbers of terrified German troops rushed out, half dressed and unarmed and yelling with terror they bolted through the barrage. Many of them were wiped out by their own gunfire. The advancing troops took no notice of them and let the survivors pass. The advance pressed steadily forward crossing Schwaben Trench, Zollern Trench and Bulgar Trench in each of which the stout Wurtenburgers put up a stubborn resistance which was beaten down.

"The advance was held up by a complicated network of trenches and strong points in which desperate hand-to-hand fighting took place. The fighting was so fierce that the 11th Royal Fusiliers on the left got far behind their barrage and also behind the Middlesex on the right who swept up as far as the Chateau, directly in front of the village, where they were brought to a halt by heavy machine-gun fire from the ruined Chateau. Here, most providentially, the last of the four tanks which had entered the action came forward and put those machine-guns out of action. It then broke down. The tank was an innovation that had just arrived on the battle scene. It was terribly unreliable but it had a tremendous effect upon the morale of the enemy who at the time did not possess such a weapon.

"This was my experience of seeing a tremendous battle being waged from a grandstand seat, so to speak. It was the most awe-inspiring sight I have ever witnessed in my whole life. One was keyed up to such a pitch of excitement that it was necessary to keep a tight grip on oneself not to rush forward and join in the melee."

Fierce hand-to-hand fighting continued all day and through the night. Fresh British troops were sent in at dawn on 27 September and drove the remaining German troops out. Thiepval Village was now in British hands. Next it was the turn of the 55th Brigade to overrun the formidable Schwaben Redoubt. This was a strategic stronghold, comprised on many trenches and strong points and lying about 1000 yards (900m) ahead along a broken slope. They were sent into action on the following morning to relieve the worn-out portions of the 53rd Brigade. The 7th Queens Battalion and the Suffolks were in the van of the attack with the Norfolks and the Essex in support.

They rushed forward and were soon engaged in hand-to-hand fighting. Bulgar and Martin Trenches were taken and the 11th Division on the right of Fitz's unit took Hessian trench. Around 3pm Market Trench was also captured and all units were now swarming up around Schwaben. The mighty stronghold was pierced by small groups in the face of fierce resistance. By evening of the 29th the British were is possession of most of the fortress including the key position of the Redoubt, point 28. Several attempts to oust the remaining defenders proved unsuccessful. The machine-gun corp was moved in in support. A hand grenade battle developed and eventually the Germans were forced to move. Many were mowed down as they tried to fall back in the open towards Saint Pierre Divion. Fresh troops were sent in on both sides and the battle continued mercilessly until Fitz's unit was relieved on 5 October. By that time the whole of the Redoubt except for one small section was in British hands and that last section was later taken by the 39th Division.

The "Short History" of the 55th Brigade's adventures recalls the scene at the end of that bloody assault. "It is impossible to give a clear account of what happened during those five days of heavy fighting. At least ten attacks and counterattacks were made during the period, the mutual bombardment was probably among the heaviest on record during the war, and gas and flammenwerfer were freely used by the enemy. The trenches were thick with German and our own dead, the ground was so churned up it was literally impossible to read a map with any accuracy, and men broke down under the nerve strain. We certainly got the better of the Germans in prisoners, the number of casualties inflicted, and ground gained."

The price of this small piece of Picardy real estate which had already cost so much blood, mainly Ulster Unionist, in the opening days of the Battle, had shot up again with the British counting their losses on this latest assault at 1,500 all ranks for Thiepval and 2,000 for Schwaben.

Following that successful action British guns were now able to dominate the German positions and it looked as if the enemy trenches directly across the River Ancre were untenable. However the Germans had built a complex system of underground shafts deep down in the chalky soil and this gave them protection from the heaviest artillery fire. Heavy barbed wire defences, thick and rusty between the front lines added to the British problems which were compounded by the worsening weather and the almost impassible mud slopes on their side of the river. In mid November as the 55th Brigade moved forward to the east capturing some villages they encountered severe fighting again.

The contemporary account in the "Short History" tells of the action on 18/19 November: "The objective was Desire Trench, 500 yards from Regina. The attack took place in a snowstorm over very bad ground. On the right the attack was completely successful; the 8th E. Surrey Regt., with the Canadians on their right, reached the objective, taking many prisoners, One Company of the 7th R.W. Kent Regt. was also successful, but on the rest of the front the attack was held up. On the next day, however, a further stretch of the trench was gained and held. A feature of this attack was the chivalry shown by the enemy. When the left of the line was moved forward, some of our wounded were found in a dugout carefully bandaged and provided with food. This is one of the rare occasions in the war that the Germans have displayed a decent feeling towards our men."

Fitz's battalion was withdrawn from the line on 19 November. Casualties over the two days were heavy. The War Diary of the 7th Queens signed by officer commanding, Lt. Col. Kent-Welch, shows 10 killed, 75 wounded and 172 O.R. (other ranks) missing in these encounters on 18/19 November. As the Battle of the Somme fizzled out the maximum allied advance was 7 miles (11km).

Fitz records what conditions were like in the final weeks of that catastrophic battle. "It is almost impossible to describe the suffering we endured in the mud, rain, sleet, fog and cold during this last month of the Somme Battle of 1916. It was simply awful. In some place the mud was so deep that men who sank into it had to be pulled out by others. The front trenches were mere gutters and attempts to deepen them only succeeded in deepening the stagnant pool within. The communication trenches were little better. The constant pounding of heavy artillery fire was almost unbearable in this nightmare chapter of this bitter campaign."

To illustrate an Irishman's loathing of war Fitz told this caustic little tale then going the rounds.

An Irish Sergeant and an English Officer were on the way up to the trenches in daylight to arrange a relief due to take place that night. It was raining heavily and a bitterly cold northwesterly wind was blowing; they were ill-clothed, hungry and tired. As they waded through quagmires of mud in which unburied dead bodies lay in profusion they had from time to time to throw themselves flat in the mud to avoid the effects of exploding shells. They would have sold their souls for a good stiff drink.

"By God, Sergeant," said the English Officer, "this is a most terrible and dreadful war and not a bit to my liking."

"'Tis indeed, Sir," replied the Irish Sergeant, "'Tis a most dreadful war indeed, as you say, Sir.   But," he continued after a short pause, "'tis better than no bloody war at all, Sir."

The 7th Queens spent the next two months in training for further battles ahead which meant that they were out of the line for Christmas 1916.   Life at the rear was rough and ready but it was like paradise compared to the front. The War Diary for Christmas Day notes a parade to Mass and Communion Service at 10.30 which was followed by an address to the troops by the Commanding Officer at 12 noon.   Christmas dinner was served at 12.30.

Fitz's limited knowledge of French, which was far beyond that of any of his Cockney comrades, caused him to be deputed to borrow from the various farmhouses in the neighbourhood some tables, eating utensils and similar articles needed for their Christmas dinner.   A lot of the borrowed items were damaged or wholly destroyed during the festive party and he was left in the embarrassing position of having to break the news to the owners and arrange compensation.

"The difficulties here will be fully appreciated by those who have some knowledge of the Somme peasantry," explained Fitz. "They were not eased by the fact that those simple, good people had always regarded the armed hordes of Britain as invaders, and could not be shaken of the fixed idea that when hostilities ceased we would remain in La Belle France as conquerors. The difficulties were, however, smoothed out with a certain amount of cash and copious quantities of army 'dog' biscuits, which the troops loathed but which made excellent chicken feed."

On 6 January, Fitz and his men were holding a line of shell holes in front of Grandcourt ready to carry out a big offensive when he realised that it was his birthday. He was nineteen years old and a seasoned veteran of a bloody war, carrying the acting rank of Sergeant and commanding Platoon No. 13 of D Company of the 7th Queens. He smiled as he contemplated his birth certificate lying in the safe in the Orderly Room of Ponsomby Barracks at the Curragh Camp and recalled his parents instructions that he must not be sent overseas until he had reached his 19th birthday, the age for active service.

It was back in the line again by mid-January. The weather was icy cold as a severe frost struck. But to Fitz and the other young soldiers it was a pleasant relief from the sticky viscous mud, rain and damp penetrating cold that had previously been their lot. The mud and the damp of the trenches led to many casualties from a condition known as "trench feet" but this very unpleasant complaint soon cleared up as the weather changed to dry and cold and through the nightly rubbing of the feet with whale oil. The cold did cause problems for some of the older soldiers whose breath froze into solid ice on their old-fashioned walrus moustaches. Upon clipping and shaving off their moustaches their upper lips were left vulnerable to dreadful cold sores and this led mostly to them requiring hospital treatment.

Chapter 6

Gallantry in the Field Rewarded

A s the Germans retreated they left behind them every
conceivable obstruction such as mined roads and sniper nests.
In the course of the pursuit many prisoners fell into the hands of
the British. Among those captured by Fitz's unit was a German
soldier found hiding in the village of Miramont after its evacuation
by his comrades. Having surrendered he proved quite useful in
the intelligence he provided. He showed his captors some of the
surprises left behind such as delayed action mines and booby
traps, which were to figure so largely in the German retreat. This
information saved many British casualties.

As the pursuit of the enemy continued Fitz was detailed to
take No. 13 Platoon, D Company on a battle patrol north of Irles
in late February. It was a "draw-fire" party and they advanced in
the open in extended order on the south end of a small village.
Other platoons advanced under cover of a large copse on the left
side of the village and along a sunken road which led up to the
right side of the village. The other two platoons were to remain
concealed until they got the signal from Fitz that all was clear.
Upon reaching the edge of the village Fitz's patrol found a newly

dug trench running along its front. It was unoccupied and no hostilities were encountered. Fitz proposed to push on as instructed. He passed on this message to his runner, Private Hughes, from Belfast, who immediately hopped out of the trench and raced rearwards. The signal was given to the other two platoons to come up on the flanks. But just as soon as these units appeared in the open they were met with merciless machine-gun fire from concealed positions. Fitz and his men were confronted by a large party of German troops who shot from the hip as they rapidly advanced out of the village. He gave the "Rapid Fire" order but it had little effect and seeing themselves greatly outnumbered he ordered his men to make a rush for broken ground to the rear of the trench. Almost all his platoon were lost in the retreat. Fitz and a companion luckily found cover behind a lone large water tank in the middle of open ground, as hails of lead whizzed by their ears and cast little puffs of dust into the air as the bullets struck the earth all around them. They were joined there by Private Hughes who had received a gun shot wound in the shoulder.

As heavy fire continued Fitz was petrified expecting a sudden startling pain at any second as a lump of steel ripped through his flesh. It was a hellish nightmare. They tried to burrow into the ground with their bare hands, tearing and clawing at the earth like madmen with bleeding fingers and broken nails. The hail of fire continued until nightfall and the water tank was riddled with bullet marks as they made good their retreat behind their own lines under the cover of darkness. Fitz and his two friends were much relieved but he was left with a gnawing sadness for the comrades he had left behind and for the many casualties suffered by the other platoons in the action.

The advance continued as the new Hindenburg Line began to define itself. During this advance the ground recaptured was littered with bodies of soldiers killed in the many bloody engagements from 1 July the previous year. The fallen of old battles were now mere skeletons, shrouded in their tunics and battle-order webbing equipment. Their rusted rifles and bayonets lay on the ground beside each set of gruesome remains. There was a critical shortage of manpower by this time as the toll of battle mounted. There were no troops available for burial parties and Fitz joined with other volunteers during their rest periods to give the dead a temporary burial until the detailed burial parties arrived to move the remains to their permanent graves in the war cemeteries. Before the skeletons were gathered and laid in shell holes and lightly covered with clay the identification discs were removed and attached to a rough wooden cross, marking the place of interment.

Fitz later noted the way in which the regular burial squads went about their work and commented about the burial and marking procedure. "Upon arrival at a temporary grave the Corporal-in-Charge gathered up the identity discs and entered the information contained on them in his notebook as the remainder of the squad opened up the grave. A heap of human skeletons was uncovered and made into a separate remains which were placed in small wooden coffins carried on hand carts. To each coffin was secured a tag alleging that it contained the remains of a certain soldier belonging to a certain regiment. All these coffins were separately interred in the war cemeteries in graves marked by a neat cross giving the regimental number, name and regiment of each soldier. The number and location of each grave was conveyed to the next-of-kin by the War Graves Commission although in thousands of cases that particular grave did not contain a single bone of their particular relative who had given his life in this tremendous bloodbath. It was, however, the best that could be done in the circumstances and no doubt offered some consolation to the bereaved."

Back in the line again Fitz received a wound in the right leg. He trudged out of the trenches late that night and he was wounded, wet and weary when he reached the hut occupied by his platoon.

He had a headache and a temperature the following morning on which a long march was planned. It was the unwritten law in the Regiment that those who reported sick on the morning of a long march, or those who fell out of line on the march, were sternly frowned upon. Fitz's leg wound problems were compounded by all the symptoms of trench fever yet he attempted the march and amazingly finished the journey - only to fall flat on his face on the roadway as the battalion arrived at its destination.

A week later he recovered consciousness in an Australian Casualty Clearing Station near Albert where with good food and medical attention and a sturdy constitution he quickly recovered. He was soon on his feet again and set off to rejoin his Battalion. After travelling for about a week by any means available to him he located his unit in the quaint little town of Bethune. The 55th Brigade had been withdrawn from the line again and were resting there. They were being held in readiness to counterattack the Givenchy ridge in the event of an expected onslaught by the Germans. The town lay well within range of the German artillery positions but this did not seem to disturb its residents. For some reason the Germans shelled only the railhead and then usually at night. Fitz and his fellow soldiers came to enjoy being lulled to sleep by the whine of the six and nine inch shells that winged their way over their sleeping quarters in the local workhouse en route to their target. Their night prayers included pleas to the Almighty that none be let fall short.

Fitz noted in his writings too that Bethune boasted of a brothel located in a large building in the centre of town. It did a roaring trade as he related. "It was a common sight to see almost complete battalions of troops - just down from the line - lined up outside the entrance awaiting their turn to enter. Order was maintained by the Military Police, as the citizens strolled by completely unconcerned. Questions were raised in Parliament in an endeavour to place such places out of bounds for the troops, with what result I fail to remember. It was a most interesting sidelight of the war."

The expected German attack on the Givenchy ridge never materialised. The Brigade was entrained for the battle zone once more at Arras for what was to be Fitz's last infantry engagement. After a period of duty in the front and support trenches the Battalion was withdrawn on 30 April for a short break from the fighting in preparation for a major offensive planned for 3 May.

On the way to the rear his company suffered heavy casualties from a direct hit and Fitz himself had a miracle escape. This happened near the village of Heninol. His unit was detailed to load equipment on to limbers that were yoked to mules outside a first aid dressing station located in a rough shelter at the side of the road beside a destroyed railway bridge. The walking wounded were squatting around in groups awaiting medical attention. Towards evening time the enemy began their usual round of shelling of the areas behind the trenches hoping to make a chance strike. Fitz was supervising the loading when he heard the familiar sound of the screaming approach of a six-inch shell. From experience he knew this was going to drop very close to where they were working. He instinctively threw himself flat on the roadway just in time as the explosion rocked the ground around him. He rose unscathed to see the place littered with dead and dying. Some were members of his company. At the end of the limber he saw the gruesome sight of one of his comrades decapitated. When order was restored the remnants of the company made their way to the rear for a brief respite from the carnage.

There was little time to mourn their dead comrades. On the night of 1 May the Brigade was moved again to the front between Cherisy and Fontaines les Croixelles and at 3.45am on 3 May, the order was given to go "over the top". This was part of a concerted attack along the British front, the object of which was to aid the big French advance down the line. Directions became confused in the darkness and the Germans mounted a heavy counterattack forcing the British back into their trenches by mid afternoon. The attack had been a disaster with nothing to show for the fierce morning's fighting and the very heavy losses suffered.

At five o'clock in the afternoon the Fitz's Battalion prepared for a feint attack on the German positions in an attempt to relieve a company cut off but still fighting behind enemy lines. It was then discovered that the artillery had run out of ammunition and were unable to give protective covering fire. The attack was delayed an hour as the Machine-Gun Corps was rushed up to give the cover.

Fitz takes up the story. "Again we were held up about fifty yards from the German front line where the remnants of my Company occupied an advance sap in the German Line. We held this position until darkness fell when we prepared to return to our front line in a series of sectional rushes to avoid the heavy machine-gun fire which was loosed upon us by the ever watchful enemy in the illumination given by the almost constantly bursting Very lights. I led the last section out and in leaping out of the trench the empty bomb bag hanging over my shoulder tripped me and I was tumbled back into the trench. I removed the bag and made my way back alone. I was the last man back into our trenches."

Fitz and his surviving comrades held the line for 24 hours before being relieved. The battalion had gone into the line about 850 strong. At roll-call in the rear area they mustered up twenty one all ranks. The remnants were billeted in one marquee. Fitz had escaped again, one of the few survivors of a disastrous episode. But not without a personal price. To his disgust he later discovered that he had thrown away a tin containing fifty cigarettes in the "empty" bomb bag!

Along with other survivors of the 3 May onslaught the Irishman was recommended for the award of the Military Medal. Fitz never received the medal for the reason, he presumed, that his Company Commander, who was responsible for putting his name forward, was killed in action shortly afterwards. But his gallantry in the field did not go unrewarded. Earlier in the year he had been recommended for his Commission and fresh from the fierce fighting in the front line in early May he was sent forward for an interview with the Brigadier-General.

On arrival at the General's quarters he found a small group of fellow NCOs from different battalions in the Brigade, who had been similarly recommended, lined up for interview. His uniform was still caked in the grime of the battlefield and he felt conscious of his grubby appearance as he surveyed some exceedingly smart looking Company Quarter Master Sergeants in the group, all spick and span in their immaculately clean uniforms never soiled by the mud of the trenches. None of them had experience of leading men into battle and as it turned out this proved their downfall. They were told that their names would come up again for consideration at some time in the future when they could prove that they had gained the necessary experience.

On entering the bell tent Fitz was received by the Brigade Major, an Irishman named MacKeown, who was later killed in World War 11. The Major handed over the file to the Brigadier-General, G.D. Price, an affable old man to the young soldier's eyes, who was also Irish, and who lay in a camp bed recovering from a minor ailment.

To Fitz's amazement the General recognised him instantly. "Aren't you the young rascal who upset my dining table one night on the eve of battle?", he asked with a knowing look. The previous chance meeting had come about when the battalion was moving in line one afternoon in preparation for an attack the following morning. Fitz had been sent up the line in daylight to acquaint himself with the sector of the front to be taken over by his company so that he could lead in the platoons under cover of darkness. The route lay across a sunken road which was entered by a rough flight of steps cut into the steep bank immediately opposite the Brigade Headquarter's Shelter. He had already led in one platoon and was on his way with the next group, unaware that between times the Signal Corps had laid some cable across the path, when he tripped over the wire and stumbled into the shelter landing under the table at which the General and his staff were having supper. He hastily picked himself up and apologised profusely for the intrusion. The grand old man's response was the offer of a glass of wine and Fitz was sent on his way with a message of good luck in his mission. Brigadier-General Price survived the war and was later to command the British troops on the Russian front at Murmansk in 1919 and 1920.

Fitz's interview went better than he could ever possibly have expected. He was asked how he, an Irishman, came to be in a South London Battalion. When asked had he any private means he replied, to a hearty burst of laughter by the General, that it would appear that his family's fortunes had been on a continuous downgrade since the surrender of Limerick in 1691. The two men chatted about the political situation in Ireland. (The Easter Rising of 1916 had been ruthlessly quelled only a few weeks previously and the leaders executed but, while the Brigade commander may have had the up to date news from Ireland, it was unlikely that Fitz was as well informed about events at home). Brigadier-General Price was highly impressed with the young Irishman's battle record and duly approved the recommendation for Commission.

The War Diary of the 7th Queens - 18th Division for June 8th, 1917, records as follows:

"Camp S17 - Control Map 51B
Training carried out yesterday.
Cpl Fitzmaurice (No 22102) proceeds to England today to take up commission.
- No 22029 Private Murtagh goes to 56 F(ield) Ambulance under escort
                   (for self-inflicted wound)".

This was certainly a case of young men going in very different directions. There is a sad touch of irony about the day's entry by the commanding officer. Fitz would have known Private Murtagh, probably very well. Had he, I wonder, his former young comrade in mind when he penned this reflection of life and death at the front while on his journey back to England?

"The acts of courage, self-sacrifice and endurance which one witnessed were beyond belief. Yet ... I had seen men, whose spirits became broken under such soul-searing tests, executed for cowardice, deserting the line or for deliberately wounding themselves to get away from it all. To shoot a man on the spot whose nerve had broken, in order to prevent a complete collapse of morale along the line, was understandable. To subject him to the humiliation and gross indignity of a trial by court martial on a charge carrying the penalty of capital punishment was indecent, inhuman and utterly savage. Under such a system a soldier could win a Victoria Cross for sublime courage and self-sacrifice one day and be shot for cowardice the following day."

Peter Simkins, Senior Historian at the Imperial War Museum in London, checked the records for me and as far as he could ascertain Private Murtagh did not face a firing squad. Only one soldier of the 7th Queen's - Private Thomas Hawkins - was executed during the war - and he was a recurrent offender.

Fitz recalled in later life the huge public outcry to this kangaroo court style justice in the field and how the King's Regulations for the Army were changed as a result. Under the "Suspension Act", which was cynically referred to as "an Act to prevent wastage of troops in the field", the soldier who broke under the terrifying test of battle was still subjected to trial by court martial but the maximum penalty was a period of penal servitude to be served after the war. At it turned out a general amnesty was granted to all so sentenced at the termination of hostilities.

Fitz also penned his definition of courage. "In the test of battle every normal man is not only frightened, he is almost petrified with fear. The greater the imagination the greater the degree of fear suffered. Courage is nothing more than the conquest and suppression of fear, or the development of a degree of will-power which is capable of rising to such supreme heights. It is sustained by a high standard of discipline."

He told of the sad plight of soldiers in the trenches. "In this welter of mud and blood, men went forward unflinchingly at a steady walking pace in the face of withering machine-gun and rifle fire and devastating artillery bombardment, to preserve their liberties, their homes and the institutions of their forefathers. Such moments tested the very soul of the soldier. Never had men set their hearts and minds to anything so desperately earnest. Fervent and frenzied prayers were mingled with hot hurried oaths as they pressed forward all along the battle line leaving columns of dead and dying comrades in their wake. Strong sturdy men were shaken by hysteria and reduced to mumbling weaklings and balanced brains were dulled into vacancy or worse by the dreadful sustained shock of it all. Broken and wearied, the survivors held fast until relieved in the face of the most excruciating bombardments, their spirits stiffened only by a sense of soldierly duty and personal honour which was sufficiently strong to prevail over death itself."

In contrast to his total admiration for the ordinary soldier in wartime he was scathing of the conduct of Chief-of-Staff, General Sir Douglas Haig. "(Meanwhile) at GHQ everything was calm and serene. It was good to know that nothing had happened to upset the constant supply of the Commander-in-Chief's special brand of toilet paper, a matter of the most profound importance in the heat of battle." He added bitterly. "On the conclusion of the war, General Haig was promoted to the rank of Field Marshal, elevated to an Earldom and handed a cash grant of £100,000. In my very humble opinion, founded on my experiences in the holocaust of the Somme, he should have been court-martialled and shot for ignorance, ineptitude and sheer bloody inefficiency. Generals, however, die peacefully in their beds."

Chapter 7

The Royal Flying Corps

B ack in England Fitz took two weeks leave before reporting to the Cadet School at the Regimental depot.   He underwent an intensive four month course at the 20th Officers Training Battalion at Church Crookham, near Aldershot. This was a different world from life at the front but it brought its own pressures.   Fitz and his fellow cadets had to accomplish in four months what the prewar Sandhurst cadet took two years to achieve.

He liked the change and took up the new challenge with gusto. He soon acquired the full knowledge of all the mysteries of Infantry Drill and avidly learned the various subjects and disciplines set down for an aspiring officer. He successfully completed the course and, on passing all his tests, he was commissioned on 28 November 1917 and, as a 2nd Lieutenant, was posted to the 8th Irish Battalion of the King's (Liverpool) Regiment. This was the nearest Fitz ever got to joining an Irish Regiment.

The Irishman was elated when he received his commission parchment signed by His Majesty, King George V, in which he was described as His Majesty's "trusty and beloved" and "in whom he reposed the greatest confidence".   The King's kind words should, he felt, dispel any lingering doubts that existed in the minds of the Sergeant-Majors he had met in his travels regarding the highly important matter of his parentage.   This tickled his fancy.

His term with the King's (Liverpool) Regiment was short-lived. Casualties in the Royal Flying Corps were, by this time, becoming increasingly heavy as a result of the fierce battles being waged in France. The War Office made a special appeal to young officers to come forward for training in this novel art, which was becoming more and more involved in engagements as the war progressed. Despite the glamour attached to its activities and the uniform, the vast majority of young army gentlemen were not in the slightest degree interested in joining the RFC.   They reckoned that their chances of survival were much better on the ground, such was the attrition rate of fighter planes and the high rate of airmen casualties.   Aeroplanes were known to them as "flying coffins". The development of the parachute was blocked on the grounds that such a safety aid might encourage the officer to bale-out rather than continue an offensive combat action when the odds were stacked against him.   Fitz spewed out in his memoirs his contempt for the "bovine wisdom" that prevailed at the War Office but as a soldier he knew little, and cared less, about the callous disregard of the British war mandarins for their flying soldiers.   The chance to become a pilot overcame any fears that existed within him.   It was the break he had longed for since his early teenage days when helping out at Aldritts little garage in the Irish midlands. He had made a number of previous attempts to join the Corps without success.   Now his opportunity had arrived and he embraced it promptly and gratefully.

Fitz's initiation into the Corps took place at its London Headquarters, the one time Cecil Hotel in the Strand, then known as Bolo House, named after the official residence in Cairo of a lovably loony Egyptian Prince. With him was his good friend, a Lancashire officer in the King's Regiment, Jack Arnold. Jack had bad luck written all over him as the nine gold wound stripes on his left tunic sleeve testified. Every one of these had been collected for wounds received in different theatres of action. He was the type in whose company people felt uncomfortable while crossing the street. He hadn't the slightest interest in flying but Fitz prevailed on him to send in an application. Jack took solace from his friend's summing up that as he was so riddled with bullet holes he would never pass the medical examination anyway, and that a few days in London would do him a power of good.

Both had satisfactory interviews and Jack was filled with trepidation that he might after all gain entry to the flying units as they both made their way to the Medical Board's Headquarters at Hamstead for medical examination. A little while after their return to Bolo House one of the Boy Scout messengers handed a chit to each man. Fitz gave a scream of delight at the contents of the note which read, "Passed fit for Pilot". At the same time Jack's face "dropped a foot" as he looked at his note. He had been "Passed fit as Observer".

Fitz was posted to the School of Military Aeronautics at Reading on 3 March 1918, where he underwent an intensive course of ground instruction before being posted to a Flying Training Squadron. Jack was also posted to the School at Reading. Shortly after arrival the friends met at the bar in the Stag's Head Hotel. Jack immediately ordered some stiff drinks. He looked mournful. Fitz tried to comfort him. "Cheer up, Jack! Maybe the war will be over before you complete your course here. Just settle down and take it nice and quietly." Jack then related his inevitable sad story. "I arrived this afternoon and reported for duty. The Adjutant filled in my name on a Training Card, neatly stamped it 'Passed through the School of Military Aeronautics' and handed me my travelling vouchers for the Pool in France tomorrow. Just like a dose of Epsom salts through a ruddy gander. They found out I was a trained Lewis-Gun Officer", he divulged as he produced the Training Card and the travelling vouchers.

Fitz discovered that Jack had made no arrangements for

overnight accommodation and he invited him back to his own lodgings. The following morning Jack departed for France. They never saw each other again but some months later Fitz received a letter from his friend. He was in a German Prisoner-of-War Camp. Predictably he had been shot down on his first trip across the lines and, more predictable still, he had collected yet another wound stripe.

The realisation of the importance of air power meant that it was developed at a rapid rate from the commencement of the war. The aeroplanes that entered the war in 1914 were hard-pressed to achieve 75 mph (120 kph) yet by 1918 it was common for such planes as the Sopwith Camel to achieve speeds in excess of 115 mph (185 kph), at much greater heights and with increased manoeuvrability.

But management of the air war machine was unwieldy and there was a long-standing rivalry between the Admiralty and the War Office. Following an enquiry under the chairmanship of General Jan Christian Smuts, a South African Boer War veteran, it was decided to reorganise the air services. On 1 April 1918 the Royal Flying Corps and the Royal Naval Air Service ceased to exist and were both absorbed into the new and separately administered Royal Air Force. The world's first independent air force had come into being.

The change in administration and in the name of the service, however, had little bearing on the day to day working of a young trainee airman. The Irishman began his practical flying training at Eastbourne Aerodrome on 1 June. He cherished the memory of his first time in the air.

"Never will I forget my first aeroplane ride! Our elementary instruction was given on the Gnome Avro Training Planes and I must admit that they were rather oil-splattered, flimsy looking contraptions. 'All set, my boy?' It was Captain Freddie Mills, my instructor. 'I'm going to give you a little flip in the air to test your air sense.' With my helmet and goggles adjusted and the safety strap around my waist, I nodded to Captain Mills. With a sudden roar the motor leapt into life. The plane trembled and started to roll across the aerodrome. Gripping the side of the cockpit I glanced cautiously towards the ground. It appeared to be slipping away and the buildings assumed an alarming prospective. We were in the air - at last I was flying!"

What an experience! It seemed so fresh and clean at the flying training centre at Eastbourne after the hell of mud and blood of the French battlefields. Thoughts of fighting in the air filled him with a thrilling sense of superiority. But such thoughts became jumbled as the landscape on the ground faded further into oblivion. One moment he could see tiny buildings and winding roads in the distance now all appeared was the horizon and the skyline. He clung more firmly to the fuselage as he noticed the sky beneath him and the fields and buildings above. Captain Mills looped and rolled and spun the little Avro until his terrified passenger lost all sense of what was happening. "What type of superman is required to control an aeroplane," Fitz wondered! He was benumbed with the thought that he would never learn to fly and that his fighting was still to be done in the trenches.

After further dual flights, however, Fitz became more at ease and with about five hours flying time under his belt he was ready to go solo. The order to go alone came in a most unexpected fashion. The Captain had put him through every conceivable manoeuvre before landing the machine close to the aerodrome boundary. He then climbed out leaving the engine ticking over. "You fly like a bloody fool when I'm with you," he said. "Let's see what you can do on your own." Fitz eased the plane away into the wind and out towards the middle of the field. He gave the machine full throttle and shoved the stick slightly forward. The nose began to rise. The oft heard instructions, "Keep your nose down laddie" kept going through his mind and again he eased the stick forward. He was some 1,250 feet up before he allowed himself to realise that he was in the plane on his own. He later reflected on his feelings at that particular moment. "That is an awful feeling - to be all alone in the sky on your first flight. Oh, how you wish that you could only be down on the field again!"

After about 20 hours experience of solo flying he was tested in the handling of the elementary machine by his Flight Commander, Squadron Leader Grange, DSC. He passed all his tests and was permitted to fly the intermediate training machine, the single-seater Sopwith Pup. His first cross-country flight was a hair-raising experience. He was detailed to fly to three aerodromes, effect landings and obtain signatures from the commanding officers of the stations, indicating a safe landing. He was 20 miles out from one of the aerodromes flying at about three thousand feet when his engine first growled and then stopped. It was heavily wooded country but he picked out a spot for landing and in a good approach he felt relieved to have evaded a line of telegraph wires that he hadn't observed in the distance. He was beginning to congratulate himself when suddenly his luck almost ran out. He discovered that he was not only attempting to land on a steep hill but also downwind. He grounded at terrific speed and careered through a fence of wooden palings which neatly sheared off the undercarriage. The plane and himself continued their forward momentum until the nose of the machine became wedged between two trees in a fir copse and they came to an abrupt stop. The plane had landed adjacent to a Canadian Convalescent Camp and Fitz was surprised to see two Red Cross men hurrying to rescue him as he clambered from the wreckage. He was bruised and shaken but did not require hospitalisation. He phoned his superiors and awaited assistance. Later that evening one of the instructors arrived from the training school. Believe it or not he also crashed while landing which was an ill wind that blew some good Fitz's way because the instructor's mishap in a similar situation eased the Irishman's blushes and the need for protracted explanations.

After about 15 hours solo flying in the Sopwith Pup, Fitz was ready to commence training on his service aeroplane, the Sopwith Camel. It had a very bad reputation in the Corps. Fitz compared it to a woman of easy virtue. "It behaved like a gorgeously attractive, oversexed Jezebel in whom little trust or confidence could be placed and called for silken, steel-like hands to keep it under perfect control. My hands, the inheritance of birth, coupled with my cavalry training and experience and the good advice given me by that dear friend of my youth, old Tom, the poacher, stood me in good stead. The machine simply wallowed in vice, being sensitive on the fore and aft control, heavy on the ailerons, considerably affected by the torque effect of the rotary engine, and more stable on its back than when in the normal flying position. Yes, a veritable Jezebel, treacherous, though capable of giving exquisite pleasure to those who had it under control!"

Fitz was nervous as he prepared for his first flight in the Camel. He knew it was an extremely difficult machine to fly. Fatal accidents in training on the Camel were tremendously heavy. Fitz remembered in one day in his training station seven bodies lay in the mortuary after crashes. He was on early morning duty and climbed into the cockpit at four o'clock in the morning more asleep than awake as his instructor Captain Knight, affectionately known as "Noisy Knight", began to explain all the controls, instruments

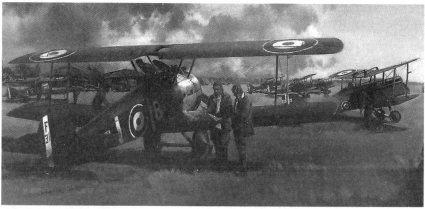

The Sopwith Camel, "an over-sexed Jezebel".

and peculiarities of the machine.   Next the chocks were waved clear and soon the plane was in the air. Having reached a ceiling of approximately 4,000 feet he tried some gentle turns before going on to try to execute some stunts. He tried the simplest one first, the loop. He carried out what appeared to him to be a loop and a half and having difficulty with the sensitive controls he found himself on his back hanging in his belt and holding on tightly to the control column.   He realised he was in an inverted spin.   It was a dreadful moment!   He thought his number was up and that he was about to meet the same fate as so many Camel pilots before. He tried various things with the controls and eventually found himself in an ordinary spin, but had lost 3,000 feet in the meanwhile.   He succeeded in bringing the machine to a level keel and was beginning to feel somewhat happier when he went into another spin in the opposite direction. He managed to right the machine again and with extreme caution he glided down and effected a satisfactory landing.   After taxiing over to the hangar he got out of the cockpit smiling with pride.   His instructor congratulated him on his performance, particularly on the stunts he had carried out.   Fitz did not attempt to disillusion him!.

The Irishman, with more experience flying the machine, came to like it very much and he had his sights set on getting back into the war action, this time in a very different capacity than before. A freak happening delayed his return.   It was late summer in 1918 and the Americans were by now heavily involved in the war with Britain their main base.   An American medical officer was making a study of the effect that flying has on the human system and Fitz was chosen as one of his research specimens, because of the mixed service and medical history revealed on his service record.   He was ordered to report for a medical examination.   Feeling in tip top shape and eagerly awaiting his call up for aerial combat he treated this diversion very lightly.   But the American officer reported a fault in his heart action and he was ordered to the Central Medical Board at Hamstead Heath in

London.   Here he was checked by two heart specialists who informed him that he was suffering from valvular disease of the heart.   He was marked unfit for active service abroad for six months. It was soul destroying news. His great ambition in life to become a fighter pilot had been thwarted.

Fitz appealed the decision but it was to no avail. He next tried the sympathy angle. If he was barred from being a pilot he would lose his flying pay which amounted to the substantial sum of eight shillings a day. This worked, at least partially, and he was allowed to continue as an airman but he could not fly at heights above 3,000 feet. "Cheer up," said one of the officers sympathetic to his appeal. "It might have been worse. It's only V.D.H.! What if it were V.D.? Now that wouldn't be so hot, would it?" He returned to his unit and was appointed a flying instructor.

London was like heaven on earth for a young officer wearing RFC pilot's wings. Fitz spent most of his leave time there. He and his young fellow officers frequented the leading West End hotels where glamorous young women flocked around them intoxicated by the alluring aura of their attractive uniforms. There was a wildly frolicsome social round and an air of carefree abandon. Fitz enjoyed it all thoroughly. "I had long since learned the art of living for the day as the prospects of tomorrow ever coming were exceedingly slender. 'Wine, women and song' was the order of the day on those gay periods of leave. There was a war on and we were very young."   He reflected later that under such conditions they as youngsters matured rapidly "without losing the gay, youthful touch which I am happy to say has never deserted me and which I have always found to be a considerable asset for which I am truly grateful".

Quickly tiring of his role as a flying instructor he managed to get a posting to the No.1 School of Fighting and Aerial Gunnery at Marske, near Middlesbrough. His Officer's Record of Service shows the date of that posting as 28 October 1918. He had been promoted to the rank of Lieutenant exactly one calendar month previously. On reporting at Marske he was detailed to a squadron of Super-Salamander scouts at nearby Redcar which was being formed for service in France. Heavy losses were being sustained by the Camel Squadrons on low flying operations, mostly ground strafing, against the enemy. The Super-Salamanders had been designed for this type of operation. It carried armoured plating underneath and around the pilot's seat as well as below the engine and petrol tanks to such an extent that it was grossly overloaded. Fitz classed it as a "perfect horror". He was posted to sail to France on 11 November. Returning to camp from a spell of leave on the morning of that fateful day he was greeted by the shouts of a near hysterical rating yelling, "The war's over, the war's over". The Armistice had been signed that morning. The American medical officer who had accidentally stalled Fitz's flying career was probably responsible for him not becoming a fighter pilot. He was also probably responsible for saving his life.

The next morning Fitz was, predictably, back in London. "London was an absolute bedlam. Traffic was completely disrupted and the most well-behaved, boisterous, good-natured festivities continued without let-up for over a week. Progress through the square mile of Mayfair was almost impossible. The police, being completely helpless, simply joined in. Not one of them was adorned with a helmet, as that portion of their attire had long since been seized as souvenirs. People everywhere were delirious with delight at the news that this long drawn-out nightmare had at last reached a conclusion."

Fitz was posted back to his original unit at Eastbourne where he impatiently awaited a decision in regard to his future. There were two possibilities facing him. One was to take part in the expedition to Archangel in Russia. The other was to be selected for a course in aeronautics. Happily for Fitz he procured the less risky assignment and was transferred to the Admiralty Compass Observatory at Dachet, near Windsor, for a special course in Aerial Navigation.

Chapter 8

Marriage

While training at Eastbourne Fitz met and fell in love with a petite noncommissioned officer in the Women's Royal Air Force (WRAF). He had experienced the good life and met many attractive young women but it was Violet Clarke who captured his heart. Affectionately known as Bill she was dark and beautiful and Fitz found her irresistible.

Commissioned officers in the RAF were forbidden by its disciplinary code to associate with, or to be seen in public with, noncommissioned members of the WRAF. Even in romance Fitz lived dangerously. The complexities of their romance were not helped by the two starry-eyed lovers being stationed at the same aerodrome. Their meetings were all the more risky on account of this because both were well known at the base and it was difficult to carry on the relationship without the affair being brought to the attention of one of his senior officers. If that happened Fitz knew it could have disastrous consequences on his career in the RAF.

The difficulties presented by the RAF's strict code, rather than dampening the ardour, enhanced the love they had for each other.

They met clandestinely and the surreptitious element of their relationship added extra spice to the romance. Their love for each other continued to blossom and Fitz and Bill were married in secret on his 21st birthday, 6 January, 1919. They did not dare to let it be generally known that they were man and wife for some time after the event.

Fitz and Violet on their Wedding Day.

Ten years later Fitz was still very much in love with Bill. He wrote after his famous Atlantic flight in 1928: "Bill ..... has been the best of pals since we have been together. Her experiences in the war have developed in her that high sense of fortitude which is such a necessary qualification for a soldier's wife. She has always had the greatest confidence in my ability or luck to succeed in the face of the greatest difficulties and dangers. She has been my inspiration and is responsible to a great extent for the successes of the many adventures which I have undertaken." But the flight changed everything and within a short time the marriage began to crumble ending in a divorce in 1930.

When the war was over the RAF shrank almost overnight. Thousands of men were demobilised and their aeroplanes scrapped. The massive wartime strength of 188 operational squadrons, made up of nearly 300,000 officers and men together with over 22,000 aircraft, was reduced to a mere 33 squadrons in the first year following the war.

Fitz loved flying and he saw his future still with the RAF. Having completed the special navigation course at Datchet and passed his examinations he was posted to No. 110 Squadron in the capacity of Squadron Navigation Officer. The unit was engaged in experimental air mail deliveries between Folkestone in Kent and Cologne on the Rhine. The Irishman was detailed to a flight and given the job of mail pilot.

The mails arrived overnight from London and were delivered to a sergeant of the Royal Engineers' section of the Army Post Office. They were then loaded on to De Havilland 9's powered by Siddeley Puma Stationary engines which allowed up to five hours' range. The navigation equipment was basic, consisting of simple compass, a bubble inclinometer, an altimeter and an air speed indicator. The development of blind flying instruments and useful radio contact was still in the future.

Fitz got off to a bad start in his new job. On his first flight to Cologne he ran into severe difficulties. Arriving over Brussels he discovered he had come to the end of the section of map he carried and while trying to get the next section out of the map case it got caught in the slipstream of the propeller and disappeared over the side. He now had no map and had never flown the route before. As leader of a formation of three planes he circled around several times hoping one of the other machines would take the cue and show the way. His signal was not understood, however, and the other two pilots followed him round and round. Fitz felt there was only one course of action open to him. He decided to proceed in an easterly direction until they sighted the Rhine and then try to locate themselves.

The formation proceeded but soon it ran into heavy rain, low clouds and a strong wind. They were in the air four hours from the time of departure and should by now have struck the Rhine, Fitz reckoned. A heavy cloud bank obscured his vision and when he had broken cloud he could not recognise any prominent landmark by which he could fix their position. He decided to make a landing in a field and check their position with locals.

One of his companion pilots had made a forced landing earlier but the other one had followed him all the way. They landed in a field of corn ready for cutting. Some locals came forward and after much difficulty they managed to pinpoint their position. They had landed near the village of Warstein and over the Neutral Zone. This was a serious blunder as both pilots were wearing military uniform and flying military planes. They made frenzied attempts to get airborne again. Fitz's companion was soon back in the air but he himself failed in the attempt and with the water in the radiator boiling over and the propeller badly damaged due to contact with the corn he had no option but to shut off the engine and await developments.

In a short while he found himself surrounded by angry farming folk carrying sticks and billhooks and looking as if they meant business. The only weapon Fitz had on board was a Very light signal pistol which he discharged into the air. To his great relief two policemen arrived on the scene on bicycles and defused the situation. Fitz pointed out to the senior police officer that he was a King's messenger and was carrying a card calling on the authorities, civil and military, in the event of a forced landing to render all the aid needed to ensure the safe delivery of the mail by surface transport. The policemen were very courteous. One accompanied him and the mails to the police station while the other stood guard by the aeroplane.

He was allowed to stop overnight at the local hotel under guard. The following day a young German officer and an escort of two soldiers arrived and, taking custody of Fitz and the mail bags, they proceeded by rail to the garrison town of Soest. That night he slept in a room with its windows barred and the key turned in the door.

The following day he was interrogated by the Garrison Commander, who politely informed him that he would have to detain him until instructions were received from the War Office in Berlin. Fitz immediately realised that he was at the centre of an international incident. The Irishman's worst fears were realised.

The nature of his custody was relaxed, though, and he was allowed to go to the public baths each day accompanied by two young German officers. A few days later an Air Force breakdown party arrived at the barracks in a Crossley Tender carrying a white flag. The officer-in-charge was allowed to visit Fitz and told him that his machine had been repaired, refuelled and ready for takeoff. Fitz handed over the mails and was pleasantly surprised to be left with a hefty supply of English cigarettes, which he shared with his captors.

As he sat in his room one night he was startled to hear the sentry on guard singing in perfect English "It's a long way to Tipperary" as he continued to pound his beat. Fitz opened the window and noticed the black and white ribbon of the Iron Cross decorating his tunic buttonholes. In conversation he found out that the soldier had been working as a boy clerk in a shipping office in Liverpool before the outbreak of war. His mother was English and married to a German reservist who had been recalled to service before the war commenced. Because he was not of military age he had been deported to Germany with his mother and young brothers and sisters. On arrival he was conscripted into the German army and won his Iron Cross on the Somme. Fitz and the sentry found they had much in common and they exchanged stories of their upbringing and war experiences during these days of confinement on German soil.

After three weeks detention Fitz finally got word of his immediate release and spent the night in a hotel in Soest. He departed the following morning for Warstein and having being provided with a passport he proceeded to the field where his machine, now repaired, awaited his arrival and from where he completed the final leg of his eventful first flight to Cologne. It was there that he learned the nature of the incident he had inadvertently provoked. The Germans had sought to exchange Fitz for some Germans detained by the Allies but this was refused. Fitz remained in custody all the while the issue was being debated.

For a short time he had become a figure of some importance on the international horizon. He had the distinction of being a prisoner of peace. It was an uncomfortable experience not knowing what was to become of him but he emerged with a better understanding and appreciation of the German people, whom he found to be courteous and considerate and much different from the picture painted of them by the British during the war.

Helping to develop an airmail service provided good experience for Fitz so early in his flying career. The object of the exercise was to see if it was a commercially viable proposition in terms of costs and usefulness. It gave the young Irishman the opportunity of flying many different types of aircraft under every kind of weather conditions. His ability and versatility as a flyer was noted by his senior officers and he was chosen to undertake the first experimental night air mail flight ever carried out in Europe. The route selected was from Folkestone to Cologne, one with which Fitz was now quite familiar. The machine used was the DeHavilland 10A Number 551, powered by two 400 hp Liberty engines. He was chosen as Second Pilot and Navigator with Captain Barrett as Chief Pilot and 2nd Lieutenant Oliver as Observer.

In early May two senior officers arrived at Hawkings from the Air Ministry carrying one small token bag of air mail, which was the total load. The DH 10 took off at

RAF Lieut. James Fitzmaurice 1919.

10.15pm on 14 May with a dozen parachute flares on board which were electrically fired through a special tube in the floor of the aircraft in the event of a forced landing - a very necessary aid in those days of frequent engine failure.   The first sign of trouble, a knocking noise in the starboard engine, became evident soon after takeoff as the craft set out over the Channel.   But the revolution counter, oil pressure gauge and radiator gauge were registering normal and the Captain decided to continue.   About 100 miles from the River Rhine they ran into very bad weather and relying on a compass course they eventually got sight of the river but there were no sign of the lights of Cologne or Dusseldorf. It was a case of a toss-up whether to turn right or left and toss-up they did.   It turned up heads and they wheeled right.   Soon below them was Cologne and the paraffin flare path laid out at Bickendorf Aerodrome guided them to a safe landing at 1.20am, just over three hours after their takeoff.

As the trio retired to a well-earned rest in a billet at the aerodrome, tests began on the cause of the knocking noise in the engine that had started alarm bells ringing early in the flight.   The following day they found out the cause, which horrified them.   A metal strap over the top of the radiator had come loose and was cutting through the bottom end of the wooden propeller blade, close to the boss, on each rotation of the propeller.   More than a quarter of the propeller had been cut through and Fitz reckoned that it was his ever vigilant guardian angel that had kept it from disintegrating.   It was more than the luck of the toss that saw them through.   Fitz converted the propeller boss into a clock base as a souvenir of their narrow escape.

As the three airmen were contemplating their lucky escapade of the night before and getting the aircraft ready for the return journey they were informed that Air Vice-Marshal Sir John Salmond, Officer Commanding the Air Force on the Rhine, required their presence at his headquarters at 2pm.   They had come dressed in the clothing of working pilots and had not brought their officers uniforms. The British officers' dress code was (and no doubt still is) very strict, all the more so when on duty overseas. Fitz recalled later the trepidation felt by him on that day as he awaited the meeting with Sir John. To make matters worse he got a couple of tellings-off because of his unkempt look from other senior officers he encountered on the way to meeting the Air Vice-Marshal. But Sir John was more interested in news of the flight than in the regalia they wore. The airmen related to him the propeller incident and he warmly congratulated them on their good fortune. He told them they would receive his personal commendation in his report, shook hands again and wished them good luck in the future.

Before leaving the airmen were told of plans afoot for carrying out Empire-linking experimental flights during the year ahead commencing with a flight from London to the Cape of Good Hope via Cairo. Sir John told them that flights would commence as soon as the necessary aerodromes were put in place on the route comprising largely of desert and jungle. The proposed flight never materialised.

Fitz carried on a daily mail run to and from Cologne and once he managed to complete two round trips between Folkestone and the German city in the one day. These were happy days with the No. 120 Squadron. The Commanding Officer, Major Stanley Clarke, allowed them operate as a Communications Squadron and his efficient running of the service meant that there were always sufficient planes and manpower to operate the service yet the timetable enabled the airmen to take good periods of leave. Fitz spent much of his free time on the continent. He made regular trips to the Aeroplane Acceptance Park at Marquese in France, where aircraft which had become superfluous after the war were sent for disposal, or as it was officially termed "reduced to produce".

He knew the officer commanding the Park and had access to various makes of aircraft he had never previously flown. On one leave break he spent ten days there flying a whole series of different machines including the Handley Page 0/400 Bomber.   While there he noticed gangs of mechanics helped by German prisoners-of-war taking brand new aeroplanes out of crates, removing all instruments, tanks and fittings and setting the remainder, consisting mostly of wood and fabric, alight.   This seemed a woeful waste to the precocious young airman.   He looked around the base and found a brand new Camel which he arranged with the chief fitter to fuel and prepare for flight. He flew the plane to Hawkings Aerodrome where he kept it for his own personal use for some time.

Fitz's Commanding Officer was given an S.E.5 aircraft for his personal use but as he was not interested in it, Fitz and a fellow officer, Wilcockson, who was with Imperial Airways from its beginnings and was later a Flying Superintendent with B.O.A.C., had it to themselves.   Soon Wilcockson tired of it and this meant Fitz had it all to himself.   When the day's work was done he would fly it to his home at Eastbourne and was back in time for work the following morning. He reckoned himself that this made him the first aerial commuter in the world's history.

By August the experimental air mail service came to an end and the Squadron was disbanded.   This took place at Lympne Aerodrome and it was marked by a huge week long breaking-up party at Lympne Castle.

Fitz was appointed to the command of the 6th Wing Working Party of the RAF based at Dover and during the next three months he was assigned the task of removing all technical and quartermasters' stores from six aerodromes along the southeast coast from Ramsgate to Eastbourne all of which had been evacuated.   Most of these were large training stations during the war and were crammed with stores, valued at millions of pounds. Fitz was informed that during the war there had been frequent changes in commanding officers, quartermasters and technical officers and this had led to large-scale deficiencies of stock at almost all the bases throughout the country.

Here was the makings of a major public scandal and it was a very sensitive assignment for a young officer. But Fitz took on the task with relish. He took command of about 200 men and 50 of the latest type of Leyland lorries, fitted with various kinds of self-loading equipment. He was detailed to write off the deficiencies and balance the books at the six bases The main emphasis in his terms of reference was on discretion. Conscience was to play second fiddle to the public good, he was told.

Eastbourne, his old station, was the first one to be assessed. The arrival of Fitz's convoy was greeted with apprehension by the senior officers and the quartermaster. But their anxieties were quickly appeased by Fitz who told them he was aware that the deficiencies in the stock were due to circumstances outside their control and that he was detailed to put matters right. An example of the mystery losses at Eastbourne was in regards to the white double naval blankets of the high quality all-wool variety. These were valued at approximately thirty shillings each and there were 2,000 unaccounted for. The remaining blankets were gathered and a small quantity of these were placed in a large wooden hut, which was destroyed in a "mysterious" fire. A court of enquiry found the cause of the fire unknown and wrote off the total number of items missing from stock. This was a typical way of balancing the books.

While engaged in this auditing work Fitz came across many crooked individuals and many sordid schemes. The looseness in the supervision of the stores left it relatively easy for those with access to materials to siphon off stock for private sale. It was a booming business and the eyes of a young officer, heretofore innocent to the existence of such activity, were well and truly opened to reality. He was shocked by the propositions and bribes offered to him by shady individuals and he steered clear of compromising his integrity with such a carry-on.

On occasions even those he helped off a hook were later seen to openly exploit the situation. At one station Fitz met an officer in charge of technical stores who was in tears because of the discrepancies at his stores. His family obligations weighed heavily on him and a lack of private means added to his woes. Fitz helped get him out of the mess in which he was entrenched. He met the same officer a year later, entering the driveway of a fashionable hotel, driving a Rolls Royce containing his wife and a party of friends in full evening dress. The officer invited Fitz to join them for a drink and as he sipped his champagne the Irishman could not but ponder on the amazing change of fortune for the former down and out. But such matters were not his affair and Fitz decided it was best to do the job to which he had been assigned and not dabble into matters which should be the concern of others.

During these months he gained much experience in stores management, control of a road fleet, staff management and an insight into the frailty of human nature. He also got in some valuable flying experience. The Sopwith Camel he salvaged from the breaking-up field at Marquese came in very handy for him now. As the mop-up operation moved from one station to the next a skeleton party was left at each base to supervise the remaining stores intended for local disposal at a later date. The money for the pay of the whole detachment was drawn on Friday mornings at whatever station was being cleared by the main body of the command. Having paid wages to the staff there Fitz put the rest of the money into small bags, one for each of the other stations scattered along the southeast coast. He used the Camel for transport to the other aerodromes where a pay parade took place on the wing of the aircraft as the engine ticked over. "Here comes Santa Claus" was the cry of the troops as he circled over the aerodromes.

Fitz closed down the last of the stations on his agenda, the Balloon Base and School of Aerial Gunnery at Hyde, and this brought his assignment to a successful conclusion. He decided it was time to part company with his trusty Camel. The machine could not be taken on charge at any of the bases at which he had operated with the working party and it was now a liability. He knew it would not be possible for him to come up with plausible answers to questions about its acquisition and use. There was only one course open to him. He must burn the machine and bury the remains, in itself not a simple operation if its existence was not to be revealed. The base at Hyde was located on the shingle on the seafront and provided what seemed the perfect spot for such a burial. The area selected for the disposal was quite small and completely surrounded by houses and a gasworks - not an ideal landing spot for the Camel. The landing was successfully completed, however, and a party of men were on hand to catch the wing tips on touchdown. The machine was "reduced to produce" and lowered into its shingly grave.

The country was now in the grip of a railway strike and orders were given to remain on stand-by, with all vehicles fuelled and

At Lympne Aerodrome 1919.

ready to roll at a moment's notice. All troops were confined to camp. One night at midnight Fitz received orders to report to Lympne Aerodrome with all his personnel and trucks. He shepherded the convoy on his motorcycle and carried his .450 revolver in a holster under his trenchcoat. On arrival he reported to the Station Commander, Squadron Leader "Jock" McCray, who was busily engaged in arranging the delivery of emergency milk supplies to London. The regular supplies had been halted due to the strike. Fitz was immediately plunged into dire trouble. The Squadron Leader observed the bulge of the revolver under his trench coat.

"By whose authority are you carrying firearms?", demanded the senior officer in his heavily pronounced Scottish accent.

"On my own authority, Sir," Fitz replied. "I did not relish the idea of being held to ransom by strike mobs and watch my convoy burned."

"Are you aware of the provisions attending the impositions of the Riot Act?", the Squadron Leader asked menacingly. After a brief moment of reflective silence he continued. "'Tis young pups like you, by your blasted foolhardiness, who'd plunge England into a bloody civil war", he bellowed.

Fitz pondered silently that maybe it was a pity that someone hadn't done so. It might have rejuvenated a country that had just won the bloodiest war in history and was now, a year later, in the process of rapid degeneration and chaos. But on reflection he understood the reasoning behind the imperial dressing-down he had received from Squadron Leader McCray. He was not, after all, an Englishman, but this sharp telling off made him realise that the English were a law-abiding people with a high sense of civic responsibility. It gave him much food for thought.

He handed over his personnel and trucks to the army service Corps and the life of the 6th Wing Working Party came to an end. It was time to test the water in civilian life. He got all his clearances and was demobilised.

Chapter 9

Joins the Irish Army Air Corps

B ack as a civilian Fitz found himself wandering around London looking for a job.   He soon discovered that there was no employer out there anxiously waiting for the moment of his demobilisation to offer him a position.   Thousands of other ex-officers were roaming the streets of the capital for over a year without success.   But this did not shake the Irishman's belief in himself.   He assessed his assets.   He was 22 years old, had an excellent standard of health, an aircraft pilot's licence and navigator's ticket, a motorcycle, that gave him mobility, a Corona portable typewriter, a very small amount of capital, his native wit and an abiding confidence in his ability to make good in the big wide world.

With the ending of the war the aircraft industry fell stagnant and the manufacturing companies had a big struggle on their hands to survive in the years that followed.   Fitz likened the usefulness of his pilot's and navigator's licences to that of a man's nipples in a nursery.   As he searched for a job he found recreational refuge in the Royal Aero Club, then located in Clifford Street.   Here he was in the company of wartime pals and the spirit of the old RFC days prevailed. The gloom and doom that had descended on the country was not allowed entry through the hallowed portals of the Aero Club where amusement often gave way to sheer frivolity in the light-hearted nature of the club.   Here he traded humour and inoffensive pranks with his deeply revered friends who included, Captain C.D. Barnard, better known as "Charlie Barley", Leslie Hamilton, later lost on an attempted east-west Atlantic flight on the *St. Raphael*, "Cod" Foster, later killed in an automobile accident in Iraq, Wallie Hope, later three times winner of the King's Air Cup Race and Dudley Watt, later shot down and killed in action in World War 11.

Another close friend was Sidney St. Barbe, who became an expert sky-writer. He was better known among his circle of friends though as a practical joker.   This attribute got him into trouble with the Department of Civil Aviation.   One day he landed at Lympne Aerodrome in his S.E. 5A single seater fighter, which he used for skywriting, and was presented with an Air Ministry form for the collection of a landing fee of seven shillings and sixpence. Sidney, who did not take the request seriously, took out his pen and simply wrote an offensive word across the face of the form. He was reported by the Sergeant Major in charge of the aerodrome to the Air Ministry at Whitehall. In due course Sidney received a very curt letter from a senior official of the Department informing him that unless he immediately wrote a suitable apology to the Secretary of State for the use of the objectionable word and paid the landing fee his pilot's licence would be withdrawn.   Sidney swiftly responded.   On a large sheet of drawing paper he wrote in the top left-hand corner in minute characters with his etching pen and with the aid of a magnifying glass the following:

"To: The Secretary of State for Air,
Department of Civil Aviation,
Gwyder House,
London.

Sir,
I have the honour to enclose my cheque for 7/6p and to
apologise for the use, on Air Ministry Form No... of the objectionable
word"

Again in the minutest characters in the bottom right-hand corner
he wrote:

"I have the honour to be, Sir,
Your obedient servant,
Sidney St. Barbe."

Then using a rubber pen he wrote in great block capitals the
objectionable word which had originally caused offence across
the whole face of the drawing paper. He attached his cheque for
7s 6d (38p), rolled up the drawing paper, addressed it neatly, tied
it up with a voluminous length of red ribbon and sent a pageboy
off to deliver it.

The official concerned was predictably highly indignant at this
latest affront and sparks began to fly. Sidney was instructed by
telephone to report to Gwyder House and was informed there
that his pilot's licence had been revoked. It was obvious to him
now that officials in the Civil Aviation Department did not share
his idea of a joke. The prank did not seem as funny in the sedate
corridors of Gwyder House as it had in the more salubrious
environs of the Royal Aero Club.   But his sense of humour
remained indefatigable as he tried to extricate himself from the
mess. He explained that he had gone to great pains to comply
with the original request. He pointed to the script at the corners
of the sheet and apologised for the habit of writing so minutely
due, he said, to his endeavours to write the Lord's Prayer on a
pinhead.   Sidney's comic side finally won the day at the Air
Ministry and that sheet of drawing paper still occupies an honoured

place in the archives of Civil Aviation, a souvenir from the early days of aviation and the colourful individuals who peopled that world.

After some searching Fitz acquired a job selling insurance with the North British and Mercantile Insurance Company.

"I did extraordinarily well in this somewhat strange world and made many friends amongst the tall-hatted, morning coated brigade who were not less than twice my age, led a boring life and earned about a quarter of my income," he recalled.

As he roamed the city streets and country lanes on his motorcycle in search of new business he felt the sight and the sound of aircraft passing overhead calling him back to a flying career. After about eighteen months of successes and failures in the world of business he was back in the cockpit. The British Prime Minister, Lloyd George, had a coal strike on his hands and trouble was also brewing on the international front. He decided to mobilise the Reserves.

Fitz got the call-up and reported to Hornchurch Aerodrome on the Isle of Sheppy. He felt good to be back again in the atmosphere of an aerodrome and to meet many wartime friends in the Officers' Mess. He was posted to his old aerodrome at Hawkings near Folkestone, where he was attached to No. 25 Fighter Squadron then equipped with Sopwith Snipe single-seater fighters.

The No. 25 Squadron was in preparation for the first Royal Air Force Pageant at Hendon Aerodrome in 1921. The unit retained its top acrobatic status right up to the outbreak of WW2, when the Pageants were terminated. The display was for permanent officers only but by chance Fitz found his name on the list which appeared in the Squadron Daily Orders. After giving a satisfactory display he was one of those chosen to take part in the Pageant. Fitz had not seen the inside of an aeroplane for well over a year and he felt chuffed at being selected to take part.

Having brought the matter to the notice of his Commanding

King George V and Queen Mary at the Hendon Pageant, 2 July 1921.

Officer, Sir Norman R.A.D. Leslie, he was persuaded to accept a Short Service Commission for four to six years. He was again posted to No. 25 Fighter Squadron and continued his duties with the unit until August of 1921 when, in the middle of the Trooping Season, he was posted to India and given 48 hours notice to catch the *SS. Princess* sailing from Southampton to Bombay.

This posting came as a great shock to Fitz. He was not long married and his wife, Bill, had given birth to their daughter, Patricia, a mere three months previously. He had many domestic financial commitments and felt the notice was too short to sort out his affairs. He appealed to Sir Norman who tried to have the order rescinded. He was ordered to report immediately in person to the Director of Personnel at the Air Ministry, Admiral Lambert. The Admiral was far from impressed with the request. He told Fitz that he'd catch the *SS. Princess* sailing for India or "be clapped in irons".

"If you tender the resignation of your Commission I'll see that you face a court martial. Get out!", boomed the Lord High Admiral.

Fitz wrote out his resignation and requested to be allowed to remain on indefinite leave pending the decision of the Air Council. He returned to London. In the course of time his resignation was accepted and once more his flying career had come to a sudden end.

His focus now turned to Ireland. The country had been in a very unsettled state for some years. Although there was little public sympathy for the republican Rising in Dublin in 1916, the manner of its crushing and the execution of the rebel leaders caused widespread revulsion. Support for independence gained a new momentum as a result, and under the military leadership of Michael Collins the freedom fighters waged a guerilla warfare against the British forces scoring some spectacular successes. In 1920 the British government reinforced the Irish police with ex-soldiers, known as Black and Tans, wearing a mixture of police and army uniform, and later with former officers known as Auxiliaries. These were not as well disciplined as the regular army and were responsible for many atrocities which were responded to in kind.

The British Prime Minister, David Lloyd George, and his government were prepared for compromise. A new Government of Ireland Act provided for a measure of home rule exercised by two parliaments. In the "Southern Ireland" election of 1918 Sinn Fein, under Eamon de Valera, swept the decks winning all but four seats but the party refused to take their seats in a new Dublin Parliament. Lloyd George offered de Valera negotiations on the future of Ireland and a truce was called on 11 July 1921.

De Valera was elected president of the second Dáil Éireann (Irish Parliament) in August and thereafter the Irish negotiating team was led by Arthur Griffith with Michael Collins, "the Big Fella", also on the team. The negotiations in London dragged on until December, when a treaty was agreed under the threat of "immediate and terrible war" from Lloyd George. The Treaty provided for an Irish Free State with dominion status and for six counties of the North to remain within the United Kingdom. It also provided for an oath of allegiance to the crown. The Dáil in January 1922 approved the Treaty by sixty-four votes to fifty-seven but de Valera refused to accept the terms.

In April 1922 anti-Treaty Irregulars under Rory O'Connor, the engineer commander of Dublin's IRA Brigade, in a blatant act of defiance against the pro-Treatyites, occupied the Four Courts. In June, after negotiations to end the standoff failed, Army Chief-of-Staff, Michael Collins, decided to go on the offensive and dislodge the rebels by force. The Civil War had begun. This time it was Irishman fighting Irishman, brother fighting brother and father fighting son.

Fitz closely studied the course of events from London. He wrote later that the Civil War "proved conclusively to the outside world that Ireland ... was God's own country populated by the devil's own people". Chief of the "devil's own people" in Fitz's eye was de Valera whom he termed "that most uncolourful personality ... a grimly dour type of gentleman who has brought nothing but grief, anguish, pain and a poverty stricken condition of life to the people of the country of his adoption".

Fitz now felt his country needed him. He returned to Dublin with his wife and baby daughter. On returning he noted, "I found my native country in a lamentable state of chaos. The newly created National Army was organised by ex-British Army Irish Officers and NCOs. Able-bodied men who were believed to be loyal to the Provisional Government were put into uniforms without even a medical examination or the formula of correct attestation under an oath of allegiance, and thrown into action against the irregular forces who occupied most of the country outside Dublin."

If confusion reigned supreme in the infant state there was no confusion in the mind of the returning former RAF officer which side he would take. He stood consistent to his beliefs in democracy. He held Michael Collins in high esteem. He also had high regard for "dear great-hearted" Arthur Griffith, now

President of the Provisional Government, Kevin O'Higgins, controversial Minister for Justice, whose family like Fitz's, lived in the Queen's County (now Laois) as well as "that chivalrous and gallant fighter", Sean McKeon, nicknamed the Blacksmith of Ballinalee. He admired Collins for his fearlessness, his inventiveness and his charismatic personality.

Collins had been the inspired though ruthless leader in the guerilla campaign that forced compromise against all the odds from London.   Yet now he was, as Irish Army Commander-in-Chief, the man responsible for restoring law and order in the newly established Free State.   Collins made the conversion from warmonger to peacemaker with remarkable ease as the political circumstances in Ireland changed radically.   Such was the pragmatism of the "Big Fella" - a man big in physique and in personality, one who could be deadly serious yet full of wit and good humour.

Fitz was delighted to recall a reputed sidelight to the Treaty negotiations in London, involving Collins and Sir Winston Churchill. After a dinner party for the Irish delegates during a crisis point in the talks Churchill is claimed to have produced a book of press cuttings dealing with his own exploits in the Boer War.   Having carefully removed his cigar from his mouth he unfolded a gummed-in copy of a poster in which the Boers offered a reward of £50 for his capture dead or alive.   Pointing at the poster he said to Collins:

"Mr. Collins, the degree of your importance is epitomised in the fact that His Majesty's Government offered £10,000 for your capture dead or alive.   As you can see the Boers considered me worth only £50."

After studying the poster for a few moments Collins replied:

"Mr. Churchill, you underestimate your real value."   After a brief pause he continued.   "I am sure you are aware that the cost of living has gone up considerably since the Boer War."

With the withdrawal of British forces in early 1922 the task of setting up a National Army began.   The Irish Army Air Service was initiated by two former RAF officers, William J. McSweeney, as officer commanding, and Charles F. Russell, his second-in-command. Both men had come to the attention of Collins and the head of IRA organisational planning, Emmet Dalton, who commissioned them for a special mission related to the Treaty negotiations. The red-haired Russell, who had worked for some time on the Canadian railway network, purchased a five seater biplane, a Martinsyde Type A Mk11, from the Aircraft Disposal Company at Croydon, near London, purportedly for the Canadian Forestry Department. But the purchase for a price of £2,600 was, in fact, funded by the Irish Self-Determination League from its office in London, and was intended for use as a getaway plane for Collins, and three of his aides, in the event of the Anglo-Irish talks breaking down. Russell would pilot the aircraft on a carefully planned course and land it at Leopardstown racecourse which

The Big Fella, the first aircraft acquired by the Irish Army Air Corps.

would be held by a party of heavily-armed volunteers under the command of McSweeney, who would give all instructions with regards to making a safe landing for Collins and his party.

With the signing of the Treaty the use of the Martinsyde as a getaway aircraft was not required and it was crated and shipped to Dublin.   It was received at Baldonnel on 16 June, 1922, and was signed for by Russell, who was given charge of civil aviation, recording it in the logbook by the name of *The Big Fella*. This was the very first acquisition of the infant Irish Army Air Corps.   Fitz later, as officer commanding at Baldonnel, attempted to purchase the Martinsyde from the government for use on a transatlantic flight attempt but his request was turned down.   *The Big Fella*, in fact, saw little service.   It was used for some years as an instructional aircraft, before being scrapped in 1935 despite its historical connotations.

Soon after his arrival back in Ireland Fitz cycled from Dublin to Baldonnel about ten miles away and presented himself to the officer commanding. He was tested in a Martinsyde F4 Buzzard, an aircraft he had not previously flown, and after an impressive flying session he was commissioned on the spot with the rank of lieutenant.

It was quite a change from the well trained, neatly uniformed and state-of-the-art arms and aircraft of the British Army and Royal Air Force to a newly formed air service with few trained personnel, poor discipline, few aircraft and the most basic facilities. Fitz was amazed and somewhat bemused by what he saw around him.

"The officer commanding (McSweeney) was an ex-cadet of the Royal Air Force whose flying experience was practically nil. This youth bore the exalted rank of Major General and was always accompanied by an equally youthful aide-de-camp, who was festooned with lethal weapons presenting a picture that resembled something out of a comic strip.

"An air of hedonism prevailed at the Aerodrome where the most amazing characters kept popping in and settling down, though they had nothing whatsoever to do with the organisation. Some of them bore exalted ranks which they appeared to have conferred upon themselves. In cases they were almost completely illiterate."

The bulk of the personnel in the new Irish Army had taken part in the War of Independence. They were the official heroes in the new Free State that emerged from the Treaty negotiations. This ragged bunch, mostly young men, had fought a dirty war against the ill-famed Black and Tans and had helped to dislodge the British hold in 26 of the 32 counties.

When the British troops pulled out they left little of value behind them. Baldonnel Aerodrome was a typical example of this. Any aircraft, piece of equipment or installation that they did not remove they left as wreckage in their trail.

The freedom fighters were left in charge. This was a new ball game for them. Never accustomed to the disciplinary constraints and lacking the formal training of the British Army many found it difficult to adjust to this strange mixture for them of peace and power. Lethal weapons were often discharged almost randomly as a means of letting off steam. Fitz was not impressed by what he saw but he accepted the situation as it was. He was prepared to do his utmost to restore order from the chaos.

Some of the incidents he witnessed were quite bizarre. He once intervened in a "friendly" dispute between two drunken soldiers armed with .303 service rifles taking pot-shots at one another behind a two-foot high double row of sandbags a mere 100 yards apart. Fitz intervened and defused the situation. Neither man remembered how the argument had started. He invited both to settle their differences over a few drinks in the mess-room but after a little time and some friendly exchanges, one of the belligerents took exception to some remark that slipped from the other man's lips and this threatened to restart their private war.

Meanwhile as the trio, seated on a leather backed settee,

continued with their peace negotiations another soldier joined them standing with his back to the fire. He made a few remarks and left. He had hardly gone out the door when a series of minor explosions erupted in the fireplace scattering red-hot coals all over the room. Before making his departure this playful young soldier had quietly dropped a handful of .450 automatic pistol ammunition into the fire as his contribution to "hotting up" proceedings. Fitz reckoned had he had a Mills hand grenade he would have dropped that in the fire with just as little compunction. This brought the heated exchanges to an end and the lives of the sparring friends were spared - at least for another day.

It was not uncommon for soldiers to return to their quarters after a night on the town in Dublin, heavily intoxicated and with city prostitutes on their arms. After retiring for their night of sweet amour in their billets they would often extinguish the electric light by indulging in some shooting practice using the bulbs as targets. This exercise resulted in a shower of spent bullets, which had penetrated the thin roofing of their billets, hailing down upon the huts in the upper camp occupied by the garrison and mechanics. This often provoked serious reprisals.

Every night a Crossley tender was despatched around midnight from the Aerodrome to the city ten miles away to transport officers back to the base. One night the vehicle turned up as usual at the appointed time outside the Royal College of Surgeons and after picking up his load, Fitz included, the transport officer decided things were a little quiet and that it was too early for some shuteye.

"Let's take a run down to Becky's and see what's the action", he piped. Becky was the famous Madame in a notorious brothel in the seedy area of downtown Dublin of the early 1920s. On arrival at this den of iniquity the whole party trooped in carrying revolvers or automatic pistols at the ready.

"What's going' on?", shouted a startled Becky to the transport officer who seemed well acquainted to the surroundings. "You know bloomin' well we have no bloody Irregulars here. I keep a nice respectable house and there's never any trouble here," she exclaimed.

As Fitz looked around he observed a statue of the Sacred Heart with a small red light burning quietly in front of it. This was a devotion to be seen in many Irish households but it looked strangely out of place in Becky's, Fitz felt.

"It's a raid"' shouted the transport officer. "Let's get goin' boys". Fitz was worried as to the real purpose of the visit but then Becky provided the answer. She suddenly provided a bottle of whisky seemingly out of nowhere and poured a liberal measure into each glass while depositing a jug of water on the table. This had the desired soothing effect on all concerned and everyone soon settled down in the somewhat stifling atmosphere of the squalid little room.

Then above the din of voices a louder voice coming from some other part of the building could be clearly heard. "Come on fella, get those hands up!" Suddenly all was quiet as a timorous response could be heard. "You can't interfere with me. I'm an American citizen."

The action was happening upstairs. One of the transport officer's pals had detached himself from the group as they entered the brothel and went on a reconnaissance tour of the upper part of the building. With a revolver in his hand he was soon confronting a lanky American in his birthday suit with his terrified lady reclining on the ramshackle bed.

As the rest of the group went to investigate Becky intervened. "Cut it out, soldier! That fella's an American sailor from a ship down at the North Wall. He's only in town for the night. Let him enjoy himself," she pleaded.

Peace was restored and Becky was so pleased that she produced a second bottle of whiskey. This proved too much for the soldiers who had had more than their fill before arriving at this night hot spot. They pushed back the table and chairs to the end of the room facing a large kitchen dresser on which plates and saucers neatly stood along the shelves with cups dangling from hooks. A revolver was produced and the room was soon converted into a pistol shooting gallery with the plates, saucers and cups as targets. The dresser was reduced to a wreckage of shattered crockery and splintered wood.   It was a miracle how no one was struck by a ricochet bullet.

In a brief interval during the shooting the lanky American could be seen sprinting for the front door.   "My Gad, I've never been in such a Gad-damned madhouse", he yelled in a Yankee drawl as he made his hasty departure.

A hat was passed around for a collection to compensate for the damage and the group then climbed aboard the Crossley tender and headed for the Aerodrome along the Dolphin Barn's Road.   Just clear of the city outskirts a tremendous explosion took place ahead of the tender.   The Irregulars had known of the nightly transport operation for officers and were in the process of setting a landmine trap for the returning group when the deadly device exploded prematurely and the ambushers were blown asunder.   The explosion left a large hole in the road and human entrails dangled gruesomely from overhead cables.

It was into this anarchical environment that Fitz had landed himself at Baldonnel.   But he was not alone in his predicament. Many of the other officers and NCOs in the new Irish Army had likewise seen service in the Great War with British Forces.   The equipment gradually acquired at Baldonnel consisted of a heterogeneous collection of British Military aircraft, all of which he had flown in the RAF.

Fitz set about his work of organising resources and training with zeal at Baldonnel but found it difficult to make satisfactory progress amidst the chaos that reigned.   He was helped by the presence of some reliable and trusted colleagues. These included Lieut. Tom Moloney, whom he had known in the RAF, Lieut. Gerry Carroll and Lieut. Bill Delamere, later to become a leading figure in Irish aviation.   There was no system of flying instructions in place, but they undertook the training of certain young officers who showed aptitude and were keen to fly. The first pilot to be trained in the Corps was Lieut. Arthur Russell, who was later killed in an aeroplane crash.

Late one Saturday afternoon in September as he and Moloney were returning to the mess after working on their machines in the hangars Fitz was approached by a newly-joined officer of whom he knew little and who gave him a certain order. Fitz questioned his authority and was told that the new officer had been promoted to the rank of captain and that the appointment would be appearing in orders that evening. Fitz and his friend wondered how this man could be promoted and told him "to go and jump in the lake". Shortly afterwards, however, they were called to the Commanding Officer's office where the appointment was confirmed. When they protested against the appointment being made except in competition with other officers they were informed frankly that it was no concern of theirs.

Fitz and Moloney were seriously contemplating resigning when a few days later they were put under orders to go to Fermoy, County Cork, where they would come under the direction of Major-Gen. Emmet Dalton, now G.O.C. Southern Command. They were delighted. Fitz flew there in a Martinsyde F4 on October 1st as part of a three aircraft unit, which included Moloney, and supplemented by a ground party. The other pilot was Lieut. Freddie Crossley. Crossley had initially been appointed as officer commanding at Fermoy but this did not find approval with his two fellow officers. He wrote out his resignation which Fitz brought by air to Baldonnel and Moloney was put in charge.

Some short time later it was learned that the officer who had been appointed over the heads of the others at Baldonnel had been abruptly removed from the service on discovery that he had served with the infamous Auxiliaries. That discovery sparked a witch hunt among all who had served with the British Forces during the first World War. Later Fitz himself was to suffer in that whispering campaign after being maliciously fingered by a colleague who held a grudge against him.

The rebels, or Irregulars as the anti-Treatyites became known, were very active in the south and they had almost complete control over the vast tracts of mountainous areas in Cork, Kerry and Tipperary. Fermoy was deep in the heart of de Valera country. The aerodrome was in a dreadful state. Fitz describes the scene.

"The aerodrome presented the appearance of having suffered an attack by a flock of locusts possessing a voracious appetite for galvanised iron sheets, wood, glass and everything that went to make up the aerodrome buildings. It had been completely stripped. The stripping had not been done in any amateurish fashion. The work had obviously been executed by skilled craftsmen and was intended for re-erection elsewhere.

"We discovered that the various buildings and station equipment had been dismantled and sold by auction and the materials scattered about in the numerous farmsteads for miles around the countryside. The auctioneer's books were finally discovered so that the location of everything became a very simple matter. The collection of this looted material, which was concealed in the most peculiar places, was the cause of an enormous amount of bad blood as many of the simple country folk who had paid good money for it to swell Mr. de Valera's war coffers, little thought that in acquiring it they were engaged in any criminal activity. They rightly felt that they had been given an extremely raw deal."

The dismantling of the aerodrome was part of a pattern of disruption carried out by the Irregulars throughout the country during the Civil War period. Several large military barracks in Fermoy were burned down and the huge Mallow viaduct carrying the main Dublin/Cork railway line was completely destroyed. The railways throughout the country were paralysed, bridges blown up and station buildings demolished. Magnificent manor houses were looted before being reduced to ashes. Telephone and telegraph systems were made inoperative.

The duties of the Air Corps team at Fermoy consisted of providing air escorts to military convoys moving through difficult mountain countryside. These convoys were engaged in cleaning up operations which called for the establishment of a military presence in the towns and in the countryside. Fitz had many narrow escapes during his term in the south.

Chapter 10

The Civil War

The new Government offered an amnesty to all the Irregular forces who would come in and surrender their arms. The Fermoy Army Air Corps contingent were called upon shortly after their arrival at the base to distribute amnesty leaflets over the mountains of West Cork and Kerry in order to bring the announcement to the attention of those who might fail to see it in the newspapers. Fitz set out in a single-seater Martinsyde Scout with a heavy load of leaflets to be distributed over the Kerry mountains. While flying over Ireland's highest peaks, the MacGillicuddy Reeks, and near the picture postcard town of Killarney, his engine failed and he had to make a forced landing in a small field in the grounds of the town's mental hospital. Fitz viewed the location with a mixture of humour and irony.

"A lunatic asylum. At long last, I felt, I had reached my true destination. It was a most consoling thought. Upon acquaintance it seemed as though the inmates were merely suffering from a degree of sanity which made them unfitted to face up to the standards of craziness that existed outside this haven of refuge."

With the invaluable help of an inmate, which supported his

theory on madness, Fitz got the engine serviceable again. The inmate, who operated his own machine shop, on his foot operated lathe made a complicated hexagon shaped hollow nut complete with perfect thread to replace one that had come adrift from the camshaft housing. After finishing work on the damaged engine Fitz dined that night in a local hotel in the company of a close friend, Colonel Michael Hogan, officer commanding the Killarney garrison.

Colonel Hogan had been involved in a daring gun burglary at Windsor Castle, near London, during the Treaty negotiations. These arms were intended for use by republicans in the event of the talks breaking down. The escapade would have succeeded but for the mistake of an accomplice who took to the drink on the night of the robbery instead of boarding the Night Mail from Euston Station for Holyhead. He took the train the following morning, was arrested, and Hogan was apprehended in the follow-up operations. He was sentenced to a ten year jail term for his efforts but was released following pressure from the Free State Government after the signing of the Treaty.

Killarney was cut off from the rest of the country and Fitz could not communicate with his home base to let them know that he was safe. He took off for Fermoy on the following evening and made the climb over large pine trees. Just as he counted his blessings at being safely in the air again he was greeted with strong bursts of machine-gun fire from Irregulars who had been awaiting his takeoff. The wings and fuselage of the aircraft were riddled with bullets but neither he nor vital parts of the machine were hit. Night was falling as he encountered engine trouble again and he was compelled to make a forced landing two miles outside the Cork town of Mallow, eighteen miles from his base at Fermoy. The following morning he found that the machine required a new engine and with the help of local Free State soldiers he had the aircraft dismantled and stored in the town's military barracks.

Fitz still could not communicate with Fermoy Aerodrome and

as he was now on the missing list for four days he felt that he had to report to base without delay. The area between the towns was in the hands of the Irregulars and the local military could not help him with transport or safe passage. Typical of the man he decided to run the gauntlet. He acquired a battered Model T Ford touring car and having destroyed any documentation that would associate him with the Free State National Army he proceeded on his risky journey.

Several trees and telegraph poles blocked the road but he found ways around them by taking alternative routes via small laneways and fields. But he came to a halt at Castletownroche, halfway between Mallow and Fermoy, where the bridge over the millstream was blown up. As he assessed his options he discovered to his consternation that the little town was occupied by a strong column of Irregulars heavily armed with Lee Enfield rifles and Thompson machine-guns. Before he could make a further move he was surrounded by some rebels and rigorously questioned by the officer-in-command. The officer was particularly suspicious because the car had no number plates and was riddled with bullet holes, something completely overlooked by Fitz.

The situation looked grim for the airman. He concocted the story that he was a Yank who worked as an aeronautical engineer and that he was on a visit to relations in Ireland. He said he was on his way from Limerick to see a relative who was very ill in Cork and had been given a lift as far as Mallow. There he had hired out the car from Thompsons, owners of a local garage. The officer was still far from convinced.

After many years of service with the British forces Fitz had acquired a distinctive English accent and despite his best efforts to Americanise it for the benefit of his captors he was finding it most difficult to do so. Sensing the officer's growing suspicions Fitz took the offensive. "You mustn't know my native city of Boston", he said. "We boast of the perfections of our English accents." Then in an attempt to impress he quoted some lines he recalled from school days:

> "Here's to the City of Boston
> In the land of the roe and the cod,
> Where the Lowells speak only to Cabots,
> And the Cabots speak only to God."

This clinched it. The rebels were convinced. After a few drinks they all shook hands and Fitz was provided with a guide who helped him manoeuvre some back roads before finally finding the main Cork to Fermoy road. His comrades at the aerodrome were much relieved to see him return safely.

That evening Fitz with a breakdown party and an escort headed back for Mallow to recover the aircraft. This time Castletownroche was negotiated without incident but a few miles further along the road to Mallow in the beam of their single acetylene headlamp

Fitz in a Bristol Fighter at Fermoy aerodrome about to embark on a reconnaissance mission over the Cork and Kerry mountains during the Irish Civil War. Sergt. Johnny Maher is in the foreground.

they saw a figure standing in the middle of the road, pointing a Thompson machine gun at the Crossley tender in which they were travelling. A fellow officer of Fitz who sat beside him in the tender quickly raised his Lewis machine-gun he had resting on his lap and discharged a burst of gunfire which dropped the rebel in his tracks. This triggered a rapid response from behind the roadside hedge and the Free State soldiers hastily took cover behind an opposite hedge and returned fire. The attacking party gradually withdrew under the cover of darkness.

Fitz went to examine the body on the road. He immediately recognised the features of the Irregulars' officer who had subjected him to severe questioning earlier in the day but with whom he had later shared a few pleasant drinks and had parted on amicable terms. He felt genuinely sorry for the dead man. He stripped him of his arms and ammunition and laid the body on roadside, where it would later be found by the man's comrades.

A comb-out of the countryside followed along the borders of Cork, Tipperary, Limerick and Waterford. Fitz, now Station Commander, was called to Limerick for a conference on air cooperation for the operation and flew there in a Bristol Fighter accompanied by Lieut. "Tosty" Gogan. Night was falling as the conference ended. Fitz's last previous night flight had been in May 1919 on the experimental mail flight to Cologne and he had never flown a Bristol Fighter at night. Although wired up, the dashboard of the machine was not illuminated for night flying. Despite protests from the Limerick Command General Staff, Fitz decided to make the flight. Just as they were almost airborne his right wheel struck a sharp ridge in the field and he knew instinctively that the wheel had buckled in the impact. When in the air he picked up the trail of the railway line from the glow of the firebox of a railway engine and, with the gleaming metals of the track easily discernible in the moonlight, he followed it until he reached the river which brought him directly to Fermoy.

Fitz noticed an "L" shaped paraffin flare path laid out for him on the aerodrome. For this he could thank the vigilance of Sergeant Johnnie Maher, who instinctively knew that he would return that night. He touched down safely despite the damaged wheel. His life, and that of his passenger, had most probably been saved by the vigilance of Maher, whom Fitz trusted absolutely and held in high esteem. In 1951 he wrote of his former loyal colleague. "I found him a gem, a most knowledgable, conscientious, hard working man ... who remained close at my elbow throughout my service in the Air Corps."

Up to this time the airmen at Fermoy had been flying without any medical officer, medical staff or ambulance. They had been extremely fortunate that there had been no serious accident to report. Their luck was soon to run out. One of Fitz's pilots, Lieut. MacCullagh, got into a spin in a D.H. 9 two seater machine while flying on a mission and crash-landed. He was thrown out onto one of the wings of the wrecked aeroplane and suffered concussion and some injuries from which he recovered in time. His observer, Lieut. McDonough, however was badly injured and died that night in the Fermoy Workhouse Hospital.

It took this fatal accident, the first one to occur in the new Air Corps, to get the authorities to respond to Fitz's repeated appeals for necessary medical staff and ambulance. Within days Dr. Theo McWeeney reported for duty complete with ambulance and medical orderlies. Fitz had not seen him since his course at the School of Military Aeronautics in Reading, in which McWeeney had been lecturing on artillery cooperation.

Some time after this incident the Rolls Royce armoured car, *Slievenamon*, fell into the hands of the Irregulars through an act of treachery on the part of a member of the crew, a Scotsman named MacPeak, who had served in the Armoured Car corps with the British Forces during WW1. He simply drove it out the barrack gates at the West Cork town of Bandon one night and handed it over to one of the most audacious and celebrated Irish freedom fighters, Tom Barry, for a cash consideration and safe conduct to one of the Scottish trawlers fishing off the south coast. Barry had also served in the Armoured Car corps in the Great War and probably knew MacPeak from those days.   Fitz had tremendous admiration for Barry, a brave and resourceful soldier, and felt it was a tremendous pity he had taken the anti-Treaty side "in pursuit of de Valera's stupid and extremely costly pipe dream".

The disappearance of the *Slievenamon* was a major embarrassment for the National Army. Air searches were carried out in the West Cork and Kerry mountains but because the armoured car operated only at night it proved difficult to find. Barry used it mainly to replenish his rapidly dwindling stocks of arms and ammunition.   His name drove terror into the hearts of young Free State Army officers, holding isolated village posts cut off from outside communication and, therefore, assistance.   On one occasion he disarmed a complete village garrison and removed from them not only their arms and ammunition but also their uniforms, which he planned to use to advantage on some other mission.   The following morning the garrison of a nearby post were alerted by the approach of a strange body of men dressed only in their underwear.

During one of these sweeps over the mountains Fitz was visited again with engine failure.   He searched for a suitable landing place as he glided his Martinsyde F4 single seater fighter downwards.   But even the largest of fields in that part of the country were small for such a delicate operation and he ended up with severe cuts over the eyebrows and an injured leg from the impact of the forced landing.   He also lost the aircraft's undercarriage in the process.

Making his way down to the railway station in a small town in the valley he discovered that every building with the exception of the station master's house had been gutted by fire. He found out from local people the location of the nearest military barracks but he could not afford to hang around because this was enemy territory and he was advised that there was a strong column of

Irregulars in the vicinity. What happened next was like something from a boy's adventure book. Fitz takes up the story.

"I could not find a bicycle anywhere and the only available animal was an old farm horse with a back almost as sharp as a razor. He had to do. I led him out and mounted sitting well back on his quarters keeping him in a gentle canter as I pushed along towards the military post grasping my rifle by the small of the butt as one would an ordinary pistol grip. I ran into a group of men coming round a sharp bend in the road and must have presented a most unusual sight to them wearing as I was a fur-lined flying helmet, the straps of which were buckled over the top of my head, goggles and a trench coat, not to speak of my rifle... at the trail on my right hip. It was now getting dusk as I galloped along the road on this noble charger.... I asked them to keep their hands up until they were well round the corner and I pushed on my way. In departing I heard one of them remark: 'By God, Mike, 'tis the bloody Russians they've brought over to fight us!' "

Fitz made it safely to the military barracks but a startled sentry, roused from a brief slumber by the noise of what must have seemed to be a cavalry charge, opened fire at point blank range. Luckily the shots missed their target and Fitz immediately identified himself.

The officer-in-charge soon had a party of troopers on bicycles sent to the scene of the forced landing. They noticed that someone had placed large dry gorse bushes in the cockpit and underneath the engine cowling and set them alight. The troopers fortunately were able to put out the fire before much damage was done. The plane was later dismantled and transported back to Fermoy by road.

The Irish Times of 5 December, 1922, told of another incident in which Fitz was involved. It reported an aeroplane being brought into action against Irregulars for the first time. It was a Martinsyde Scout piloted by Fitzmaurice and came to the aid of national soldiers who were ambushed while travelling between Drimoleague and Dunmanway. "About sixty fully equipped armed men sighted the military in two lorries and prepared to ambush them. They took up well covered positions behind high fences on the roadside. When the lorries were passing intensive fire was opened on them. One soldier was killed. The troops replied with fire but realised they were outnumbered and that their attackers were in an excellent position and sent for reinforcements. Fresh troops duly arrived backed up by an aeroplane."

The report goes on to relate how Fitzmaurice located the attackers near a wood at Leap, descended to a few hundred feet and when over the ambush party, nose-dived in their direction. Fitz opened fire and dropped bombs on the ambushers causing consternation in their ranks. The successful employment of air support was noted with deep satisfaction in army circles.

He may have had innumerable close shaves during his days at the Front in WW1 and again in aerial escapades and ambushes during the Irish Civil War, but Fitz considered that his luckiest escape from death or serious injury happened in the most unlikely place and circumstances of all - while relaxing in the lounge of the private hotel in which he lodged in Mallow. It was run by a charming lady, Mrs. Seagar, who looked after him and the others in her care like a mother. One day Moloney and himself were seated opposite one another in leather upholstered chairs in front of a glowing fire. It was a very cold day and they had just returned from Cork in a Crossley tender, having been ambushed both on the way out and home. Moloney always carried a Lewis machine-gun with him on such missions and had just removed the ammunition drum from the gun, which he held between his knees with the barrel pointing towards the floor between Fitz's feet.

Fitz takes up the story.

"My colleague was busily extracting, with a table knife, the live round that is always left in the feed-arm after the gun had been fired. He had pulled back the cocking handle to its full extent and was trying to scoop out the round when his hand slipped, and the cocking handle flew forward, firing the round now rammed home in the breach. The bullet struck the seat of the chair between my legs giving me a severe jolt as it hit the springs upon which I was sitting. It whistled round the room and we finally found it embedded in the wainscoting. I was lucky not to have been killed. I felt it would have been utterly ridiculous to die in that fashion after all I had been through."

Fitz was promoted to Captain in early 1923 at the return of Tom Moloney to Baldonnel and was appointed to the command of the detachment stationed at Fermoy Aerodrome.

He had a problem with some civilian workmen at the camp and tiring of their antics he chased them off the airfield with a Lewis machine-gun. The incident was brought to the attention of his superior officers and questions were asked in the Dail (Irish Parliament) about the affair. Fitz, steeled from his safe emergence from so many menacing encounters in the past, was not to be deterred from doing things his way and he soon earned a reputation of being teak tough but totally fair.

As the year progressed the Civil War gradually petered out. But the country's troubles were far from over. The Government under William T. Cosgrave introduced a policy of retrenchment and this included a reduction in the size of the Armed Forces. This was bad news particularly for the old IRA officers who had proven their worth in guerilla warfare but had not the education nor the formal military training to be absorbed into a peacetime establishment with the exalted ranks to which they had become accustomed. An ultimatum signed by some of the most revered veterans of the Black and Tan campaign, who were well connected with the leaders of the Treaty Party, was delivered to the Government. The mutineers had a considerable amount of arms and ammunition at their disposal and it was feared that their action would influence other officers to join the mutiny. The situation was fraught with danger.

Fitz, during this tense period, was astounded by the visit of his Corps Commanding Officer, Jack McSweeney, to Fermoy

Aerodrome driving his own private automobile, the back of which was crammed with sub-machine guns, automatic pistols and ammunition. McSweeney, of whom he had a poor opinion, was accompanied by his usual escort and both were in mufti. He questioned Fitz as to his attitude and that of his officers to the mutiny. Fitz bluntly told him his allegiance was to the State. He also said that he had sent a message to HQ through his radio officer (Lieut. "Tiny" Flanagan) telling of the arrival of his visitors and was awaiting a reply. This was merely a ploy to hurry his visitors on their way and so avoid a possible awkward confrontation with his unwanted guests. He had no message sent but had arranged for a coded signal to be handed to him a quarter of an hour later. A piece of paper was duly handed to him a little later in the presence of his embarrassed guests. Fitz told them that he did not know the contents and that it would take a little time to decode the signal. He suggested that as it might contain some reference to his visitors it might be his painful duty to put them under arrest. To obviate such unpleasantness he suggested that they should leave the camp immediately. After some refreshments they duly left and a relieved Fitz threw the spurious radio message into the fire.

The mutiny was brought to a peaceful conclusion by the intervention of Paddy McGrath, a Free State Government Minister and later of Irish Hospitals Trust fame. In order to mediate he resigned his Cabinet post and succeeded in brokering a deal between the Government and the disaffected officers without resorting to bloodshed. McSweeney was discharged from the Corps and was followed by a number of other officers, who either resigned or were likewise discharged from the service.

The crisis had been averted but it had sown the seeds of discontent amongst the troops. With the approach of summer Fitz decided to move the time of reveille by one hour, from 6am to 5am. He got word that "troublemakers" were stirring the pot and that there would be a nil turnout for reveille on the following

Monday morning when the new order was being brought into force. He felt that it was time to nip the revolt in the bud and he detailed his second-in-command to take the Church Parade on Sunday morning informing him that he would dismiss it upon its return to camp.

After service Fitz found the troops lined up in two ranks on the parade ground in front of the hangers and there he spelled out to them the seriousness of their projected action. He then requested all who wished "to persist in this foolishness" to take a step forward. First one soldier stepped forward and the remainder of the parade followed. He repeated the exercise with a similar result. To the consternation of those on parade he then produced two heavy automatic pistols from his greatcoat pockets and threatened that the first man who moved would be shot dead. Having turned out the guard, who surrounded the men, he had the whole command, excluding officers and NCOs as they had not taken part in the act of defiance, marched into a large empty transport shed and had the doors locked. The ringleaders were marched off separately to the guardhouse and by lunchtime the erstwhile defiant soldiers, now leaderless and left without food, were in the process of cooling off.

Just after lunchtime Fitz was informed that two Benedictine priests who were conducting a religious retreat in the town wanted to see him. Over a cup of coffee they told him they had called seeking his support in getting as many of his men as he could to attend the closing service of the retreat that evening. They were amazed to hear that all his men were under close arrest. One of the priests, a former British Army Chaplain, asked for permission to speak to the men. The soldiers were mesmerised to see these two white-robed figures apparently floating through the open doors of the transport shed on beams of sunshine. Were these messengers of death sent to give them the last rites of the Church before execution?, some wondered. They were relieved to hear the good Father give them a short talk on military discipline and

Planning a mission at Fermoy Aerodrome circa March 1923.   The aircraft are a Martinsyde F4 fighter, Bristol fighter and D.H.9 bomber.

the necessity of obedience in all things to their superior officers. Fitz then followed up by delivering a good telling-off laced with a little humour and, having been given an undertaking of good conduct in future by the men, he arranged for lunch to be served. The men filed out gratefully to partake of their belated meal and Fitz never heard a whisper of dissent from them afterwards.

In due course Fermoy Aerodrome was closed down and the whole unit was recalled to Baldonnel in early 1924. He was appointed officer-in-charge of No. 1 Flying Training Squadron and Chief Instructor to the Corps. He enjoyed the challenge and found the work of organisation and of delegating tasks absorbing. It was a tremendous responsibility for a young officer and it was a rewarding experience.

Col. Charles Russell was now in charge at Baldonnel. Fitz had deep respect for, and was on friendly terms, with Col. Russell, who had just very successfully concluded the job of organising and directing the Railway Repair, Maintenance and Protection Corps which laid the foundation for the Corps of Engineers. His other good friend, Tom Moloney, now promoted to Commandant, was second-in-command. Carroll and Freddie Crossley were now Captains and soon had the Aeroplane and Engine Repair Shops functioning efficiently. Captain Bill Hannon was in charge of Stores Accountancy. In addition to their ordinary duties each qualified pilot took his group of trainee pilots into the air on flying training.

One of the chief instructors was Captain Oscar Heron, who had a distinguished air combat record in WW1. He had served with the RAF's No. 70 Squadron in France and was top ace in October 1918, when he scored nine enemy aircraft hits. This earned him promotion to the rank of captain, he was appointed a Flight Commander and won the Belgian Croix de Guerre. He may well have been on his way to challenging the record hits of the RFC's top scoring aces, Mick Mannock, who hailed from Cork, and James McCudden, whose family came from Carlow, had not the war come to an end a short time later. Heron was tragically killed in an acrobatic demonstration when his Vickers "Vespa" spiralled to the ground at a flying display in the Phoenix Park in 1933.

Under Russell's enlightened leadership great progress was made at the base in the organisational and flying training functions and there was a pleasant camaraderie among the staff.

The Air Corps took part in the first Irish Army manoeuvres in and around the town of Kildare and the Curragh in September 1925.   Tom Moloney commanded the Red Air Force and Fitz was in command of the Blue.   On the opening morning of the manoeuvres tragedy struck.   Commandant Moloney was killed instantly during war games. He was flying low at full speed across "enemy" lines, presumably spotting infantry concealed under trees, and hit the top of a tall oak tree.   The machine did two quick rolls and hit the ground with the engine full on.   Fitz was flying about 100 feet above him and witnessed the disaster.   The observer had a remarkable escape and recovered in hospital.   Fitz had lost an "exceedingly close and good friend".

Since the discovery of a former hated Auxiliary in the ranks all who had held commissions in the British Army were treated with great distrust by some politicians and most old IRA officers who referred to them as the "Exers", a derogatory term in Irish army parlance.   Fitz was far from impressed by this carry-on.   "In the estimation of these morons Irish history commenced in 1916 and the rewards of office and employment were the special prerogative of these zealots, their relatives and friends."

Non technical officers were appointed supposedly for ground duty work but, in fact, their main function was in gathering intelligence on the background of the former British Army officers in the corps. The snooping campaign was aimed at uncovering officers who had helped the British military establishment in Ireland during the Black and Tan campaign.

Fitz became aware that he was the subject of a witch-hunt

because of false information supplied by an officer and an NCO, who had served under him, that he had been in the Auxiliaries, the notorious officer branch of the Black and Tans, in Dublin Castle and had committed some very serious offences during the War of Independence.   With the covert help of an officer friend he had been given access to his confidential file in the office of the Director of Intelligence. This contained the malicious statements made against him which allegedly involved him in the burning of the North Dublin town of Balbriggan by the Black and Tans, and also of the robbery of a bank and the murder of a parish priest.

One night after returning to his house at Baldonnel at about 3am Fitz was surprised to see two officers of the Provost Marshal's staff in his sitting room. They had instructions to place him under close arrest and he was removed to Arbour Hill Military Detention Barracks. The following morning he was charged with the simple offence of "making away with by selling the property of the Minister for Defence, to wit: some sheets of galvanised iron and two water tanks". As close arrest in the case of an officer, except in the case of an accusation of a most heinous crime, consisted of confinement to quarters in the escort of a brother officer, the motive of his detention was patently obvious to him. Yet for lack of any evidence the authorities hesitated in preferring the false and unfounded charges of a far more serious nature of which he knew he was being investigated. Fitz dispatched a highly indignant letter to the Chief-of-Staff and within a week he was released and returned to his own station where he was held in open arrest for sixty days before being freed without being brought to trial.

One evening about a month later Fitz was informed that he was to appear before a court martial the following morning at 11 o'clock. Knowing the nature of the witch-hunt against him he decided to take the precaution of making his trial as public as possible so that the people in the street could judge for themselves what was happening in their army. He telephoned the news editors of all the Dublin newspapers and, without disclosing his name, informed them of an interesting court martial that was taking place the following morning.

Next day the Judge Advocate General was alarmed when he heard that a battery of journalists had arrived to report on the trial. He reluctantly allowed them entry. Fitz was again charged with the lesser offence of doing away with Government property. He conducted his own defence and, after clearing a few legal points to his satisfaction, he contested the charge. He pointed out to the court that the property in question was recovered loot and of no use to the Service. He told the judge that he had disposed of the goods for the sum of £20 and placed that amount, in addition to £10 of his own money, in the troops' sports fund. This was borne out by the production of bank statements. He was found 'not guilty'.

Not happy with the finding he claimed that his personal honour had been impugned and the verdict was duly changed to 'honourably acquitted".

In a meeting with the Adjutant General the following morning Fitz sought retribution against those members of the Force who had made false statements against him. He told the AG that all his movements during the period 1919 to 1921 would be accounted for by the Air Ministry in London. The meeting ended as Fitz launched an attack on the secret police tactics being employed by the Irish Army. He experienced little further trouble from that source.

Chapter 11

Looking West

itz's qualities as an officer and his expertise in aviation matters did not go unnoticed by his superiors. He was promoted to the rank of Commandant and appointed second-in-command of the Air Corps in late 1925, on the tragic death of his dear friend, Major Tom Moloney. On the transfer of his commanding officer, Colonel Charles F. Russell, to Army General Headquarters a year later, he became acting Officer-in-Command at Baldonnel.

There was great satisfaction for Fitz in knowing that his talents were being at last acknowledged and he enjoyed the favours that accompanied his rise in the ranks. He was an accomplished horseman and now he had more time to renew his love for horses and in hunting wild fowl with a gun and dog. He had the odd flutter at a race-meeting and relished the occasional high stakes card game with friends. This more relaxed lifestyle was fine for a while but soon Fitz began to look around for something more exciting to occupy his ever restless disposition.

For a new adventure he looked upwards and westwards. The Atlantic had been crossed nonstop by air from west to east (by Alcock and Brown in 1919) but the feat had not been achieved

Fitz and friend - hunting wild fowl in the Wicklow mountains.

the other way round.   From as early as 1924 he had harboured the ambition of challenging the Atlantic in the westerly direction.

The more he examined the problems the more apprehensive he was about the possibilities of a successful attempt - and the more excited he became.   "This was something to test the soul and spirit of a man not acting under the powerful stimulus of war, for the real spice of adventure is to be found only in walking coldly and calculatingly into the unknown," was how he expressed his titillation at the prospect of achieving what human endeavour had as yet failed to achieve.

His first consideration was the question of using a single or multi-engined aircraft.   To the layman it would appear that the more engines employed the greater the chances of survival on such a long and hazardous journey.   But reality as Fitz saw it was that aircraft design of the period ordained that a multi-engined machine was not capable of maintaining height in the event of the total failure of one power unit.   It merely allowed for an extended glide and added only a matter of minutes of longevity to the flight. Such a brief relief was an insignificant factor in an Atlantic attempt on the Great Circle course over almost 2,000 miles of water between Ireland and the nearest point on the American continent, Newfoundland. In the circumstances, therefore, the single engine aircraft was, paradoxically, a safer bet as multi-engines simply offered that many more possibilities of disaster according to the number of engines used.

The main difference in the degree of difficulty between flying the Atlantic either way lay in the prevailing winds backing flights from the west. Further there was an added advantage flying from a practically uninhabited North American coast which swings sharply away to the southwest from Newfoundland to a more densely populated European coast, better charted and running due north and south.

Meteorological information in the 1920s, and for some decades afterwards, was patchy and weather forecasting unreliable. Nothing was known of the upper air conditions and what little was known of surface conditions from shipping using the Great Circle route indicated a preponderance of adverse weather blowing up mainly from the west. Conditions were known to be most treacherous at the westerly end of the Great Circle track where the warm Gulf Stream meets the ice-floes from the north. Fitz likened this meteorological phenomenon to "a witch's brew in Hell's Kitchen".

Because of the considerably greater degree of difficulty and the consequent longer flight time, a much greater load of fuel was required in flying from east to west to cover the same distance. This made takeoff a much more dangerous undertaking on the bumpy grass airfields of the period. There was also the consideration that the longer the flight the greater the chance of unforeseen storms brewing up along the way. Bad conditions on reaching landfall on the bleak Canadian coastline would make it virtually impossible to fix position, especially at night.

There was also the problem of erratic magnetic variations known to confuse compass readings near American landfall on the Great Circle route.   Fitz was well aware of this added complication. "As meteorology is indelibly interlinked with the problems of navigation there was the question, using a simple magnetic bowl compass, of the position of the isogonic lines, or lines of equal magnetic variation, when off the Grand Banks of Newfoundland. The isogonic lines shown on the sea chart swing sharply away to the north converging very closely so that large differences in magnetic variation occur over short distances along one's track and the very sparsely inhabited coast swings sharply away to the southwest.   Therefore unless one was aware of one's exact position at all times over this particular area - a sheer impossibility working on dead reckoning and without radio - it would be possible, believing you were flying due west, to be actually travelling in a southwesterly direction parallel with the coast, when fuel could become exhausted and you would be forced to 'ditch' with the usual fatal results."

All these meteorological and technical difficulties were compounded by the absence of navigational aids that are taken for granted in aircraft today.   In his book *Bremen Ireland-America 1928* Fitzmaurice mentioned the standard instruments in use at the time and their functions.   "We had to rely entirely on an inadequate bowl-type magnetic compass, a very rough type of Askania turn and bank indicator, an air speed indicator, engine revolution counter and altimeter.   The first of these instruments gave us an indication of direction which enabled us to maintain a definite course.   The second told us of the altitude of the machine in relation to the surface of the earth, that is to say, whether we were on a straight and level keel, turning and banking.   If the air speed indicator showed an increase in speed for constant revolutions indicated on the engine revolution counter we were down, and vice versa.   The altimeter enabled us to maintain a constant height."

Fitz had taught himself blind-flying by practice on a trial and error basis on the old Reid and Sigrist turn and bank indicator with the airspeed indicator set into its face. But flying the Atlantic the more difficult way was a different proposition to what he had attempted previously. Would his endurance see him through in a protracted period of solo blind-flying in the turbulent atmosphere liable to be encountered flying westward from Ireland demanding such intensive concentration levels? He had grave doubts. This combination of meteorological and navigational hazards was a lethal mix, he knew. The more Fitz considered an east-west attempt the more frightening the notion became. It brought on spells of most disturbing nightmares, he later admitted.

He was also confronted with difficulties of an entirely different nature. The main one of these was finance. He did a canvass of his well-heeled friends but to his bitter disappointment he found that, except for one individual, the only person that appeared even vaguely interested in helping him make aviation history was himself. The exception was his good friend, Oliver St. John Gogarty, surgeon, writer and supreme wit, whom he greatly admired. After being snubbed on the home front, Fitz and his friend sought support for his project in the US. There was little response. Gogarty approached a wealthy and eminent Irish-American who offered him £100 - a derisory pittance!

Fitz remained determined to make the flight. He turned his attentions on the Martinsyde Type A Mk11, the first aircraft acquisitioned by the Irish Air Corps. This was a bomber that had been converted to carry a pilot and four passengers and, and as has been previously mentioned, was the stand-by aircraft in London intended to whisk Michael Collins to the safety of Ireland in the event of the collapse of the Anglo-Irish talks in 1921. Later christened *The Big Fella* because of the Collins' connection, the two-bay biplane was powered by the very reliable Rolls Royce Falcon 111 engine. It was a similar machine to the one used by Raynham and Morgan on the first ever Atlantic west-east attempt in 1919 which ended in failure. Because it was of no practical use to the Air Corps it had done very little flying.

Fitz was satisfied that the Martinsyde would be ideal for his Atlantic attempt and he had it eyed out for such a purpose for quite some time.   He was particularly happy with the Rolls Royce engine.   "The name Rolls Royce was, is and always will be a guarantee of perfection in aero engines as it is in automobiles. What a gorgeous feeling of affluence one experiences propelled by one of their products.   If one must die, it is consoling to do so in the best of company."

He decided to make his move and approached the military authorities and offered them the nominal sum of £1,000 for the machine.   Although the plane was of little use to the Air Corps, the authorities refused to part with it.   They were completely unsympathetic to Fitz and his plans.   He was left embittered by the negative response both from the army and the public.

"Ireland was not interested in supporting such a project. I was later to discover that while it was interested in sharing in the glory of such an accomplishment, it was prepared to put every possible obstacle in my way and later to deny me the financial awards attaching to such an accomplishment which I had necessarily to forego because of the circumstances attending the success which ultimately came my way.   In the final analysis they even refused to give me a job.   If you have the misfortune to do anything useful for Ireland they do everything possible to destroy you.   Then when you are dead they dig you up and laud your praises as a bolster to their own mediocrity."

This could well have been his epitaph because despite going on to achieve a place of honour in world aviation history for himself and for Ireland, his country turned its back on him in life but when he died it gave him a state funeral reserved only for those who had served their country with great distinction.

It seemed ironic to Fitz that it was an Irishman, newspaper magnate Lord Northcliffe, proprietor of the *Daily Mail*, who motivated the early challenges of flying the English Channel and the North Atlantic itself.   Following a meeting with Wilbur Wright at Pau in France in 1909 he offered a prize of £10,000 for the first successful flight of the Channel, which was accomplished on July 25 of the same year by French aviation pioneer, Louis Bleriot. Lord Northcliffe offered a similar prize for the first nonstop crossing of the North Atlantic in a heavier-than-air machine which was achieved in a west to east direction by the British airmen, Captain John Alcock and Lieutenant Whitten-Brown ten years later, in 1919, in a converted Vickers Vimy bomber.

The spur of a hefty payoff reactivated interest in the North Atlantic route in 1926 with the offer of $25,000 by a wealthy New York financier, Mr. Raymond Orteig, for a flight from New York to a European capital or from a European capital to New York.   In addition the city of Philadelphia offered a similar prize for a flight from a European capital to that city.

The first to take up the challenge was the famous French war ace, Rene Fonck, with three companions in a Sikorsky S.35, built by the famous Russian designer, Igor Sikorsky, who had been domiciled in the USA since World War 1.   The machine was powered by three Gnome-Jupiter engines totalling a massive 1,260 hp.   Fonck was accompanied by a White Russian exile, Islamoff, a fellow Frenchman named Clavier and an American named Curtin. The machine crashed on takeoff from New York on 21 August 1926 and Islamoff and Clavier were killed.   No further attempt was made that year.

The Atlantic challenge was taken up with gusto in 1927.   The first serious attempt at the east-west crossing was made by Frenchmen, Nungessor and Coli, who took off from Paris at 05.19 on 8 May.   The aircraft, *L'Oiseau Blanc, (The White Bird)*, a single-engined biplane, disappeared over the Atlantic and the aviators were never seen or heard of again.   There was no radio aboard and the disaster remains a mystery.

Charles Nungessor, like Fonck, was a revered war pilot and had been officially credited with having destroyed forty-five enemy

Irish Army Air Corps officers pictured at Baldonnel in 1926: (left to right) "Tosty" Gogan, Jacky Hume, Oscar Heron, Ned Stapleton, Bill Delamere, James Fitzmaurice, "Danzer" McKeon, Ned Fogarty, Freddie Crossley, Dr. Theo McWeeney, Sergt. Barnes, Arthur Russell, Gerry Carroll, Brian McSweeney, Frank McGrath, and Tim Prenderville.

aircraft. Fitz had met him once at a British Air Force mess in France. The famous war ace had impeccable old world manners and reminded the Irishman of a child's storybook hero, a chivalrous knight of many past glories. There was a bitter reaction in France to the tragedy, particularly to the death of Nungessor. The criticism was directed mostly at American meteorological expert, Dr. Kimball, whom the French press blamed for giving a misleading weather forecast. This caused further tension in French-US relations already strained because of the insensitive behaviour of some unthinking American tourists in a country which had been so badly scarred by the war.

Despite the number of failures and mounting tragedies every flyer of note, it seemed, wanted to get into the act. One after another they hastily completed their plans vying with one another for places in aviation record books and lucrative contracts as a result.

Less than two weeks later, on 20 May at 12.53 hours, Charles Lindbergh in his Ryan aircraft, The *Spirit of St. Louis*, set off solo from New York and after an incident-packed flight landed at Le Bourget Airport, Paris, at 22.21 hours on 21 May having covered a distance of 5,750 Km. It was the first solo crossing of the Atlantic - a magnificent feat in flying skill and navigation. The French took the young American to their hearts and gave him the welcome they had prepared for their beloved Nungessor. All the bitterness that had been brewing for some time, and had blown up a mere fortnight previously, was smoothed out by the Lindbergh achievement.

Americans greeted their young flying ace like an all-conquering hero on his return. New York, synonymous with flair, flamboyance and ticker-tape parades among the towering skyscrapers, gave Lindbergh the biggest victory reception ever witnessed. This was seen as the most celebrated feat in aviation since Wilbur Wright watched his brother, Orville, make the first sustained mechanically powered flight in history in their creation, *The Flyer*, at Kitty Hawk,

North Carolina, almost a quarter of a century previously. Lindbergh's success signalled a major boom for the industry, especially in the US where, in the first twelve months after the flight, applications for pilot licences trebled and the number of airline passengers quadrupled.

At the same time as the talented young Lindbergh was making his preparations to fly from America to Europe another American who had the same idea was the subject of ridicule throughout the US.   Charles Levine, scrap dealer and millionaire by the age of thirty, had arranged for Clarence Chamberlin to pilot the Bellanca WB-2, *Columbia*, manufactured by the company of which he was managing director.   But because his flight plans hit one difficulty after another, legally and otherwise, he was derided throughout the country.   Lindbergh had flown from one side of America to the other, crossed the Atlantic to win the Orteig prize, and was almost on his way back, and still the Levine aeroplane was waiting on the flying ground with its owner enmeshed in fresh wrangling. Few felt he was a serious contender.   But at dawn on 4 June, Chamberlin climbed aboard the *Columbia* at Roosevelt Field, New York, and onlookers, including his bemused wife, watched in disbelief to see Levine climbing into the cockpit as his companion. The machine took off, rose and flew due east.   Levine **was** flying the Atlantic, destination Berlin.   After 43 hours in the air and 6284 km later the *Columbia* ran out of fuel near Eisleben in Saxony. It was a world nonstop long distance record – a marvellous achievement – and it greatly impressed the Germans.   The airmen were warmly greeted on their arrival at Tempelhof airport in Berlin. Among the throng waiting to greet them was a former World War 1 German fighter pilot, Hermann Koehl, who now worked with Lufthansa.

Germany was going through a period of political turmoil and the wounds of World War 1 were slow to heal.   There was a passion among the Germans to restore their nationalistic pride so damaged by the war.   This was a period of economic boom worldwide and it greatly helped investment in aviation development.   While aviation activity was fed by nationalistic fervour in other countries, it was nowhere more apparent than in Germany.   Massive foreign investment had helped the country make a dramatic economic recovery and because record-breaking flights helped boost a country's status, German industrialists and financiers viewed aviation accomplishments as a way of putting their country back on the international map.   One of the most formidable and prestigious records still to be achieved was flying the Atlantic east to west.   Hermann Koehl, was to play a prime role in its achievement.

The frenzy in the skies continued.   On 29 June, Commander Richard Byrd, U.S. Navy and hero of a thrilling survey of the North Pole, piloted the aircraft, *America*, from Roosevelt Field, the same New York airport as the *Columbia* had used, with Paris as his destination.   He and his three companions flew over Le Bourget airport, where a huge crowd had gathered to greet them, but because of dense fog, were not aware they were so close to their target and, losing their bearings, flew about aimlessly for hours before finally landing in the sea, near the beach at Ver-sur-Mer, Calvados, France.   They had been forty hours in the air and were almost out of fuel but luckily managed to make it to safety. Another attempt by Americans, William Brock and Edward Schlee, from Harbour Grace, Newfoundland, to London was successfully completed without any major hitches.

Meanwhile plans for an east-west Atlantic attempt were well advanced in Germany.   The person spearheading the operation was famous aircraft designer and manufacturer, Professor Hugo Junkers, who had his base in Dessau.   Prof. Junkers had been the first to build an all-metal aeroplane and, despite the restrictions imposed on German aircraft manufacture after the war, he managed to keep abreast with aircraft development internationally by manufacturing planes under licence in Russia and Sweden. Minds became concentrated on the modified Junkers W33 and long-range flying tests were carried out.

A Prussian aristocrat and aviation enthusiast, Baron Von Huenefeld, heard about the tests and threw in the backing of Germany's largest shipping company, the North German Lloyd, for whom he managed their public relations wing.   The Baron became heavily involved in the planning of an aerial assault on the Atlantic. Fulfilling his PR duties for his employers he had the planes named the *Bremen* and *Europa* after ocean-going liners operated by the North German Lloyd.

In the endurance tests the *Bremen*, which was manned by Capt. Hermann Koehl and Junkers test pilot, Fritz Loose, a Chechoslovakian, force-landed after three hours due to engine trouble.   Benzol fumes filled the cabin and rendered Koehl unconscious but Loose managed to land safely and Koehl recovered later.

The *Europa*, manned by Cornelius Edzard, from the city of Bremen and Johann Risticz, a Hungarian nicknamed "The Bear" and also a test pilot with Junkers, managed much better and remaining in the air for over 52 hours set a new long-flying record. The sponsors were delighted and decided to go ahead with an east-west Atlantic attempt.

An 800m (2624 feet) strip of concrete was laid to assist takeoff at Dessau and by early August all was ready for the twin attempt. The *Bremen* representing North German Lloyd had Koehl and Loose again as crew and Von Huenefeld went along as passenger. The *Europa*, sponsored by the Hearst newspaper group, had Edzard and Risticz again at the controls with Hearst reporter, Hubert R. Knickerbocker, as passenger. The two aircraft took off successfully on 14 August but almost immediately ran into heavy rain and high winds. The *Europa* was soon in trouble over the North Sea and returned to the city of Bremen where an emergency landing was made in a field, without engine power and in the pitch dark. The damage was extensive but the three occupants were safe.

Koehl and Loose pressed on despite knowing they were losing

time all the way across England and over Ireland. They suddenly ran into fog as they faced the Atlantic and this proved to be the last straw. Neither could claim expertise in the art of fog flying. The instruments went berserk and the *Bremen* became utterly unmanageable in what flyers call the "death spiral", of which little was known at the time. Koehl finally managed to get the aircraft under control again after a close brush with disaster. It was his experience as a night flyer that came to the *Bremen's* rescue. The airmen decided to abandon the attempt and weary and despondent they turned and headed for home, making a good landing at Dessau after 23 hours in the air.

Meanwhile Fitz, despite his inability to whip up support, financial and otherwise, for an Irish transoceanic bid, through all this time remained determined to get involved in some capacity with a record breaking attempt. Frustrated by efforts to raise funds at home and in the US he turned his attention to London for help. From his RAF days he had many friends and contacts in aviation circles there. One of these, Handley-Page, top aircraft designer and manufacturer, helped him secure the support of oil magnates, Lord Wakefield and Lord Greenwood, and between them he was assured backing to the tune of £11,000, should he be able to raise the balance needed in Dublin. The machine he proposed using was a modified 0/400 Handley-Page bomber. But after a determined bid to package the deal and make it a runner, he eventually failed to bring the project to fruition.

While in London he met old acquaintances, Lieutenant-Colonel F. Minchin, Leslie Hamilton and Capt. Frank Courtney. All three were busy organising east-west attempts. Fitz asked Minchin and Hamilton to consider a takeoff from Ireland and invited them to inspect the facilities at Baldonnel.

"If I could not take part in such an undertaking, at least I would succeed in proving that Ireland was a logical terminal for this most important route in commercial aviation," he observed.

Hamilton owned a Vickers Virginia Amphibian and both he

and Minchin promised to fly over to Dublin. Fitz later received a
telegram telling him to expect the flyers in a matter of hours. His
friends duly arrived but it was not until one week later. Apparently
on takeoff something directed their attentions towards Dover and
its white cliffs. Their money ran short so they gave joy-rides at
10/- (50p) a time to raise funds to pay their hotel bills and to
secure petrol and oil. After working their way around the south
coast of England and into Wales they proceeded to Baldonnel.
On their arrival Fitz noticed another old RAF buddy in the third
seat of the Amphibian, "Cod" Foster, who was home at the time
from Mesopotamia. They all wore Jack Tar type sailor hats, such
as were the fashion for children's parties, and large dark sunglasses.
As they shut off the engine Hamilton, who was in the pilot's seat,
shouted "Let go the anchor" and Minchin in the front seat dropped
a sea anchor onto the tarmac, shouting "Aye, aye, sir".

Such carefree antics from men about to undertake a most
hazardous undertaking recalled for Fitz what he termed "the true
spirit of the old RFC - eat, drink and be merry, for tomorrow you
die!".

After a few days of merrymaking in Dublin the airmen flew to
London. Minchin and Hamilton had assured the Irishman that
they were satisfied with Baldonnel and that they would use it as
their base for takeoff. Shortly afterwards, on 31 August, 1927,
his two friends and a wealthy lady passenger, Princess Lowenstein-
Wertheim, took off from Upavon Aerodrome in Salisbury to fly to
Ottawa in *The Saint Raphael*, a Fokker F.7 high-wing monoplane
powered by a new Bristol Jupiter engine. Fitz received the news
of the attempt in a phonecall from the London Press who asked
him to keep a lookout. He was disappointed that the intrepid
flyers had not used Baldonnel as they had promised, but his prime
worry now was their safety. He sent a signal to all the coastguard
stations to keep a lookout. He finally got a report from a station
off Wexford stating that a machine similar to the one he had
described in his message had been sighted. It circled over the

coast for a while before setting off to the west. The monoplane was later sighted over Slyne Head Lighthouse, on the Galway Coast. It was last spotted when, halfway across the ocean, an oil carrier noted its position and features. It was never seen again. Fitz was deeply upset at the loss of two close friends of many years.

Before the fate of *The Saint Raphael* and its crew was finally determined the daily newspapers of Wednesday, 7 September 1927, on both sides of the Atlantic reported that a transoceanic flight had been undertaken the previous day from Maine USA in an attempt to beat the world's long-distance record by flying to Rome. They also reported that no less than five further attempts were expected to start that very day and listed the machines and the personnel taking part.

The attempt under way was the monoplane, *Old Glory*, piloted by Lloyd Bertaud and James D. Hill and accompanied by an American newspaperman, Philip Payne. Ready for takeoff that day from the American side were the *Royal Windsor* crewed by C.A. "Duke" Schiller and Phil Wood and the *Sir John Carling* piloted by Irish-Canadians, Capt. T.B. Tully and Lieut. J.V. Medcalf.

Off the Newfoundland coast Bertaud and Hill dropped a wreath from the *Old Glory* into the ocean in tribute to Nungessor and Coli with the inscription: "You showed the way". Eighteen hours after takeoff several Atlantic liners picked up an SOS message from the *Old Glory*. Four liners, *Transylvania, California, American Merchant* and *Carmania*, all rushed to the rescue but nothing was found. Mr. Hearst, US newspaper magnate, immediately offered a reward of $25,000 (then £5,000) for the finding of the missing plane and its three occupants. It was all to no avail.

While fears for the *Old Glory* grew another west-east attempt was quickly following-on. *The Sir John Carling* left Newfoundland on Wednesday, 9 September, on the final stage of its flight from London, Ontario, to London, England. The aircraft and its pilots were never seen again. Both members of the crew were Irish born.   Tully was born in Carracastle, County Mayo, and at the beginning of WW1 he joined the London Yeomanry and later the RFC.   He was wounded at the Dardanelles, was mentioned in despatches, received the Air Force Cross and was presented to the King at Buckingham Palace.   A pioneer of the aeroplane excursions at dawn to Cader Idris he secured second place in the aerial Derby at Southport in 1919.   In Canada he was chief pilot to the Northern Ontario Government patrol.   Medcalf, who also learned his flying with the RFC, was a native of County Mayo and had gone to Canada in March 1927 to take up a post with the Canadian Provincial Air Service.

On the European side it was all systems go for Capt. F.C. Courtney's second attempt on the flying boat, *The Whale*.   On Saturday, September 3, he had taken off from Cattewater Seaplane Station in the Sound near Plymouth en route to New York via the Azores and Newfoundland.   There were three others on board. But halfway to the Azores he was forced to turn back due to bad weather and came down safely at Corunna, Spain.   Courtney had planned a second attempt from Corunna but later abandoned the plan due to continuing poor weather conditions.   Capt. Hinchliffe with his *Miss Columbia* was in readiness to take off from Cranwell, Lincolnshire, but like Capt. Courtney his plans were also thwarted by the weather.   Despite bad conditions there was a strong determination to go ahead with a first-ever attempt from Ireland by Capt. McIntosh and Capt. A. Joynson-Wreford in the *Princess Xenia*.   Fate was to play a hand in ensuring that Fitz was soon to get his chance at making aviation history.

Chapter 12

The Princess Xenia

As summer turned to autumn in 1927 the media and public interest in new aviation records was frantic. While most of the world's attention was focused on the North Atlantic challenge, aviation appetites were being whetted by a variety of other ventures as well. The American airmen, Brock and Schlee, in their *Pride of Detroit* had made the successful crossing of the Atlantic from Harbour Grace in Newfoundland to Croydon in England on 27/28 August and the following day proceeded in their attempt to fly around the world in a record 28 days. By 6 September they had arrived in Calcutta.

In the meantime four Royal Air Force all-metal seaplanes were preparing to leave Plymouth on a test flight to Australia and back. Grabbing public attention too was American Naval Commander, Richard Byrd, who with another famous American airman, Floyd Bennett, was first to fly over the North Pole the previous year in a Fokker Trimotor. He was, through all this time, engaged in the process of planning a flight over the South Pole, a feat which he and a crew of three eventually accomplished in 1929 in a Ford Trimotor. There was also growing interest in the forthcoming prestigious international race in Venice for the Schneider Cup for the greatest speed reached by seaplanes over a triangular course of 150 miles. Speeding up the air mail service added spice to the competitive edge within a vibrant aviation industry. The aeroplane represented the future and the race for new records gripped the public imagination.

The fascination in aviation was at its height but at the same time the rate of attrition in experimental flying was so great that there was a growing outcry particularly in relation to long-distance "stunt" flying. The media focused in on the spate of deaths on North Atlantic attempts in the early days of September 1927 and pressure mounted on Governments and aviation authorities to ban any further attempts. Backers of the *Royal Windsor* forced the pilots, C.A. "Duke" Schiller and Phil Wood, to abandon their planned attempt from Windsor (Ontario) to Windsor (England). The *Westminster Gazette*, main sponsor of Capt. Courtney's westward attempt, threatened to pull the plug on his effort. Capt. Rene Fonck gave up on his plans for a transatlantic flight when his crew of two US Navy pilots had their leave revoked. The Navy Department also announced that they were withholding authorisation for any Navy personnel from engaging "in flights of this nature".

By 9 September the *Pride of Detroit* was in Hong Kong on its round the world flight but there were strong representations made by hundreds of their relatives and friends to the US Navy to refuse Brock and Schlee "the right to cross the Pacific Ocean except by steamship". US President, Calvin Coolidge, backed the Navy's stance and intimated that he intended to conduct "a thorough investigation into the circumstances of the flights with the object of determining whether flying over wide stretches of ocean could not be made more safe and certain".

Purses of $25,000 (£5,000) offered to the first fliers to land in Boston or Philadelphia after a transatlantic hop from Europe were withdrawn. Thirty balloonists in Detroit for the start of the Gordon

Bennett Balloon Race passed a resolution "that future flights of this nature be limited to dirigible airships, or large flying boats possessing seaworthy hulls and accommodation and supplies adequate to sustain life in the event of an emergency landing. The resolution added, "aeroplanes which fundamentally are for service over land should not attempt over water flights, except for short distances. Most certainly aeroplanes are not suitable, nor are they adaptable, at the present time for transoceanic commercial service".

Feelings were running high against further attempts in England and Germany as elsewhere yet aviation record breaking activity continued apace in both countries. The Junkers plant at Dessau was particularly busy. The loss of the *Europa* was a big setback to plans but Koehl and Von Huenefeld had hoped for another crack at a westward flight in 1927. Two later attempts to get away before the winter were thwarted by unfavourable weather and with the authorities casting a cold eye on such projects it was decided to put plans for an Atlantic crossing on ice until the spring of 1928.

Another German flyer, Otto Konnecke, was forced to abandon plans to fly from Cologne to Philadelphia. Instead he decided to fly his Caspar Works biplane *Germania* to Japan and back and this news was welcomed with great satisfaction in Germany where it was seen as "further proof of Germany's prowess in the air".

Meanwhile in England, despite pressure from all sides that he drop the idea, American millionaire, Charles Levine, continued to press ahead with his plans for a westward attempt with Capt. Hinchliffe as pilot on the aircraft *Miss Columbia*. Unfavourable weather had stalled the attempt from Cranwell, Lincolnshire, but despite impassioned pleas from technical and meteorological experts, Levine persisted with the plan until he was finally forced to relent and in mid-September he announced his decision to defer the attempt until the following spring.

This left only one transatlantic contender in the field, the Fokker

F.7A monoplane, *Princess Xenia,* piloted by Capt. Robert Henry McIntosh. Fitz had invited McIntosh to use the facilities at Baldonnel and flying a Martinsyde Scout he was in the air to greet the arrival of *Xenia* from Bristol and showed the way for the big monoplane onto the Baldonnel runway at 6.15 pm on Sunday, 4 September.   Capt. Maurice W. Piercey, a well-known test pilot and organizer of the project, was pilot with McIntosh also seated in the cockpit. The plane carried four passengers including Capt. Anthony Joynson-Wreford, who was to be the navigator and assistant pilot on the transatlantic flight, and Mrs. Piercey, wife of Capt. Piercey.

McIntosh, a Lancashire man and unmarried, was one of the most experienced pilots in the world with over 12 years and 6,650 flying hours clocked up.   Trained as a war pilot he had worked with Imperial Airways for many years and had flown the English Channel more times than any other flyer.   He was known as "All Weather Mac" because of his reputation for arriving on time irrespective of the weather conditions.   Less than two months previously he had had a hair-raising experience when piloting an Imperial Airways machine from Paris.   While still over France he ran into a thunderstorm which put his wireless apparatus out of action.   He climbed steeply and then descended as near to the ground as he could but he was still unable to avoid the storm. He passed Berck at an altitude of fifty feet and flew along the coast to Boulogne where he set out across the English Channel.   The gale blew stronger and forced him back again and he made a forced landing at Berck by the light of lightning flashes.

Joynson-Wreford was a cousin of Sir William Joynson-Hicks, the British Secretary for Home Affairs. On *Xenia's* arrival he was greeted by his wife who gave her version of the reason why the trip was being undertaken to the waiting press. "Bluntly it is to show the Americans that English pilots can do big things too and to show them that as English pilots were the first to cross the Atlantic from west to east, so will they be the first to cross from east to west ... The object that Capt. McIntosh and my husband have in view in making this great flight is to help the nation as much as possible. I am proud of my husband and when they have succeeded I will be the proudest woman in the world."

Captain Piercey intimated that it was the intention of all concerned to get on their way as soon as possible and that instructions had been given for a fill-up early the following morning for a possible next day takeoff. Meanwhile a final check would be made on the aircraft and the landing ground would be inspected.

The flyers were driven around the aerodrome by Senator Oliver St. John Gogarty in his Mercedes and were pleased with what they saw. A stone wall at the lower end of the runway was knocked down overnight so that the length of the 1,400 yards run could be extended by another 500 yards.

McIntosh told the press that he was out to break three records:

1. First to cross the Atlantic east to west.
2. To make the longest flight on the return journey and
3. To be the first to cross the Atlantic and return in the same aeroplane.

The lion's share of the financial backing came from New York millionaire, Billie Leeds. He was married to Xenia, daughter of the King of Greece, hence the name of the aircraft.

Slight problems were detected with the engine on the Monday and necessary adjustments were made by two Bristol aircraft engineers. A final test trip was made and all was in readiness for a takeoff on the following morning (Tuesday, 6 September) subject to two main considerations - the weather and Charles Levine. The American had considered using Baldonnel as a takeoff point and had requested information by telephone and telegraph regarding length, accessibility and suitability of the aerodrome. But he was now at the Cranwell base in England and was ready to start from there pending good weather reports.

McIntosh and companions were keeping a close eye on

developments at Cranwell.   They were determined not to be outmanoeuvred by Levine.   Joynson-Wreford told reporters bluntly that the American was not going to beat them in the race westward. "If he starts at 5am in the morning we will be off within two hours. We have three hours start on him at least and, in addition, *Princess Xenia* can travel faster than his plane.   We admire Levine for his pluck, but whatever happens he is not going to beat us."

The weather remained unfavourable for a crossing as the early days of September slipped by.   The flyers at both Cranwell and Baldonnel were becoming more restless by the day.   McIntosh re-echoed Joynson-Wreford's vow that they were not going to let the American steal a march on them, irrespective of the weather. "If Levine starts we start also.   That is definite.   We are not going to be beaten at the last moment," he told reporters at Baldonnel.

As wild weather persisted over the Atlantic and the newspapers were full of reports of missing planes the vigil continued.   *The Irish Times* reported that while awaiting a favourable weather report McIntosh "took Commandant Fitzmaurice up on a trial spin as a compliment to him for his help in connection with the preparations."

Then on Monday, 12 September, the news broke that the Irishman was to replace Joynson-Wreford on the flight.   The reason given for the Englishman's late defection was that owing to a war wound in his left knee he would not be fit, over such an extended period of time, to efficiently operate some of the controls which had to be worked by the feet.   But, whatever the reason, Capt. Piercey and McIntosh, found an ideal and willing replacement in Fitzmaurice.   Further test flights were carried out and Fitz's friend and ally, Sergt. Johnny Maher, was now a main advisor to the airmen.

McIntosh's period of leave from Imperial Airways was fast running out.   His request for further time off was turned down. He was becoming more restless with each passing day while awaiting a satisfactory weather report.   During this testing time

Autographed photograph of Comdt. James Fitzmaurice and Captain R.H. McIntosh pictured the day prior to the abortive transatlantic attempt.

for him the Irish Prime Minister, William T. Cosgrave, paid a courtesy visit to Baldonnel but McIntosh admitted later that while the visit was appreciated he was not disposed at the time to listening to speeches.

Fitz was sceptical of receiving a good weather report so late in the year because the equinoctial gales had already made their appearance over the Atlantic and he knew that these could produce winds from the west, southwest and northwest reaching velocities of 100 mph or more at altitude. The disappearance of Nungessor and Coli and later Minchin and Hamilton in an aircraft of very similar type to the *Xenia* did not inspire any great confidence in their chances of success. But he admitted later that he had put on a "bold front".

Everything possible had been done to ensure that the aircraft was fit for the trip, every detail was covered in the tests and the course was fully charted. As McIntosh's frustration grew so did the likelihood of him making a faulty judgement on the weather reports. With time running out for him there was a growing danger that he might settle for something less than the ideal and finally when what looked like a favourable report came through on 16 September he decided "to have a go".

McIntosh was in confident mood as he climbed aboard the aircraft. "The flight has been planned with the utmost care and the charts, prepared by Capt. Collins of the Air Ministry, are the most complete ever used by Atlantic flyers. We both have wide experience and have flown in every conceivable weather. I have been at sea for more than four years and eighteen months of that time was on the Atlantic. I know intimately the kind of weather we are likely to meet. We are going into the flight with our eyes wide open, realising that there is a certain amount of risk, but we have endeavoured to reduce that to a minimum. I have complete faith in our ability to do the journey."

Despite his misgivings Fitz was not a man to let this opportunity of achieving his longtime ambition pass him by. If McIntosh was

having a go then he would "have-a-go" too.   But all did not seem
right.   "We had the feeling of over-trained heavyweights entering
the boxing ring in a stale condition," was how Fitz described their
mood.

The final weather report was received at 10.40am from an old
acquaintance, Capt. Entwhistle, the Chief Meteorological Officer
at the Air Ministry in London, and it was on the strength of this
that the airmen decided that the start was definitely on.   The
report forecast a depression for 200 miles off the west coast, with
a wind of 15 miles an hour and fairly good visibility. For the night
journey fairly good conditions were expected, but on the
Newfoundland side fog would be prevalent over scattered areas.
Taken all round this report was considered favourable especially
as visibility averaged two to eight miles and the cloud base was
1,000 to 2,000 feet up.

A big crowd was gathered at Baldonnel for the takeoff. Shortly
after 1pm Capt. Piercey gave the word to "get aboard" and after
Fitz had said brief goodbyes to his wife, Bill, and little daughter,
Pat, who held up the red-cloaked doll she carried for her daddy to
kiss, the airmen climbed aboard.   In the cabin they changed their
shoes for fur-lined knee-boots of soft leather, put on leather air
helmets, goggles, headphones and the throat instruments for
communicating with each other.   Fitz wore a light leather jacket
over his uniform while McIntosh wore a heavy leather coat.   The
food for the journey consisted of some cold chicken, hot coffee
in thermos flasks, a bottle of brandy and some sandwiches that
had been prepared by Bill.   The aircraft, heavily laden with 800
gallons of fuel on board, also carried a collapsible rubber boat
with two paddles and a red kite with 500 feet of light twine which
would be flown from the boat to attract attention in case of
accident.   On board too was a parcel addressed to a person in
Philadelphia and a letter for New York complete with "By Air Mail"
label.   Fitz took with him a golden sovereign given him before
takeoff by a friend, Bill Galvin of the Royal Hotel, Valentia Island,

The final checks are made as Capt. McIntosh prepares for takeoff.

The wheels begin to turn as the *Princess Xenia* sets out on her transatlantic attempt from Baldonnel.

The *Princess Xenia* in the air above Baldonnel.

as a good luck charm.

Captain Piercey from a position of 100 metres in advance of the plane gave the signal and at 1.36pm the single Bristol Jupiter engine roared into life and the wheels started rolling. The *Xenia* made a perfect takeoff and two minutes later a Very light was fired indicating that they were on course and able to throttle the engine down to cruising conditions. Two Air Corps aircraft took to the air to accompany the *Xenia* to the west coast.

An upbeat Piercey then faced the assembled press and questions on the advisability of such flights and the hostile public reaction were asked. He readily brushed any criticisms aside. "The fact is, inasmuch as Atlantic conditions cannot be produced overland, it is essential if we are to continue the development of aviation that first of all we must conquer the Atlantic, and re-conquer it repeatedly, so that it will become as common to fly the Atlantic as it is the English Channel." Piercey, who praised the officers and men at Baldonnel for their assistance particularly Capt. Crossley on the technical side and Capt. Carroll for his help in drawing up navigational charts, went on to tell reporters that the biggest problem in crossing the Atlantic was not mechanical but navigational. A plane could easily be blown off course and there was no instrument at the time available which could accurately tell the amount of such drift. "It must be appreciated that whereas in a ship one can stop to take bearings, in an aeroplane this is not possible. This necessitates navigation by dead reckoning," he explained.

He was confident about the success of the flight and its importance in terms of aviation development. "The *Princess Xenia*, excepting downright bad luck in the breaking of some vital part, will reach Newfoundland, and finally New York, her destination, if the knowledge of navigation at present available is adequate. The information that Capt. McIntosh will be able to give on this subject when he arrives will be invaluable for the future of transatlantic aviation."

Five and a half hours later the flight was over and the airmen and their plane were back on Irish soil. It was not the breaking of some vital part or navigational problems that aborted the flight. It was the weather. They had run into bad conditions almost from the start and it was not a good omen when the two Air Corps planes were forced to return to base after losing track of the *Xenia* as it zig-zagged across the Irish midlands in very poor visibility. As predicted conditions off the west coast, having left Galway and the Aran Islands far behind, were poor. But they pressed on expecting the weather to improve. Instead of improving, conditions worsened. Yet still they persevered. "What shall we do?", McIntosh asked his copilot on the intercommunication system in which the sounds were taken from the larynx and received on earphones. Fitz was busily engaged in taking drift readings. "Let's hold our course for an hour and then we'll decide," he replied.

But visibility was fast disappearing as the turbulence worsened and the plane was being badly rocked about. McIntosh was kept busy battling with the controls. The aircraft was almost forced down a few times onto the surface of the raging ocean. A certain roughness had developed in the engine as decision time approached. Having being given a wonderful sendoff and with so much national and personal pride at stake quitting was not an easy decision to take. But they were about 300 miles out over the Atlantic and continuing would have been suicidal. Their only chance of survival was to head for nearest land. Fitz went to the cockpit. He leaned down to the aperiodic compass just in front of them, lifted the clamps and turned the vernier ring right round through 180 degrees.

Mac was worried at the idea of returning but he, like Fitz, knew they had no other choice. It was not plain sailing to get safely back to land. Fitz went to the rear of the plane and with a hacksaw cut through a copper pipe on a large petrol tank containing 250 gallons of fuel, fitted a piece of rubber hosing and pushed it through the drift gauge bearing plate-hole in the bottom of the machine. He then went forward and turned on the cock in the petrol system and the fuel began to empty from the tank.

They were flying dangerously low brushing through the cloud base in heavy rain with a strong southwesterly wind hustling them back to the coast where they were in grave danger of flying smack into a mountain or a cliff face. Fitz got his drift fairly accurately, though, and had a good idea of the direction and velocity of the wind so that he knew he could not be far out in their dead reckoning position at the time they turned for home.

The compass course he set would bring them in over low-lying country to the south of Galway, he reckoned. Both flyers kept a keen lookout for landfall. Fitz prayed that his dead reckoning was correct. It was! They struck the coast in a low-lying stretch of country but they were unable to recognise any features below them because of the poor visibility. It would have too risky to go inland because they were flying so low and the danger of flying into suddenly rising ground was too great. They turned south in the hope of finding a stretch of sand at the mouth of the River Shannon on which they might make a forced landing.

As they flew south the weather eased and they could make out the conformation of the coastline more easily. Fitz went back to see if the petrol tank was empty. He picked up the end of the rubber hosing and suddenly a gush of petrol containing tetra-ethyl of lead hit him smack in the eyes. It completely blinded him. He remembered that the oil company's men, who filled the machine, had worn rubber gloves to protect their hands while handling this particular fuel. If it could damage the hands, he thought, what would it do to such a delicate organ as the eye? He was petrified. Mac looked backwards and in the light of his torch he could see Fitz rolling around in agony. But he could not leave the controls to help his friend. Fitz groped about searching for fresh water, found it and proceeded to bathe his eyes with a wet handkerchief. Slowly his sight returned, to his great relief, and except for a stinging sensation he soon could see clearly again.

Mac was relieved to be rejoined by his copilot and navigator, as he hadn't an idea where he was. The Shannon estuary loomed up and Fitz spotted a suitable landing area. Mac brought the *Xenia* safely down on shingles at Beale beach not far from the County Kerry holiday town of Ballybunion. It was almost 7pm and just before dusk.

The airmen were safely back on "terra firma" but while observing the scene they noticed that the wheels of the *Xenia* were beginning to sink in the waters of the incoming tide. Luckily there were many willing helpers on hand. These came from the surrounding countryside and, never having seen an aeroplane close-up before, they stood enthralled at the sight of the *Princess Xenia* and her strange looking human cargo. Soon they had the machine safely on higher ground where stones were piled up around the wheels to keep her in position. She was moored by the tail with a rope tied to a bag of stones and canvas sheets were draped over the engine. Fitz rewarded them with the bottle of brandy that had been aboard the plane and asked one of their number, Bill Deenihan, to contact the gardai at Ballybunion.

Garda Sergt. Larry Fennelly was settling into his duties for the night when Bill dismounted from his bicycle after the five mile spin and rushing through the front door of the police station, he announced the news of the mysterious landing at Beale strand. The Sergeant wondered was he being fooled but decided to check out the story just in case and set out immediately to the reported landing spot in the company of the local correspondent for *The Kerryman* newspaper, Paddy O'Sullivan. Sergt. Fennelly, who in later years was promoted to the rank of Garda Superintendent, remained with the machine while O'Sullivan ferried the two airmen to the Central Hotel in Ballybunion in his Model T Ford car. Later that night a military guard under the command of Capt. Con Brosnan arrived from Ballymullen Barracks in Tralee.

The airmen were wet through and through and shivering with

the cold as they brushed their way slowly and dejectedly through a gathering of locals and late summer holidaymakers at the Central Hotel en route to the bar. "In our soaking clothes we must have presented a weird sight to those good people who had no idea where we had come from," Fitz later recalled. He placed his charts and navigational instruments on the bar counter and ordered drinks of hot punch, with a base of Irish whiskey. The only money they could muster was the gold sovereign Fitz had been given by his Kerry hotelier friend prior to takeoff. It had been a good luck charm after all!

News began circulating in the hotel as to the identity of the weird looking visitors. The flight had been the topic of conversation there all evening and soon the "untouchables" became honoured guests of one and all. The people were overjoyed that the airmen had had the good sense to turn back in the impossible conditions and were safe and well. They were immediately fitted out in comfortable attire and their wet clothes were sent away to be dried. After warm baths they spent most of the night bantering with their new found friends in the comfortable surroundings with the hot punch reviving their drooping spirits. All through the night they listened to the howl of the raging gale and the streaming rain as it lashed relentlessly against the windows of their cosy refuge. The airmen felt it was good to be alive.

Capt. Piercey travelled through the night by car with Oliver St. John Gogarty at the wheel and accompanied by Engineer Shipley and Sergeant Long. After a close inspection the *Xenia* got the all clear. Fuel men arrived from Limerick and drained a further 250 gallons from the tanks to lighten her load for takeoff. On Sunday evening Capt. Piercey took the pilot's seat with Fitzmaurice alongside and with Shipley and Long as passengers the aircraft was flown back to Baldonnel. McIntosh had caught a chill from his endeavours and stayed on for a few days at the hotel in Ballybunion to recover.

The arrival of the monoplane had whipped up enormous public

interest in the area, quite unaccustomed to such sights. On the Sunday over 300 motor cars were clustered on Beale Strand and an estimated crowd of over 5,000 was present to see the *Xenia* take to the skies again that evening.

As the inquest on the failed attempt raged both McIntosh and Fitzmaurice were determined to have another crack at the Atlantic crossing perhaps even within a couple of days. At first it seemed to them that it was generally accepted that they had fought the brave fight and had failed honourably. It was universally agreed that the weather forecast had been grossly misleading and that the persistence of the storm well into the night indicated that they had used sound judgement in quitting when they did.

But both men were conscious of the detractors too. These mostly congregated in small groups and chatted in hushed whispers. Fitz lashed out at the backbiters while at the same time he tried to put the failure in context. "The fireside fusiliers and the armchair critics who never had, or never would, set their safe posteriors in the seat of an aircraft had it all beautifully worked out. We were just plain yellow. We simply had no intention of ever going anywhere, they said. We became figures to be despised and were held up to opprobrium. We were ostracised and denied the company of our fellow men. I treated it all with the contempt which it merited. I knew well that nothing succeeds like success and that even then, one enjoys the plaudits of the sycophants for a limited time only."

Both men prayed for another opportunity. But unforeseen problems and the lateness of the year ruled out any further attempts in 1927. Sand had penetrated the engine of *Princess Xenia* which required a major overhaul to make it airworthy again. For "All Weather Mac" it was the end of his aspirations to Atlantic fame. But fortune was to favour Fitz with a second chance!

Chapter 13

The Winter of 1927/'28

F itz was sent on a senior officer's course at the Curragh Military
Camp shortly after the failed flight with McIntosh.   He saw it
as a form of punishment for bringing disgrace on the army.   This
would keep him well removed from the temptation of making
another attempt.

But still the desire burned within him to have another "go".
When work finished on Saturday mornings an aircraft flew from
Baldonnel, less than 20 miles away, to fetch him back.   This left
him free to his own devices until reveille on Monday morning.
Each weekend was spent in plotting another attempt.   After a
while, however, his weekly transport to and from Baldonnel was
stopped by his superiors despite his protestations that as a pilot in
receipt of flying pay it was incumbent on him to keep his hand
and eye in, in the matter of handling aircraft.

Fitz was kept aware by Waldemar Klose, a German living in
Ireland, of the intense activity in planning for a new German assault
on the Atlantic taking place at the Junkers plant in Dessau.   Klose
was resident manager of North German Lloyd, whose operations
in Ireland were handled by the Limerick Steamship Company.   The

two men had met initially when Fitz flew an aircraft to Oranmore, in County Galway, to greet the first liner (which was owned by North German Lloyd) to call to Galway Bay for the purpose of disembarking passengers. Klose had questioned him exhaustively about facilities at Oranmore aerodrome and its suitability for a takeoff on a heavily overloaded W.33 Junkers low-wing monoplane. Later an aeronautical expert from the Junkers works came to inspect facilities both at Oranmore and at Baldonnel.

Hermann Koehl, who was to pilot the *Bremen*, and Baron Von Huenefeld, the main promoter of the project, convinced the company's technical team and the project's backers that it made good sense to use a base in Ireland for takeoff. Apart from the probable difficulties of making a start from Germany due to the ban on Atlantic attempts by the authorities there and the public outrage fanned by the press, it seemed logical because it was a waste of crucial flying hours flying over known territory, especially against the head winds in a westerly crossing. Koehl and Von Huenefeld were on the lookout for an experienced flyer to join them on their transatlantic attempt. They were very aware too of the necessity of full cooperation from the Irish authorities and the Irish Army Air Corps. Fitzmaurice was the key on both accounts. He had vast experience and he held a crucial position as officer-in-command at Baldonnel.

Captain Hermann Koehl was low-sized and stocky, more like a sea captain than a bomber pilot. As tough as nails, resolute and fearless he was loyal to a fault to country and friends and totally absorbed in the development of aviation in all its aspects. His underlying friendly and jovial disposition was largely concealed behind a reserved and often stern appearance.

He was born in Neu-Ulm in Bavarian Swabia on 15 April 1888. He followed his father, an artillery captain, into the army. At 22 he was commissioned in the Muenchen Cadet Corps and entered WW1 as a sapper officer but was wounded in the early stages. He went on to win the *Pour le Mérite*, the German equivalent of the Victoria Cross, for daring exploits as a fighter pilot.

As a trainee pilot he got a baptism of fire when crash-landing on his first solo flight. At the end of 1916, by then an echelon leader, he got embroiled in a battle with two French Nieuport pursuit planes. His machine was shot to pieces and he received a serious wound in the upper thigh. He glided over the front lines back to his own trenches.

He was hospitalised for most of the following year but recovered and was promoted to captain in command of a bomber squadron. While on a reconnaissance mission over French lines on his first night flight in his new command on 20 May 1918 a shell knocked his twin-engines out of commission and he made a forced landing safely - but this time behind enemy lines. He tried to make his way back to his own lines and evaded capture for four days. Within sight of the German lines his lack of French gave the game away and he was arrested and sent to a distant prisoner-of-war camp. He was confined for 16 months during which time he was involved in numerous escape attempts.

Then on a beautiful moonlight night in September 1919 he made a daring solo escape by scaling a roof and climbing down to a deserted courtyard. He calmly walked through the streets of the town and sitting down at nightfall he checked his direction from the North Star and the moon. Two train journeys brought him to the River Rhone and the border where he swam to Switzerland and freedom.

In 1924 Koehl joined a small airline, Junker-Luftverkehrs. In 1925 he was in charge of the entire management and organisation of tests on the land route between Berlin and Warnemuende. An extension of the night flights by seaplane from Warnemuende to Stockholm followed. He spent all his working time on night flying operations. Lacking capital and with subsidies stopped Junkers-Luftverkehrs were forced to merge with another German airline to form a new company - the German Lufthansa.

Koehl was put in charge of the night flights department and

enjoyed the work but hated the job because of the red tape involved. He looked around for a new challenge which led him to team up with the Professor Hugo Junkers' transatlantic project and Baron Guenther Von Huenefeld.

The Baron, born on 1 May 1892 in Koenigsberg, Prussia, was a slim gaunt aristocratic figure, blind in his left eye with a rimless monocle in his right eye. He invariably wore a little naval cap perched on the side of his head and smoked a cigar. He had serious health problems from his early years and had missed out on the many physical activities enjoyed by other teenagers.

A man of great vision and charming personality he managed to overcome his physical failings by steely determination and persistency. He was a poet and patriot, a philosopher and a romantic, and despite recurring kidney trouble and a weak heart, he managed to complete a course of philosophy and literature at the University of Berlin. He took some private flying lessons but because of his poor eyesight and frail health he never became a pilot. Instead he became a motorcycle despatch rider until shrapnel injuries to his legs left him hospitalised for many months.

In 1916 he joined the diplomatic corps and served in Sofia and Constantinople. Later that year he became Imperial German Vice-Consul in Holland, which led to a close friendship with Crown Prince Wilhelm. This friendship with royalty caused him much resentment by the anti-imperialists in the postwar years.

By 1926 the Baron had developed an incurable stomach cancer and underwent surgery that year. During his long convalescence period he occupied himself in his chief interests, writing, politics and aviation, in which he had a long time fascination. He went on to work for North German Lloyd as public relations officer. His job and his interest in aviation led him to the Junkers transatlantic project in Dessau. Here he met Professor Junkers, company director, Gotthart Sachsenborg, and Capt. Hermann Koehl. He saw the project as an opportunity of striking a blow for his beloved Fatherland in the exciting and fast developing world of aviation and he arranged the backing of North German Lloyd. He and Koehl got on well together from the start and a close friendly working relationship evolved between the pair.

During the winter of 1927 Klose confided in Fitz the news that the Germans had planned to try again in the early spring but this time they planned to take off from Ireland using only one aircraft, the *Bremen*. In a letter to the Irish Government, Klose outlined the plans for the proposed flight being organised by Baron Von Huenefeld, "Director of North German Lloyd". This letter was acknowledged by Foreign Affairs on 23 December and it is noted in National Archives that it was referred to the Department of Industry and Commerce.

Klose confided in Fitz that his cooperation was central to their plans and that they would like him to take part in the flight as copilot. The *Bremen's* previous copilot, Fritz Loose, had left the team to attempt a crossing via the Azores in a trimotored Junkers G24. Because of the hostile reaction in Germany and elsewhere to any such flights Klose asked Fitz not to disclose the Germans' plans to anyone.

The Irishman was delighted to be asked to join the German effort but he knew from experience that circumstances could change by the springtime of 1928 which might rule him out of the German plans. He still had other possibilities to explore and was determined to use every trump in his hand in order to be involved in some way in a westerly flight into history. As he awaited developments from Germany he continued in his efforts to secure a suitable aircraft and to whip up support for his proposed all-Irish attempt. *The Irish Times* and *Irish Independent* carried letters from him strongly emphasising the benefits to Ireland of such an undertaking.

He wrote a letter in late 1927 to Sean McKeon, the famed freedom-fighter nicknamed the Blacksmith from Ballinalee, who was now Quartermaster-General with the Defence Forces and an influential voice in the army and with the Government because of his heroic exploits during the War of Independence. He outlined the benefits to be derived for the country in being the first to achieve the westward flight. He also suggested ways in which the £10,000 required to fund the attempt could be raised. The letter read:

"A successful flight across the North Atlantic ocean from east to west has not yet been accomplished. Next spring British, French, Italian, German and Dutch airmen will fight for the honour of first place in the aerial race from east to west. The following reasons are put forward for an all-Irish flight which if organised immediately should be the first to accomplish the feat.

"(1) Enormous influence upon our international prestige such a flight would have by drawing attention to the New Ireland leading the way in the hazardous pioneer work of this new science.

"(2) The aid to the development of our National Esprit de Corps the flight would prove by directing national attention and enthusiasm towards the accomplishment, in the face of big foreign competition, of a gallant and valorous feat.

"(3) The laying down of a noble tradition for the air arm of the future.

"(4) To secure the recognition of Ireland as the port of arrival and departure of the transatlantic aerial services of the future.

"The machine considered most suitable for the undertaking is the Fokker F V11 type, an aircraft similar to the *Princess Xenia* but fitted with the high efficiency reinforced wing and equipped with three Lynx Radial air-cooled engines. The engines have already been offered free of charge by Mr. Siddeley of the Armstrong Siddeley company.

"A sum of £10,000 will be required to finance the expedition and effect insurance on the lives of the crew. It is suggested that a committee consisting of the chief-of-staff, the Q.M.G. and an officer qualified to assist in the organisation of the technical details of the flight should be formed immediately to raise and handle the finances for the undertaking. Colonel Russell, who is willing to co-operate, is suggested as the third member of the committee.

"There are two sources from which the necessary finances can be procured:

No.1:   Irish-American money raised by such people as Mr. John McCormack and the Bishop of Baltimore.   It is considered that no difficulty would be experienced in raising the money from this source quickly.   In view of the urgency of the matter this is considered the best source from which to obtain the funds.

No.2   General national subscriptions.   With regard to this method it is thought that the following sums could be raised: General Army sub. £1,000, General Garda sub. £1,000, General Civil Service sub. £500, various other organisations £1,000, military tattoo and flying display £3,000, Irish press £700, anticipated private sub. £1,000, Dublin sub. £1,000, Cork sub. £500, Limerick sub. £300.

"The chief value of the flight lies in our being the first to do the crossing.   Providing the machine is ready and has completed her tests by March next we are in a better position to pull off the venture than any of the European competition as we have a 500 miles start of anyone jumping off from the nearest suitable aerodrome in England which will allow a machine of this type to take off.   This is a very big consideration.

'In considering the matter it should be borne in mind that the French, German and British machines are now ready for the job and already awaiting the favourable weather conditions which will not prevail until next spring.   The matter should, therefore, be put in hands immediately and endorsed as soon as sufficient money is available to pay the deposit which is required with the order."

Fitz met General McKeon on the morning of 23 November and discussed the proposal with him.   McKeon said he would write immediately to John McCormack, the world renowned Irish tenor and admirer of Fitzmaurice, seeking financial assistance and disclosed that he would be also taking up the matter officially with the chief-of-staff.

The call for support of an all-Irish effort bridged the bitter political divide and one of Fitz's best supporters was Sean Lemass, who was to succeed de Valera in 1959 as leader of the Fianna Fail party and Taoiseach (Prime Minister).

On 3 November Fitz had written to Fokker aircraft manufacturers in Amsterdam requesting information on a suitable aircraft for a proposed transatlantic flight. More information was sought about the Irishman's plans and Fitz wrote to the company again with further details on 15 November. He stated that he required one of their machines for a nonstop flight from Dublin to New York via Newfoundland. Fifty hours fuel would be required to allow a reasonable factor of safety in range. The personnel would consist of two pilots only, clothed in the usual flying kit and carrying life-saving suits, four gallons of water together with the usual food supply for the journey and seven days emergency rations. He asked that a wireless set weighing approximately 180lbs be included, if possible, in the equipment. He also gave some details of Baldonnel, that it had a "firm smooth surface of boulder clay on limestone allowing a run of 1900 yards into the prevailing winds". In case it be necessary, he added, he was having two slipways erected similar to that used by Commander Byrd for the takeoff of the America. He asked for the company's advice on whether three Siddeley Lynx engines or the single Bristol Jupiter engine should be used. Personally he said that he favoured the three Lynx engines provided that they could guarantee sufficient fuel for the journey.

This stated preference for a multi-engined aircraft is interesting in light of his strong views stated later in favour of the use of a single engine on such a flight.

In any case Fokker opted for the single Bristol Jupiter engine in their F.V11 machine. In their letter dated 29 December the Fokker company offered the full package for just under £5,000. They told Fitzmaurice that they could not guarantee a flight of 50 hours as he had requested.   They advised him not to make a nonstop flight to New York and suggested that he make a first landing in Newfoundland "unless extraordinary weather conditions would be encountered which would allow a nonstop flight".

The Bristol Aeroplane Company wrote to Fitzmaurice on 24 January 1928 telling him that, while they were aware that he preferred a geared engine they felt that they had not had sufficient flying experience with geared engines to enable them offer one for a transatlantic flight unless he proposed to delay his attempt until later in the year.   They offered him a standard series V4 ungeared engine with a price tag of £1,550 less special discount "for him" of 20%. Managing Director, Sir Stanley White, advised Fitz that his company would insist on supervising the installation of the Jupiter engine into the aircraft at the Fokker plant.

The Irishman was also watching developments in England as the early days of 1928 passed.   Capt. W. R. Hinchliffe was in contact with him informing him that he was obtaining an American aircraft for an east-west attempt. Levine and the famous Imperial Airways pilot, after deciding against a westward flight in late 1927, had embarked on a flight to India instead.   A forced landing in Austria ended the project and Hinchliffe had returned to England to prepare for an Atlantic assault on his own account. Hinchliffe had vast flying experience with nearly 90,000 miles clocked up. He was awarded the Distinguished Flying Cross for his feats of bravery during WW1. In 1917 he had been shot down in action over France and was badly injured, losing an eye.

Fitz went to London and meeting Hinchliffe was told of his plans in some detail. He invited his flying friend, as he had done with others in the past, to take a look at Baldonnel.   Hinchliffe came to Dublin with Captain Joynson-Wreford and said he was eminently satisfied with the aerodrome. Fitz remarked later that during the English pilot's visit to Baldonnel he could not help noticing that about every two hours his visitor removed the shield he wore over the damaged eye as he cleaned out what was still a seeping wound.   He left Fitz under the impression that he had intended using Baldonnel for his takeoff.   He also left him wondering who he was going to take with him on the flight!   The mystery was soon to be solved in the most tragic of circumstances.

On 13 March Hinchliffe's monoplane *Endeavour*, a Stinson Detroiter similar to the machine that American pilots Brock and Schlee had used the previous year in their round the world attempt, took off from Cranwell with the Honourable Elsie Mackay, daughter of Lord Inchcape the shipping magnate, as a secret passenger. Fitz received a phonecall from the editor of one of the British national newspapers telling him of the surprise takeoff.   Very reminiscent of the Minchin and Hamilton effort, he sent out signals around the coast seeking information on the whereabouts of the aircraft.   At 1.30pm, almost five hours after takeoff the plane was spotted over Mizen Head, County Cork, heading west and with snow falling.   It was seen passing over a steamer later in the afternoon about 170 miles off the Irish coast.   Hinchliffe and his passenger were never seen again.   Later that year Lord Inchcape settled a gift on Mrs. Hinchliffe and her two daughters of £10,000, to be held in trust and administered for their benefit.   This was the sequel to one of the saddest chapters in aviation history.

The latest tragedy was followed by renewed hostility to any further efforts.   This was most vehement in Germany where newspapers warned against "such playing with human life".   They recommended a general prohibition by law on transoceanic flights.

Capt. R.H. McIntosh commented that Hinchliffe knew that "there were twelve foreigners preparing to make the attempt so he was determined that England should be there at the start.   It was a gallant deed," he said," but it seems to me incontrovertibly, not that the east-west flight should not be made, but that it should be made in a suitable machine.   I am convinced that there is only one craft for the job - a multi-engined all-metal flying boat capable of riding out a gale on the open sea, of flying with one engine out of action, and with a range of about 3,000 mile."

At least a dozen people had lost their lives over the Atlantic in a period of ten months.   Seven of these were on flights in the westerly direction and others, including McIntosh and Fitz, were fortunate to survive attempts.   The Irishman was forced to admit, but not publicly, that "it did seem that such an undertaking was absolutely impossible" with the machines and equipment then available.

Paradoxically, yet typical of the man, it was his inbuilt need to achieve the seemingly impossible, that made the Atlantic flight now even more of an attraction for him.   He wrote of this sense of elation.   "One is stimulated by the knowledge that the joy of achievement is all the greater when the successful accomplishment ... is performed in the face of what is regarded overwhelming odds."   He lambasted the "sensational" press for their "hysterical outbursts" and restated his determination to make the flight.   "Let those who so wish, still keep their pocket wisdom for the benefit of the mediocre and console them for their mediocrity.   The world goes forward and this job has to be done."

In Germany Baron Von Huenefeld and Capt. Koehl continued to make preparations in secret.   With Atlantic attempts under such a cloud the North German Lloyd company shied away from their official sponsorship which meant the Baron had to seek new sponsors for the proposed flight.   He put his own life savings of 10,000 marks into the project but found it extremely difficult to get anyone interested in the interest free loans he offered. Eventually he found 11 sponsors willing to back the venture with loans ranging from 2,000 to 10,000 marks each.   Significantly eight of these came from the city of Bremen and by mid-February the aircraft *Bremen* was registered in the Baron's name.

The Baron and Koehl now embarked upon a secret mission to Ireland to examine the suitability of Irish airfields for their flight. They travelled on board the steamer *Dresden* and in Ireland linked up with Herr Klose and their host for the entire visit, Commandant James Fitzmaurice.   The airfield at Oranmore in County Galway

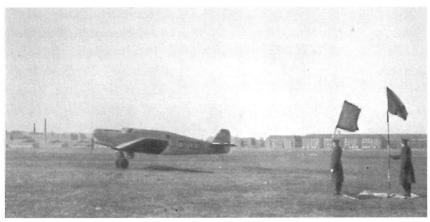

The start from Tempelhof on March 26th 1928 at 8.08am - first stop Baldonnel.

was considered because of its strategic position near the west coast but the runway was too short for a heavily loaded takeoff. The main Army Air Corps base at Baldonnel was deemed more suitable because of its accessibility, its facilities, the availability of Air Corps technical staff and the standard and length of the runway there. It was decided to use it as the starting point.

Preparations at the Junkers plant continued under utmost secrecy fearing a backlash from aviation authorities. But the *New York Times* of 15 March had the news that Capt. Koehl was to try a transatlantic flight "this spring". The *Irish Independent* of 17 March followed up with a story on the visit to Ireland of Capt. Koehl "accompanied by a German nobleman" and revealed that the Germans were planning an attempt from Ireland. It was no longer a secret and Koehl, chief night flyer with Lufthansa, was questioned by his superiors about the intended flight. He was evasive with his answers and this tested the patience of the Lufthansa officials. They told him the company would not support the attempt and would not allow him extended leave for the trip. He was reminded that the air force credentials he held as pilot were not recognised passenger aircraft credentials. Instructions were sent out to detain any aircraft attempting an ocean crossing, clearly aimed at the Junkers' project.

As destiny day fast approached the German newspaper, *Achtuhr Abendblatt,* branded the plan as a thinly veiled scheme to start a world flying service by the Junkers company.   The authorities kept a watching brief on happenings at the Junker's plant. Koehl, aware of the constant scrutiny into his flying activities by aviation officials, decided that the time had come to set the next phase of the plan into motion.

At Tempelhof airport, Berlin, early on Monday morning, 26 March, a time when the least surveillance was in operation, Koehl casually registered a trial flight to Dessau. At 8.20am the *Bremen* took off with mechanic, Arthur Spindler, as copilot and the Baron, who had boarded secretly, as passenger.   On board also was a small wooden cross of Connemara bog oak which Herr Klose had purchased for the Baron on his trip to Galway a short time previously. Spindler was an important crew member on this flight because he had a commercial pilot's licence, unlike Koehl, and his presence could have saved an embarrassing situation had anything gone amiss with their plans to leave the country.   Spindler was not in Koehl's transatlantic plans, however.   He had not the experience of Fitzmaurice as a pilot or navigator and furthermore the Irishman's position in charge of the Air Corps was vital to the success of the operation.

Nine hours later the aircraft was spotted in the skies above Dublin. Fitz, on seeing her hovering above Baldonnel, went up in an Air Corps machine, a Baby Moth, and made two landings to show Koehl where to come down. The *Bremen* made a perfect landing. The nine hundred mile flight had been an ideal test for her. She had experienced some head winds and patches of poor weather over Hanover and Amsterdam but had passed all tests with flying colours.

A veil of secrecy enveloped the *Bremen* for the next few days. There was speculation in the press that Koehl and Huenefeld were ready for immediate takeoff depending on the weather and that

The *Bremen* at Baldonnel being prepared for the flight.

Spindler would go along as copilot. But a week after arrival *The Irish Times* revealed that the two Junkers mechanics, Paul Lengerich and Alfred Weller, who had arrived at Baldonnel a few days before the arrival of the *Bremen*, "had now concluded their work on the machine". That revelation certainly did not match up with suggestions of an earlier takeoff. The German mechanics were assisted by four Air Corps mechanics, Sid Peacock, Leo Canavan, George Barton and Fitz's loyal confidant, Johnny Maher.

Koehl was not a man to stand on ceremony. He found it uncomfortable trying to fit his portly frame into the pilot's seat because of the armrest. Johnny Maher recalled many years later how the Captain overcame the problem. He grabbed a fire-axe from the side of the plane just behind the cockpit and chopped off the armrest. Sergt. Maher was disgusted because had he been aware of the problem, he could have seen to it that a neat job was done by Air Corps staff.

Maher found that the Germans, who knew little English, were worried about the security of their plane at Baldonnel. "The peculiar thing about the Germans," he said in an interview later, "is that they didn't trust anybody. Every night they used put a canvas cover over the aircraft. They hooked it up with special clips along the side with wire. Weller would come along and put a seal on it and seal it with a Junkers pliers. Every morning they would religiously inspect the seals to see that none of them were broken." He was very impressed with them, however, and said he had never met such positive people about their work.

The task of extending the runway at the aerodrome was also well in progress. It was now patently obvious that it was not the weather that had delayed the attempt. After all the effort and finance that had been invested in the project by those concerned and the absolute attention to detail by Capt. Koehl, there was no possibility that the Germans were going to be rushed into making an overhasty start because of outside pressures. In a cryptic statement in *The Irish Times* of 31 March, the Baron announced that he and his colleagues would not allow "external circumstances" to interfere with their "carefully prepared plans". Significantly Spindler left Dublin quietly en route back to Germany the following evening, Sunday, 1 April, which in Ireland is known as "All Fool's Day". Klose had set out for Germany two days earlier. Information from within the German camp was so restricted that *The Irish Times* of March 31 ran the headline "Atlantic Flight Mystery". Meanwhile it was reported that French pilot, Maurice Drouhin, was considering a separate attempt from Baldonnel, and there was speculation that this could result in a transatlantic race from Ireland. The French plan did not materialise but the report did add flavour to the "mystery". It was like a jigsaw puzzle with the news hounds trying to put the pieces together.

Chapter 14

The Takeoff

Unknown to the press Fitz was the missing piece of the jig saw. Plans for an all-Irish attempt had fallen through yet again for want of backing, financial and otherwise. Klose had kept him informed of developments at Junkers and that it was all systems go for the proposed attempt from Baldonnel in the late spring. Fitz was still very much central to their plans and on their arrival at Baldonnel the Baron and Koehl confirmed the earlier invitation from Klose. But the public announcement on him joining the Germans in the attempt was delayed subject to permission being granted him by his superiors.

As soon as he was told of the pending arrival of the *Bremen*, Fitz applied to the Chief Staff Officer at GHQ requesting a month's leave and permission to go abroad. This was responded to by an inquiry requesting the name of the country to which he proposed travelling. He replied it was the United States of America via Canada. He was next asked what form of transport he proposed using. Fitz replied "air transport". The fat was well and truly in the fire! To his amazement permission was granted - but there was a sting in the tail. He was told that if he went by air he did so

at his own risk. He was asked to sign a declaration to the effect
that if he lost his life on such a journey his dependants would
have no claim on the State and that all such pension rights were
forfeit.

Fitz agreed to sign but he was far from happy about the
implications. He was, after all, a married man with a young
daughter, and to take part on such a risky mission without adequate
cover for his dependants would have been totally irresponsible.
The insurance premiums quoted were so high as to be prohibitive,
up almost a quarter on his flight the previous year. His friends
rallied round him to help find the cash needed. The Germans
were reported to be insured for £2,000 each at Lloyds and that
the cost was shared between North German Lloyd and Hamburg
American Line.

On Monday, 2 April, the *Bremen* had a trial flight over Dublin
with Koehl and Fitz in the pilot cabin and Huenefeld as passenger.
The flight was watched by a number of journalists and press
photographers who were allowed into the aerodrome for the first
time. Fitz took over the controls for a time in the trial that lasted
over an hour. He was very impressed with the action of the
Bremen. "I was absolutely fascinated with her from the first
moment I became airborne in her ... She was what she looked - a
beautiful stable aircraft possessing the most perfect flying
characteristics. Like Koehl and myself she had withstood the
buffeting of the turbulent weather that is to be experienced over
the Atlantic off the west coast of Ireland, and had survived to
come back into the fray again for the purpose of a final tilt with
this allegedly invincible opponent."

The *Bremen* was a full cantilever, all-metal, low-wing monoplane,
typical of the Junkers aircraft of the period. The W.33 had been
specially designed for freight carrying. She was powered by a six-
cylinder in line, water-cooled Junkers LV engine, developing just
over 300hp at 1,500 revolutions per minute. The cockpit was
neatly designed to give her a clear line in keeping with her overall

good looks. Her weight was just over 5,500 lbs but this would increase to 8,140 lbs gross for the Atlantic crossing, which included the three airmen, provisions, 20 gallons of oil and 500 gallons of a fuel mix of petrol 60 benzol 40 which had been shipped in from Germany prior to the arrival of the plane in Dublin. The name *Bremen* appeared on both sides of the silver-coloured corrugated duralumin fuselage with the registration markings D1167 clearly visible on both the fuselage and wings.

Koehl and the Irishman carried out a number of other test flights. Fitz in his writings described these tests: "These hops were joyous little affairs filled with the tingle of anticipation and with the thrill of novel intricacies of a new aircraft. The *Bremen* is one of the best ships that it has ever been my good fortune to fly. I found her to be exceedingly stable not only in level flight but in gentle banks. The aileron control was so light that it was possible to turn the ship in the air by a gentle touch of the finger. On the cross-country hops which we made in order to test our navigation instruments I found that it was possible to remove both my hands and feet from the controls and the *Bremen* would remain in level flight without deviation for a considerable period of time. Needless to say these features filled me with a sense of great satisfaction for after many hours flying and after the tired nerves have become almost stupefied from lack of rest, a plane which has many peculiarities in flight is liable to become especially treacherous."

Speculation grew by the day that the Irishman was to join the Germans on the flight and the much anticipated confirmation finally came through on the evening of Friday, April 6. *The Irish Times* of the Saturday headlined "Irish Pilot on the Bremen - Special Leave for Commandant Fitzmaurice." The *Irish Independent* had headlines "Ireland an Official Partner in the Venture" and "Air Force Honour".

The work on extending the runway for takeoff had been completed. A work party of twenty soldiers had been busy for some days working on the new stretch of runway from the hangar.

Under this arrangement the *Bremen*, instead of having to be taken some hundreds of yards to the place from which the *Princess Xenia* took off six months earlier, could start immediately on leaving the hangar.   The extended runway was 1,300 yards in length and tyres were placed at intervals on either side to outline its edges. A stretch of sixty yards of concrete was laid from the starting point between hangars "B" and "C".   This was followed by a small bricked-in piece of runway leading on to a stretch strengthened by railway sleepers bedded in clay.   The remainder of the runway was over a rough textured grassy surface.

A stone wall at the western boundary of the aerodrome was removed which allowed a further 150 yards at the other end. The removal of the wall caused a huge rumpus because it was the property of the owner of the adjoining field.   It cost £200 to replace for which the *Bremen* team were later held responsible. But it was worth the price because the decision to add the extra distance at the end of the runway proved a crucial safety consideration in the actual takeoff.

Every 100 yards was marked with a 50 gallon drum numbered from the beginning to the end of the runway.   A red oil drum signified the point at which the aircraft should have reached a certain speed so that takeoff could be safely effected in the distance still available.

Decision time was fast approaching and as yet Fitz had found no insurance cover. Attempts were made to get him included on the Lloyds insurance but a reply from the underwriters was delayed because of the Easter Bank Holiday weekend.

Fitz eventually found a way out of his difficulty.   As he later explained.   "Fortunately in a talk with my old friend, St. John Gogarty, I got him to approach the then President of the Executive Council, William T. Cosgrave, asking him to send me a letter for delivery to the President of the United States, Calvin Coolidge. When the President's aide-de-camp arrived in my office and handed me the letter with the President's compliments, and asked me to deliver it to the President of the United States, my leave was automatically cancelled. I was an officer on duty on a select state mission. The requisite witnesses were present to note the fact. The highly expensive insurance policy was not now necessary. I was, therefore, all set to go as soon as conditions were suitable."

The wraps of secrecy that up to now shrouded the project could safely be removed. The Irish, German and US press snapped up every detail of the preparations. Fitz facilitated reporters with the use of a hut in the aerodrome and interviews with the main players in the unfolding drama were allowed. Big crowds came out from Dublin and from other parts of the country each day to get a glimpse of the *Bremen* and the intrepid airmen.

One such person was Valentine McCarthy, who was a boy of ten at the time and who went on to carve a prominent name for himself in the business life of Ireland in the decades that followed. He related to me his memories of the great buzz of excitement surrounding the coming of the *Bremen* to Ireland. There were lots of articles in the newspapers and he avidly read everything about it. Without his parents' permission he walked all the way from the South Circular Road to Baldonnel on the Saturday previous to the flight, a distance of about ten miles. He arrived at the gates of the aerodrome a very tired boy. He walked up to the entrance but was stopped by the sentry and asked where did he think he was going. Val told him he had walked the whole way out from the city. "Sir, could I see the *Bremen?*'," he pleaded. "That's impossible", snapped the sentry in reply.

Young Val moved away in tears and sat on the ground beside a wall contemplating his bad fortune. He was still sniffling when this beautiful car drove up alongside where he sat. The gates were opened and just as the car was proceeding an officer sitting in the back noticed the young boy crying and asked the sentry what was the matter. The sentry told him how he had walked all the way from the city hoping to see the plane. The officer told

Val to sit into the car which was driven across the base and straight to the hangars.   The officer was Comdt. Fitzmaurice.

When the hangar doors swung open a wide-eyed Val looked on in wonder.   "It was a most beautiful sight as the sun came beaming in on the bright silver wings."   Fitz took him by the hand, led him up the ladder and put him sitting in the pilot's seat. "You are the last person to sit in that seat before we fly," Fitz said to him.   "If we succeed in crossing you can tell of your experience for the next fifty years".   Val was thrilled.   Fitz ordered a soldier on a motorcycle to bring him back home.   There he was met by his relieved parents who had been searching everywhere for him. Valentine went on to own one of Dublin's finest food outlets, Shiels of Moore Street, he founded the retail association RGDATA in 1942 and was its president for 15 years.   He also founded the Londis retail group and was a director with the Irish Sugar Co. and the Institute of Industrial Standards amongst other things.   He has many happy memories of his long and successful career but his favourite memory was the day he met Comdt. Fitzmaurice and saw the *Bremen*.

With the ardour for a westward flight across the Atlantic cooled off in other countries, the *Bremen* was, for the time being at least, left all alone in the field.   This gave its crew the opportunity to wait for really favourable weather.   But with the project now an open book and events being closely followed throughout the world, Koehl could sense the pressure building up for an early takeoff.   During these waiting days he received a message from Lufthansa that his employment with them had been terminated. This was a bitter blow for him and also angered the Baron greatly.

The early days of the second week in April were wet, windy and miserable and reports of weather conditions off Newfoundland were most unfavourable.   Torrential rain made the aerodrome unserviceable for any type of aircraft.   The *Bremen* looked lost and forlorn standing with her head facing to the west on the bleak Baldonnel landscape.   Takeoff was impossible and, in any event,

Supervising the loading of fuel for the flight.

weather experts advised that it would be suicide to attempt the crossing under the conditions prevailing on the Atlantic. These days passed slowly for the three adventurers. Koehl and Fitzmaurice kept themselves busy reading and rereading the charts and checking out the aircraft. The Baron kept himself occupied by writing poetry and learning English.

There is a saying that behind every great man there is a woman. This was certainly borne out in Fitz's case. His wife, Bill, proved a rock of strength, especially in those frustrating waiting days and in a contemporaneous account of the famous flight the Irishman was profuse in his praise of the part she had played. "She did everything to add to our comfort and peace of mind during the restless days that we wandered about feeling very much like caged lions. Never once did she allow the slightest note of fear to creep into her voice; in fact she accepted my proposal to fly the Atlantic as stoically as though I had casually mentioned the fact that I was going to fly to London.   Her fortitude and bravery added greatly to my peace of mind during these days."

Capt. Koehl and the Baron had also the highest of praise for Mrs. Fitzmaurice.   She made them feel at home from day one and they were very appreciative of her kindness in those tension filled days.   Fitz's sister, May Fitzmaurice, recalled the Germans first meeting with Bill.   She had been peeling onions for the dinner when they arrived in her home with her husband.   The chivalrous Baron took her hand and kissed it before Bill had time to wash off the smell of the onions.   It was most embarrassing for her at the time but the incident was the cause of much mirth for her afterwards.

By Wednesday, 11 April, there was a significant improvement in the weather which resulted in the aerodrome surface drying up quickly.   The eagerly awaited forecast from Captain Entwhistle of the British Air Ministry's meteorological service, that would signal the green light for the flight, at last came through.   The airmen had a final conference with Professor Martin of Dunsink Observatory on astronomical matters and returned to Baldonnel awaiting affirmation of the satisfactory weather forecast.   Fitz received the confirmation he awaited shortly after midnight.   Word was immediately passed on to Koehl and the Baron who were resting.   Fitz was elated.   He said he was "as cheered as a boy who had just learned that the little old red schoolhouse has been burned down."   Waving the report he dashed into the officers' mess and called out: "Crack goes the whip, off go the horses, round go the wheels."   Takeoff was scheduled for 5am.

Fitz slept soundly but it was a short night for him and at 3.30am he was up, fully refreshed and ready to meet whatever the new day was to bring.   Before he slipped off he kissed his young daughter goodbye as she slept in her cot.   "Little Pat was sleeping the sleep of the just but I feel sure that had she known at 5 o'clock in the morning I was about to hop off across the Atlantic, she would have immediately insisted that she be allowed to go along."

Koehl had a restless night. Thoughts of the perils of the flight he was about to undertake and of what a successful crossing would mean for the Fatherland agitated his mind. "In spite of all the daring attributed to me I am, as far as it is possible, very thoughtful and careful. Again and again the thought crossed my mind, had I made a mistake anywhere? The takeoff presented the greatest worry."

Time and time again his thoughts were for the Fatherland. "You, my dear Germany, I want to serve and help. And you, my nice world, I want to conquer."

As morning approached he was psychologically prepared for the risky mission, just like a brave soldier getting ready for an attack at the battle front. "Now let everything come - the mighty elements, gales, waves, darkness and fog - I will fight them all, or die in the struggle."

The German mechanics, Weller and Lengerich, worked through the night checking and rechecking every detail. They supervised the loading of the fuel and coated the wings and tail with paraffin oil as a protection against icing, which proved a vital consideration during the flight. At 4am fifty Irish Free State soldiers pushed the *Bremen* from hangar number 3 to the takeoff point nearby. They placed a two-wheeled dolly underneath the tail to support it in a takeoff position. This would discard itself as the plane gathered speed on the runway. With such a heavy load on board this simple appliance would be helpful for a safe takeoff.

Koehl, like Fitz, was a Roman Catholic. After making their confessions and taking communion they quietly had breakfast in the officers' mess. Koehl was first to appear. He was wearing his flying helmet and a light blue-grey overcoat over his flying suit. He strolled jauntily to the plane looking quite relaxed with hands in pockets and a broad smile on his face as he saluted to the crowd which included President Cosgrave and his wife, the German Consul-General, members of the cabinet, army and police chiefs and many other dignitaries.

Michael Burgess, Boyle, Co. Roscommon, was a Garda on duty at the aerodrome helping to control the big turnout of spectators that morning. Although retired from the force for over forty years he still vividly recalled for me that the crowd were "very excited but well behaved, many of them had Rosary beads, and some of them were shaking holy water at the plane and its crew".

Koehl had a briefing with the mechanics before climbing into the cockpit where he carefully checked the controls and instruments. He got out again and inspected the aircraft for the final time. He climbed the incline of the wing once more and at 4.55am was seated in the left-hand pilot's position.

Next the Baron appeared and after a salute for the President he set about overseeing the loading of provisions for the trip. These consisted of beef (unsalted) sandwiches (6 each), five flasks

The final preparations...

of tea, one flask of coffee, five flasks of beef tea, two dozen oranges (peeled) and two dozen bananas (peeled). He gave this message on behalf of Koehl and himself to reporters:

"On leaving the Irish Free State, Capt. Koehl and I wish to give expression to the deep and sincere gratitude which we both feel. We have found here both counsel and active help. More than that, we have found complete human understanding and great sympathy on the part of all civil and military authorities, as well as among the Irish people themselves.

"We count it a most unusual pleasure and honour to start our flight together with the Commandant of the Irish Air Force, whose officers, subalterns and privates have aided our preparations with exemplary comradeship. May God, into Whose omnipotent hands we have placed the success of our enterprise, fulfil for this island and its people, with their inspiring history, our grateful prayer for a happy future". He had already presented a silver cup to the Air Corps officers "as a token of gratitude for kindness and facilities rendered".

Meanwhile a smiling Fitzmaurice, wearing a heavy flying suit over his Free State uniform, was being wished well on his way by his fellow officers and friends. It was the same uniform he had worn on the *Princess Xenia* flight and his lucky charm, a gold four leaf clover, was still in his tunic pocket. President Cosgrave had a brief chat with him and Mrs. Cosgrave had words of encouragement for the airman's wife, Bill.

The Baron was, by now, seated in the cabin and Koehl, waiting patiently in the cockpit for Fitz to say his fond farewells, gave the signal to Lengerich and Weller to turn the propeller. After a long loving goodbye kiss to his wife the Irishman took his place in the right hand seat of the dual-controlled aircraft.

The airmen had been hoping for a backing wind to help the *Bremen*, dangerously overloaded with fuel, get off the ground. There was not a puff of air to help them. They were totally dependant on the power of the motor to make the break with

"Mother Earth". Fitz exchanged his lucky charm for a tiny inch high silver doll with the Baron who also had been given a small gold cross and some typewritten prayers by wellwishers. The Baron told Fitz his little doll had brought him safely "through a world war and off six operation tables".

The mechanics gave the "All Clear" and the chocks were jerked away from the wheels. Koehl nodded to his copilot and Fitz replied with a wave of his hand. One more fleeting glance down the runway; then a peep into the cabin to see if the Baron was all set. All was well. Koehl and Fitzmaurice looked at each other and nodded. The gas lever was pushed forward and the throttle was opened wide.

The *Bremen* gathered speed quickly over the concrete apron and the railway sleepers but it slowed again along the grassy upslope, gathering momentum again as it cleared the top and hastened along the downslope to the boundary fence. It had speed in hand as it swept by the red marker and all seemed right for the takeoff. Suddenly Fitz spotted a sheep sauntering across the runway in the path of the plane. This unexpected visitor was a recipe for disaster. Koehl could not see the wandering animal from his side and was startled when the Irishman lunged forward and grabbing the control column from the pilot he eased it back. The aircraft barely cleared the sheep and hit the ground again with a sickening thud. The Baron, looking through a small window in the bottom of the fuselage, wondered what had caused the bump as he watched the ground beneath him speeding past.

Koehl now had to work feverishly to regain the momentum. He kept her down until the last possible moment ensuring the maximum speed thrust and with only yards of runway remaining he asked the *Bremen* the $64,000 question. She duly responded. Slowly she rose touching the stunted hedgerows on the aerodrome's perimeter and barely clearing some big oak trees. The plane began sinking again as a conical shaped hill appeared directly ahead. Koehl eased her into a gentle flat turn as the left

wing-tip almost touched the side of the hill.   Any splutter of the
Bremen's engine or any slight error of judgement on Koehl's part
and the heavily-laden aircraft, with its 500 gallons of lethal cargo,
would have become an instant fireball in the hedgerow or on the
side of the hill.   Koehl and Fitz clasped hands again and both
touched the engine revolution counter as one would pat the neck
of a horse after clearing a formidable obstacle.   The *Bremen* was
on her way.

As the machine sped on full throttle across the Irish midlands,
familiar terrain to Fitz, his thoughts were for his wife, young
daughter and his many dear friends.   He wondered how his own
dear Bill felt on returning alone to their little daughter, Pat, still
sleeping soundly no doubt.   Her parting words were a source of
comfort to him now as he sped to an unknown destiny.   "Good
luck, Fitz," she had said, "**I know** you'll make it."

He felt it a shame that he had left his old friends in the Air

On her way - the *Bremen* begins her journey into aviation history.

Corps without telling them how much he appreciated their friendship. "For a moment I almost wished that I could wave to them once more but the trail of mist was closing in behind us."

Fitz wondered what his colleagues, Koehl and the Baron, were thinking. These were his silent companions on the adventure. Speaking with one another was impossible above the noise of engine and elements but that did not matter much anyway to the pair in the cockpit since Fitz had little German and Koehl had only a few words of English.

Mountain tops and church spires could be seen breaking through the thick blanket of ground fog over central Ireland. About one and a half hours after takeoff the airmen could see Galway beneath them and a little later they were flying over Slyne Head Lighthouse waving to the keeper, as he stood on his observation platform, and watching the great Atlantic swells as they lashed the craggy cliffs along the west coast below. It was a beautiful clear morning over the Atlantic, very different from the weather that had forced both the Irishman and the Germans back the previous year. Koehl kept the *Bremen* five hundred yards above the water and headed west at a constant speed of 200 kph (125 mph).

Brendan Ellis arrived at Baldonnel that morning just in time to be late to see the *Bremen* take off. He was a schoolboy at the time and, with his father and younger brother, had been to the aerodrome twice before and had met the three aviators. His father knew Fitzmaurice, whom Brendan recalls really looked the airman's part - in contrast to Koehl, whom he remembers as a friendly portly fellow who seemed always to have sweets in his pockets to dish out to the youngsters. Huenefeld, complete with monocle, and who seldom spoke seemed a little "weird" to a young lad's eyes.

On one of these visits Fitz asked Brendan, "Do you like dogs, sonny?". The teenager was shocked by the accent - a very exaggerated upper-crust English sound. Having recovered his composure Brendan replied that he did like dogs. Fitz asked did he have one? Brendan said "No". "Then I'll get you one, sonny", said Fitz. Brendan didn't believe that the aviator would live up to his promise but two weeks after the flight a lovely Irish Water Spaniel was delivered to his door.

Brendan confesses that he was not particularly fond of Fitz, especially the way he sounded, yet in time he became one of his greatest fans as a world class aviator. He also became an avid admirer of the *Bremen*, which was "light years ahead of everything else at the time", and of the aircraft's creator, Professor Hugo Junkers.

Brendan had been in the *Princess Xenia* the previous autumn before its flight. He boasted to his schoolmates of being in the plane and of knowing Fitzmaurice. He was so disappointed when the machine had been forced back and became the butt of nasty schoolboy remarks about his hero being "funky".

Most commentators have put forward the view that the Irishman was a last minute choice for the Bremen flight. Brendan revealed to me that his father, through contacts in the Fitzmaurice family, was aware that Fitz had been invited to join the Germans on a pending transatlantic attempt prior to Christmas 1927. A tentative invitation was certainly extended by North German Lloyd representative in Ireland, Waldemar Klose, in late 1927 which supports Brendan's claim that Fitzmaurice was, indeed, earmarked by the Germans many months previous to the flight.

His memory of the day of the flight was one of gloom. "It seemed to me a most depressing morning. There had been a huge crowd at Baldonnel but they were all gone when we got there. All we met was one soldier. He told us that they were gone and had killed a sheep on takeoff. That was a terrible omen. The whole place seemed depressed. I went home feeling they were gone and that we would never see them again."

Chapter 15

The Flight

As the Irish coastal outline faded into the distance behind them, smoke bombs were dropped to calculate wind speed and direction. When the charts and instruments indicated that they were holding their course Fitz and Koehl would exchange nods. When it was necessary to make a correction Fitz would mark the number of degrees deviation of the wind on the chart. When it was favourable they climbed to get the best advantage. When it was adverse Koehl would bring the aircraft down to 50 feet. Throughout the day the drift checks were made, their ground speed was calculated and the DR (Dead Reckoning) position noted.

Occasionally gathering clouds of a local storm could be seen on the horizon and these were skirted in the daylight hours. Fitz recalled these early hours. "The long rolling swells of the ocean seemed to smooth out and during the evening the sea looked like a sheet of glass with hardly a ripple on it."

Everything was going as well as could possibly have been expected.

"It all presented a most majestic sight. As we glanced at the great circular horizon we gained an immense appreciation of the

The *Bremen* leaves Baldonnel on her famous flight.

vastness of the mighty ocean and the puniness of our frail machine.

"Here and there ahead of us and to the right and left huge local downpours gave the appearance of vast solid columns reaching up from the ocean surface supporting the extensive banks of dark cloud reclining in the sky. Several isolated snowstorms looked like giant marble pillars fulfilling similar functions.

"It all presented a resemblance to an interior view of a high vaulted domed and arched cathedral of colossal proportions, the dome and arches being supported by gigantic vari-coloured columns and pillars, the whole illuminated by giant sunshafts flooding through great windows and apertures in the sides and ceilings. It looked so completely unearthly that it brought one close to God."

Throughout the day the Baron, isolated in the rear cabin between two huge fuel tanks, serviced his companions with supplies of food and drink. He had access to the cockpit only through a small opening and was kept updated on the plane's estimated position and other information through short notes scribbled on pieces of paper by Koehl and Fitzmaurice up front.

During these blissful, if uneventful, hours Fitz contemplated the development of transatlantic flying and the great advances that would be made in the years ahead. "I pictured a giant multi-engined airliner leaving Ireland. In the cabin were seated men and women, voyagers of the future to whom the ocean means but a barrier between the nations and to whom the aeroplane represented the most rapid means of overcoming the obstacle. A spacious cargo compartment was loaded with important freight, negotiable securities, money and bank notes. Below the pilot's cockpit would be a radio-room in which one of the two radio operators would keep in constant communication with ground and ship radio stations ascertaining and checking the position of the plane at all times both day and night. These reports after being handed to the navigator would be used by the pilot on duty for checking his instruments.

"As the darkness came I could visualise the passengers entering their berths in a similar manner to which the train passengers do at night. During the long hours of the day the passengers were either occupied by reading or eating light nourishment which was provided from a small electrically operated compartment in the rear of the passengers' salon.

"The failure of any one or even two of the power plants would cause but a momentary readjustment of the other motors in order to take the additional load. I could see the motors installed in such a manner that they would be easily accessible to the flying mechanic who would attempt to make repairs, if possible, while the plane was in flight."

The casual observer nowadays, accustomed to the reliability and comfort of long distance flying, might scoff at such modest predictions but when one considers that these thoughts were conjured up in moments of silent meditation on the very first successful westward flight ever made across the Atlantic after a litany of failed attempts, and were penned a short time after arrival on the American side in 1928 when long-distance flying was still strictly the reserve of aviation pioneers, one can just as readily understand why his ideas were scoffed at then too - but for so

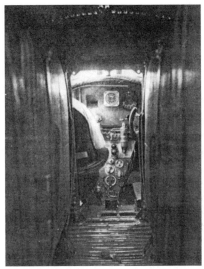

The passage way between the main fuel tanks from where the Baron operated as steward during the flight.

very different reasons.

Koehl and Fitzmaurice had agreed to alternate on the controls, three hours on and three hours off during the day with half-hour stretches at night. During one of Koehl's stints at controls in these daylight hours of peace and relaxation Fitz caught up on some missing sleep lulled by the sweet note of the engine. After a catnap of about half an hour a sudden roughness in the engine and a backfire jerked him from his slumbers. There was no need for alarm, however. Koehl was merely

The cockpit of the *Bremen.*

testing the mixture control to ensure the most economic use of the fuel.   A gentle touch and all was well again.

There was no sextant aboard but the flyers were able to calculate their approximate progress from noon according to the sun calculations.   Their watches were already ahead by 1h 45m and they estimated at that time they had passed the 30th meridian. They were happy to note that their speed was over 104mph.   The winds were light and variable and it became sunnier as the morning turned to day and as day turned to evening. At 21.00 GMT according to dead reckoning they were more than halfway across.

After about twenty hours of incident free flying in mostly favourable weather the doughty travellers suddenly became aware of a worrying change in conditions.   Temperature dropped, more threatening cloud formations built up all around enveloping them in a dense murky fog and the wind blew up violently against them. The change at first was gradual but soon the airmen found themselves in the eye of a fierce Atlantic storm.   Their weather report, spot on so far, had forecast little likelihood of fog off Newfoundland but the airmen knew that this had to be "Devil's Kitchen" and there was no way back.

Koehl explained his feelings.   "If we encountered similar condition on our night flights, we either turned back or landed carefully.   Here it was impossible to turn back. We were too far from the saving coast of Europe and very probably in the vicinity of Newfoundland. I had fought through a gale at night and without moonlight, but my previous experiences were child's play compared with what was threatening now"

They took the machine up to 6,000 feet in an attempt to rise above the storm and also, realising they were approaching land, to avoid hitting unseen mountain ranges jutting into the clouds. The plane, still on a westerly course, continued to be rocked and buffeted as it hobbled along now in pitch-black darkness.

With the sun no longer their guide and visibility down to zero outside the airmen were reduced totally to instrument flying. Very few pilots had developed this skill but Captain Koehl had made a deep study of the art and had vast experience in flying by instruments only or blind flying as it is known. The German was the recognised expert and he had an able assistant. The Irishman was, after all, one of the pioneers of night flying in Europe. He had vast flying experience over many years, in varied types of aircraft and in all weather conditions including fog and storms. This was the supreme test of their skill, nerve and endurance. There were not two other airmen in the world as well prepared to take up the challenge.

Fred Hotson in his book on the *Bremen* assessed the role of both pilots during these decisive periods of blind flying. He also listed the instruments on their respective panels. Koehl was captain and the one with the intimate knowledge of the Junkers' handling characteristics. Hotson emphasised that he was also "the one with the blind flying experience" and "it was he who had the critical blind flying instruments on his side of the panel". There was an airspeed dial, a magnetic compass and a turn and bank on either side. Koehl in addition had two extra instruments, one to indicate climb and descent, and the left-right indicator of the Askania remote compass. He also had an additional curved glass inclinometer as an effective backup. Hotson made the point that when visibility was down to zero there was no routine alternating at the controls. Fitzmaurice, he stated, would be engaged in increased cockpit vigilance. He would monitor his set of instruments, particularly the turn indicator and at half hour intervals attend the simple but vital matter of giving a half-turn to a Teclamet grease gun lubricating the engine pump. Failure to do so could result in putting the water pump out of action which could cause engine failure.

Hotson's excellent account of the flight tends to undervalue Fitz's role as copilot when the chips were down. If, as Hotson suggested, there was no routine alternating at the controls when visibility was zero outside, it might be interpreted that the German ace remained at the controls throughout the critical periods. Fitz's own account tells how Koehl and himself did, in fact, alternate at the controls during these most testing times in the flight. "At the end of each spell we were exhausted, both physically and mentally, and we had the feeling that the instruments were actually grinning at us".

If the alternating was not routine at these times it was because common sense would suggest that instead of clock-watching for break time both Koehl and Fitz instinctively knew when best to change roles. These men were not clock-watchers and were certainly not short-changed in common sense. It is clear that the two men worked closely together as a team throughout the flight but particularly during the critical periods of blind flying, each relieving the other from time to time and each dependant on the other.

Because of the good forecast that had signalled their departure from Baldonnel the airmen had anticipated that they might be spared the worst of the "witch's brew" off the Grand Banks. The forecast from the British Air Ministry had indicated, however, an arc of low pressure progressing south from Newfoundland to New York and that there would be wide regions of rain between Labrador and New York. Koehl wrote later that "I knew from all my past observations that an east-west flight could never be carried out without flying through a low pressure area and so we did not let this circumstance influence our decision whether the flight should or should not be made". They hoped and prayed that the storm might but be of short duration. Yet it continued lashing against them mercilessly hour after hour with the grim possibility of disaster striking at any second. Their machine was making little progress as the furious tempest rocked it up and down and tossed it from side to side. The do-or-die struggle was under way between the raging elements and the courageous battle-hardened aviators in their trusty *Bremen*. They were now in the same situation, no doubt, as that which had confronted previous pioneers on the transatlantic westerly route, none of whom had lived to tell the tale.

The Baron takes up the story. "By this time the storm rose to such fury that the plane appeared to make no headway. Cloud and fog patches raced past. The furious sea sought to tear itself asunder. Memories of the first stormy flight of the *Bremen* bore in on us. Now she was simply not flying any more, but dancing ... What an eternity! Will this darkness never end."

Fitz lamented the absence of a radio. Its inclusion was sacrificed for the sake of getting extra fuel on board. Such equipment was heavy and unreliable but now it would have given them a lifeline. He felt sure that it was a grave mistake not to have one on board. Had they contact with the ground or with ships below they could ascertain their exact position and the weather conditions ahead of them. Had they a radio they would make it to New York as they had planned, he reckoned. But now they did not know their position or whether they were over land or sea and could not be certain of the precise direction in which they were travelling.

They carried a large-size barometer secured to the outside of the cockpit, which had to be carefully watched for indications of ice formation on the wings and tail. If this happened it would be the end of the adventure. The upper clouds the airmen knew were a freezing zone, so they came down to a lower altitude where the ice flaked off. The decision to coat the wings and tail in paraffin oil prior to the flight was a vital factor in helping the flaking process and preventing the ice packing on the extremities.

The Venturi tube operating the gyro wheel of the turn and bank indicator froze up and put the instrument out of commission. Fortunately they had a spare which Fitz managed to fit with a couple of butterfly nuts in rear of the engine exhaust stacks, where the warm air from the exhaust prevented a similar occurrence happening again.

They decided to alter course to the southwest in the hope that they could escape the storm area and once in the clear they could change direction again to the west and come in over Nova Scotia.

Then the cabin lighting system suddenly failed.   All the instruments had luminous dials, however, and the crew had electric torches so it was more of a discomfort than a disaster.   Worse was to follow.   In flashing his torch to locate his chart, Fitz noticed that the floor of the cockpit was covered in oil.   He checked the main oil gauge.   It showed that the tank was less than a quarter full.   He turned the cock on the reserve tank to the main and after a while the gauge showed that it was full.   But when he shut off the cock he was alarmed to see the gauge on the main tank dropping again to its former level.   He pointed out the problem to Koehl.   The German ace pilot later admitted to the Baron that at that point he said three "Our Fathers" to settle himself.

Fitz decided to investigate.   He had to get to the main oil tank underneath the dashboard and in the confined space of the cockpit that was not an easy matter.   He opened the roof of the cockpit cabin and standing on his seat he first pushed his body through the opening with his face and upper body taking full force of the slipstream.   Slowly he forced his legs into the opening between the two large petrol tanks in the rear of the cockpit and eased himself forward until he managed to get his head under the wheel of his control column.   Flashing his torch he could see that everywhere was covered in oil.   In his cramped position he could not discover the leak but assumed that a bad one must exist between the tank and the engine.

He worked his way painfully back to his seat and scribbled a note to Koehl.   It read: "We are losing oil somewhere - Get to land as quick as possible, we are losing oil very badly".

If the machine was losing oil at the rate it seemed to be then time was fast running out for them.   An alarmed Koehl wrote in reply that he was heading for landfall and changed course to northwest.

Some time later they discovered, however, that the oil leak scare was a false alarm.   The gauge showed the rate of flow, which was a slow trickle, from the reserve into the main tank and was not a measure of oil in the tank. The oil found on the floor came from the tachometer cable. Koehl admitted in his account of the incident that the needless scare was caused by an oversight during preflight tests. "We had never practised filling the tank from the reserve during our test flights and thus owed this hour of bitter torture to our negligence."

This oil scare received extensive reportage afterwards and some accounts erroneously stated that Fitz had fixed the leak with insulation tape. Even the Baron in his *Report from Greenly Island*

The note passed from Fitz to Koehl during the oil leak scare.

got it wrong. He wrote: "After some minutes groping about he (Fitz) found the oil leak and repaired it. The oil gauge remained steady and we carried on". That indicates the state of confusion caused by the phantom leak. It certainly did not help the aviators in charting their course during the storm that raged into the night.

The level of concentration needed to survive this endless struggle in the dark combined with the lack of sleep was now beginning to take its toll on both pilots. Fitz in *The Three Musketeers of the Air* told of his weariness as the long night dragged on. "So great was our fatigue that for moments I would drop off into slumber only to awake with a start and my heart pounding madly against my ribs."

After what Fitz termed "interminable hours of endless flight" the thick fog suddenly disappeared behind them and above they could see a welcoming star-studded sky. Koehl described the scene. "These were stars, many stars, and they glimmered like the lights of as many lighthouses. Every now and then they, or we, disappeared in the sea of clouds." The multitude of stars above cast their reflection in the sea below and this gave the weary airmen an unreal feeling "like floating in a bowl of stars". It took them a little time to adjust to their new situation. They had no idea where they were but at least now they could check their course with the Great Bear and Pole stars, the same as mariners had done for many centuries.

Koehl ordered a southwesterly course by Polaris and during the next few hours of steady flying both wearied pilots took brief naps. The clouds at last cleared from their path and strange shapes could be seen below. From their lofty perch over 6,000 feet up these seemed like icebergs. Fitz, through his binoculars, could identify in the "stygian darkness" what appeared to be a vast snow-covered forest. They came down and on despatching some white flares their discovery of land was confirmed. Fitz signalled to Koehl who, with a broad smile, acknowledged that they had reached the North American continent and that the land below had to be Labrador. Their only course now, they reckoned, was to continue flying in the direction in which they were heading and wait for the dawn.

As daylight broke they could now see more clearly a huge expanse of snow covered forest and mountains. "Where were the long white concrete roads, the broad aerodromes? Where were the great factories? It seemed we had broken in upon the silent sepulchre of desolation. Not a puff of smoke, not a beaten path over the trackless wastes of white snow. Not even an animal or bird ... could be seen," Fitz wrote later.

But they had reached landfall and that made them happy. They now realised that during the night they had strayed hundreds of miles north of their course and had been positioned somewhere between Greenland and Labrador before realising their plight.

As they continued their flight they marvelled at the bleak forbidding landscape. They crossed a deep river valley running southwards and over "long drawn-out lakes", as Koehl described them. It was now 14.00 hours GMT on Friday, the 13th. What a day to tempt fate!

They flew southwards, following the course of a river, coming down sometimes to under 50 feet (15 m) and searching along its banks for any sign of human habitation. No trace of life could be seen in this remote wilderness, this wonderland of snow and ice. They altered their course to the east in the hope of reaching the coast and possible salvation.

More hours of flying in the same direction through several snowstorms and over large frozen lakes added to the exhaustion and frustration of the *Bremen* crew. Their tired minds conjured up images of big modern cities in the distance complete with aerodromes on their outskirts. The visions evoked feelings of joy and elation but these turned to ones of frustration and bitter disappointment when finding out on closer examination that what they had seen were simply scrub trees surrounded by snow - cruel mirages of fatigued minds.

"We seemed to be over a land forgotten by God. Nothing but snow, snow, snow everywhere", Fitz recalled.

They had calculated that there was sufficient fuel for 40 hours flying on board leaving Baldonnel. But now they were over 30 hours in the air and with greater than average consumption during the night the fuel situation was becoming a major concern. Although there was no way to assess accurately what fuel remained it was obviously starting to run dangerously low, perhaps sufficient for only another two hours or so they reckoned. They still could not pinpoint their exact location but they knew that hopes of reaching Mitchel Field, in New York, over a thousand miles away, had long since vanished.

While forging their way through a heavy blizzard and with spirits drooping again Fitz saw, through a rift in the snow storm immediately below, what appeared to be a ship held by ice in a large frozen lake. He yelled at Koehl: "A ship! A ship!" But just as suddenly it disappeared again. Throttling back the engine they came down lower and again found what he had seen a little earlier. It was not a ship but a lighthouse on a small island and surrounded by a frozen lake or sea. They noticed smoke coming from the chimney of the living quarters and a husky dog team lay harnessed to a sleigh just outside. The men of the *Bremen* almost wept with joy and relief.

Huenefeld remembered the moment of redemption. "We skim over the lighthouse. Now men and dogs are moving about. We are safe".

Fitz and Koehl shook hands silently and prepared for a landing. They knew this was going to be a tricky operation. In the middle of the island there was a large frozen pond. They decided to put down there because otherwise all to be seen were jagged rocks and heavy snowdrifts. A smoke bomb was dropped to determine the direction of the wind, which they estimated was blowing at the rate of about 40 mph. They circled round, turned into the wind, throttled back and began a slow and cautious approach.

Fitz in his memoirs takes up the story. "We got Von Huenefeld to lay on the cabin floor wedged between the two big petrol tanks behind the cockpit, his monocle firmly screwed into his eye. As we approached the edge of the pond we switched off the engine, eased the control column gently back and dropped straight onto the ice, which broke leaving us standing on the propeller boss, the tail of the machine vertically above us.

"Koehl got slapped against the dashboard receiving a severe cut over his eye. Von Huenefeld presented a remarkable spectacle. He was perched immediately above us, between the tanks, giving us a jaundiced look through the monocle which did not budge from its setting.

"We were now almost hysterical with joy, and all three of us burst out laughing. We shook hands congratulating ourselves on our luck and tried to force our way onto the ice. Koehl and I, who were first out, immediately collapsed, our legs having become so cramped that we could not stand up for several minutes. After we had collected ourselves we set out to extricate Von Huenefeld from his precarious position.

"As soon as we got him out the force of the wind swept him off his feet and he fell into the icy cold water. We retrieved him and hustled him in the direction of the lighthouse. By the time we got him propped up in front of the roaring fire he was as cold as a block of ice."

After 36 $\frac{1}{2}$ hours in the air they were on mother earth again. It had almost been a perfect landing despite the bone-shaking experience and the unflattering resting position of the plane with its nose in the ice and its tail in the air. The Baron recorded that Koehl had set "the machine down perfectly on the frozen surface, the shortest and best landing I ever experienced." The ice had held until the plane had almost come to a halt but then gave way under the braking wheels which caused the machine to tilt forward on stopping. The only apparent damage done to the *Bremen* was a broken propeller. The small lake of ice on which Koehl set down the plane was later discovered to be a reservoir, which supplied fresh water to the islanders.

For the few inhabitants of this remote, forbidden, windswept island perched between Labrador and Newfoundland in the Strait of Belle Isle in the Gulf of St. Lawrence, this was a day to remember. Situated only two miles from the Quebec mainland, to which it is joined by ice during the long winter months, and three miles from the western borders of Labrador, it was little known except to sailors who used the strait as a shipping route for the St. Lawrence. Within hours of the *Bremen's* landing Greenly Island was to become world famous.

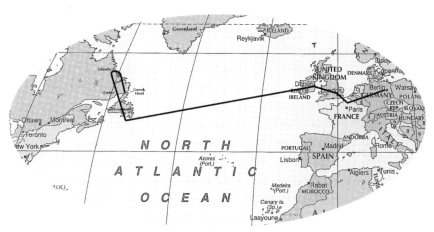

The flight path of the *Bremen*.

Chapter 16

The Agony
and the Ecstasy

The *Bremen* flight grabbed the headlines of all the top-circulation dailies on both sides of the Atlantic. The story particularly captured the imagination of the American public. The huge ethnic German and Irish population in the US, and particularly in New York, took especial delight in the prospect of proudly honouring their heroic countrymen and in sharing in the reflected glory of their achievement. The massive interest evoked in the 'Big Apple' by the flight of the *Bremen* was almost unprecedented, similar to the excitement evoked by the Lindbergh flight to Paris in the *Spirit of St. Louis* the year before. The *New York Times* alone recorded receipt of 11,663 telephone calls on 13 April from a public anxious for news of the flyers. The *Boston Globe* received more than 4,000 similar calls on that fateful Friday.

The *New York Evening Graphic* of 12 April had sounded caution to its readers on the chances of success of an east-west Atlantic attempt. "American flyers, Lindbergh among them, have consistently repulsed suggestions, accompanied by golden promises, to attempt the dangerous east-west crossing. **From the first they recognised its peril. Of late they have called it**

impossible".

Such negative thoughts were far from the minds of reporters for other New York newspapers. This was one of the major "feel good" stories of the century. They made the most of it. Big coverage was given to the elaborate welcome being arranged in the city for the triumphant aviators when they arrived. Grover A. Whalen, Chairman of the Mayor's Committee for the Reception of Distinguished Guests, headed the welcoming group which included representation of the City of New York, the military authorities, Nassau County, and German-American and Irish-American organisations in the city.

The *Brooklyn Daily Times* was littered with articles on every aspect of the story. One of the main reports told of the huge crowd waiting excitedly at Mitchel Field in Long Island, New York, the intended destination of the *Bremen*. "New Yorkers in holiday spirits stood in groups about the field, waiting to be the first to welcome the aviators.... Two false alarms provided large thrills for the crowd when, within a half hour of each other, two Junkers monoplanes of identical build circled the field and made perfect landings. As the crowd, breaking through police lines, rushed the field it was discovered that the first plane, No 87, had only travelled the distance of one mile from Curtiss Field to join the welcomers.

"When the excitement of the first false alarm had barely died down another Junkers plane was sighted, and again the crowd went wild. This time the passenger was discovered to be Miss Herta Junkers, daughter of the inventor, who had also come from Curtiss Field."

The newspaper also reported that nine planes were waiting at Curtiss Field and six at Mitchel Field, ready to welcome the transatlantic flyers at first word of the approach of the *Bremen*. The 29 year old Miss Junkers, who was accompanied by her 19 year old brother, Erhard, was to be the only woman in that party. On the fuselage of her plane were painted in huge black letters

"Welcome Bremen" while the American flag decorated the other side.

Irish National Archives show that the Irish Government were eager to make capital from a successful attempt. The Department of Foreign Affairs sent the following message by cablegram at 3pm on 13 April to Professor Smiddy, Minister Plenipotentiary of the Irish Legation in Washington: "Very urgent ... Bremen flight ... Commandant Fitzmaurice is officially on leave but travelling in uniform. Nevertheless you should go to New York ... meet him ... facilitate him getting all possible recognition ... successful flight."

Eagerly awaiting the *Bremen's* triumphant arrival at Mitchel Field was the captain's uncle, Joseph Koehl, a music teacher based in Manhattan who was accompanied by his daughter. He was confident that his nephew would not fail. The New York *Evening World* of 13 April reported that Mr. Koehl had composed a march to honour his now famous nephew. It was titled "Mitchel Field or Heaven". The last time he had seen Hermann had been in 1922 when he had conducted the music at the captain's wedding in Ludwigsburg. Hermann had told him at that time: "Uncle, some day I'm coming over to see you, and I'm going by air, and so fast that it will astonish you."

The same newspaper ran a huge headline "No Report of German Plane" on its front page. Other headlines told of "Coast skies scanned for Atlantic flyers due to arrive today" and "Monoplane should have reached Newfoundland or Nova Scotia soon after midnight - Big welcome planned".

There were extensive accounts of the scene that awaited the flyers at the Long Island aerodrome. The *New York World* headlined that 25,000 people had waited in vain at Mitchel Field. "By train and automobile the crowds came from New York and from all parts of Long Island until at noon roads to Mitchel Field were glutted with cars and a crowd of surging humanity estimated at 25,000 was massed on the borders of the field.... There were few references to the "jinx" of Friday the 13th and these were overshadowed by the confident belief that German thoroughness and efficiency and "Irish luck" would win out this time with the Atlantic spanned at last in a single flight by plane from Europe to America."

Among the huge throng at Mitchel Field was Mayor Jimmy Walker of New York. *The Sun* reported that as the long day of waiting wore on the more the doubts began to surface and the upbeat mood of the crowd slowly gave way to an air of pessimism. But Mayor Walker roused their spirits again. "The Mayor struck the keynote when as aviation experts began to shake their heads gravely and express fears that the *Bremen* no longer could be in the air, he issued a statement expressing the personal conviction that 'he knew they were coming'."

Such was Mayor Walker's assessment of the importance of the occasion and his confidence in the success of the flight that he decided to stay the night at the field believing that it was his "official duty" to do so.

The British press was rather more subdued in its reporting of the flight. This being a German-Irish attempt, rather than a British one, it did not command the same interest in the editorial offices of Fleet Street as it did in America and elsewhere. Yet the *Daily Express* managed to overcome the narrow nationalism evident in some other London dailies and was generous in its leading article in its praise of the bravery of the aviators involved. "The three airmen, two Germans and one Irishman, who began yesterday their attack on the east-west crossing of the Atlantic, carry with them the good wishes of two continents. The risks of that enterprise have been proved in tragedy after tragedy, which is one of the reasons why red-blooded men will always be ready to run them."

"A few years hence the passage will be commonplace, but these are the pioneer days, when those who essay the great adventure take their lives in their hands, with the full knowledge of all the odds against success. The more honour to them, and the heartier the desire that their gallantry may be rewarded. When it comes to bravery of this high quality there is no question of nationality, but only an instinctive and universal cry of 'Good Luck'."

The London Letter in *The Irish Times* of 14 April mentioned Fitz's efforts to organise an all-Irish attempt in previous years and that the plan never got off the ground because of the refusal of the Free State authorities to fund the project. The article also referred to discussions he had had with English experts in the Royal Aero Club, where he was well known, concerning the development of private flying. His English associates had complained of the red tape hindering progress in this regard in their country to which Fitz is reputed to have replied: "We have the same thing in Ireland only there we call it green tape." The same column reflected the popular feeling in the British capital. "News of the departure of the German and Irish aviators is received with mixed feelings of admiration for the bravery of the men and fears for their safety. Up to now attempts to fly the Atlantic have borne nothing but a record of tragedy. But it is hoped that this present expedition may accomplish **what most people consider impossible.**"

The big aviation story in the French newspapers was not of the *Bremen* but of the awarding of the Legion of Honour to Capt. Costes and his copilot Lieut. Le Brix after their round the world flight which took over six months to complete. But the Parisian dailies also found good space for articles on the *Bremen* flight.

The *Brooklyn Daily Times*, typical of the big circulation dailies in the US, was dominated by the story. Its front page banner headline told of two reported sightings of the *Bremen*, both of which turned out to be false and, as a result, caused bitter disappointment by dashing the dearly held hopes of a successful crossing. The story ran: "The report of the sighting of a plane high over Brocton, Mass., was received shortly after 1pm and followed by almost exactly two hours by a report from the

Canadian steamer, *Arras*, of the sighting of a plane over Nova Scotia. The elapsed time would be logical for a plane's flight from Nova Scotia to Massachusetts. If both reports are correct, it is evident the Bremen followed a course south of Newfoundland, made for the coast of Nova Scotia, and from that point headed for Long Island over a direct route that would bring the plane above Brocton".

This news was cabled round the world. It was the cause of rejoicing in London, Paris, Berlin and Dublin. The report was passed on to Fitz's wife, Bill, by an officer at Baldonnel. The great sense of relief she felt was soon shattered, however, when she was informed a short time later that it had been a false sighting.

Fitz's loyal aide in the Irish Air Corps, Johnny Maher, in later years reflected on the long night's wait for verified news at Baldonnel. "The two Germans, Lengerich and Weller, arrived over at my house at 8pm that night and we had a few drinks. We then went down to the mess. Word came through at 12 o'clock (midnight) or 1 o'clock that the machine had been sighted over Nova Scotia. Weller, who had with him a picture of Capt. Koehl in full German uniform, went up to Col. Russell, and handed him the photograph. Col. Russell, friend and mentor of Fitzmaurice, said: 'No, I wont take the photograph as yet because by our reckoning they (the airmen) could not have got anywhere near Nova Scotia.'" Weller had been given the photograph by Koehl with the instructions that he was to present it to the officers at Baldonnel if he succeeded but he was to burn it if he (Koehl) did not succeed. The German mechanic was somewhat taken aback by Col. Russell's rejection of the photograph but the Irish officer's doubts proved subsequently to be well founded.

Baldonnel aerodrome was buzzing with excitement and anticipation through the long hours of waiting. All but a few officers waited up all Thursday night for any news. Among those in the officers' mess throughout the vigil were Col. Dan Hogan, Army Chief-of-Staff, and Gen. O'Duffy, chief of the Garda Síochána

(Civic Guard).

Arrangements were made in New York to broadcast bulletins on the flight on a short wave station WGY especially for reception in Germany where the print media were also closely following developments. Word had come through to Berlin that the plane had arrived safely at Mitchel Field. The news was circulated to other European capitals and for a brief while ecstasy reigned. But it was another false dawn.

Newspaper offices in London and Paris were besieged for news of the flight and all were becoming wary of unconfirmed reports of sightings of arrival from the American side. On the Friday the newspapers offices in the Irish capital were again besieged for updated bulletins by a public fast becoming pessimistic for the welfare of their brave hero and his gallant German comrades. But a false report in the evening meant that most people in the city went to bed on the night of 13 April believing that the three airmen had reached America safely - only to have their hopes shattered the next day.

Mrs. Fitzmaurice could not sleep as she waited and worried through the long vigil. The longer her wait the lesser the chances of her husband's survival, she knew. Yet she remained hopeful. "What more can I do, but hope," she said to friends. The Fitzmaurices' seven year old daughter, Patricia, played in the yard of their home with her alsatian puppy, given to her by Capt. Koehl and the Baron, and which she had given the name, Bremen, blissfully unaware of the growing concern for her father's wellbeing. Capt. Koehl's wife, Elfriede, also kept vigil throughout the night. She awaited news in the editorial rooms of the *Local Anzeiger*.

Back on Greenly Island the three airmen were being hospitably cared for by the French Canadian lighthouse keeper, Johnny Letemplier, and his large family. Johnny managed the Canadian government station assisted by his nephew, Albert. The Letempliers provided some rope which was looped round the tail of the *Bremen* projecting into the air. Slowly it was lowered on

Fitz's daughter, Pat, at the wheel of her father's convertible prior to the flight.

to the ice and, when the machine was back on even keel, the engine was covered.   Next the airmen, with the assistance of the Letempliers tried to pull the machine off the ice but In the attempt the undercarriage got damaged.   Capt. Koehl was furious when he saw what had happened and put a halt to any further efforts. Up to his knees in icy water he drained the radiator.   The machine was then secured.   He wrote later: "With strong ropes we fastened the Bremen down to North American soil".

All day, while the airmen slept in the lighthouse, a steady stream of visitors came to Greenly from the mainland to view the aircraft. One of the first visitors was Alfred Cormier, who operated the local telegraph office from his home at Blanc Sablon (Long Point) on the Quebec mainland nearby, which was still linked by winter ice to the island.   He returned to his village and tried to make first contact with the outside world.   The landline to the west was out of operation, which was a common occurrence during the winter months, but Cormier managed to make contact with a Marconi station at Point Amour, 18 miles to the east of Blanc Sablon, in Labrador.   The operator there, W.F. Barrett, imprinted his name indelibly on the unfolding drama by transmitting the news of the *Bremen's* landing on Greenly Island to stations in Newfoundland and Nova Scotia and from there to points in Canada and the US. The news spread along the wires like wildfire.   The world was soon to know of the fate of the *Bremen*.

Word got through to St. John's, Newfoundland, at 6.30pm EST. The message read: "German plane at Greenly Island, wind southeast, thick. - W.F. Barrett."

The US Lines' steamship, George Washington, was at sea and was among the first to hear of the *Bremen's* landing from the Point Amour broadcasts.   Great Britain got its first reports from the ship.

Associated Press flashed the message across the US, Canada and Europe.   The first report in Germany of a safe landing was received in the early hours of Saturday morning by a wireless

Greenly Island from the sky - (insert) the lighthouse where they slept.

operator in Munich who was monitoring US transmissions. In Dublin President Cosgrave was wakened during the night to be told of the news. So too was Mrs. Fitzmaurice. She was naturally thrilled. "It was the greatest ambition of his life to fly the Atlantic east to west for the first time and he would never have rested until he did it. He said he was going to do it and he has kept his word," she told a reporter of *The Irish Times* who delivered the news.

The flyers were anxious to make direct contact with the outside world. Having rested and taken some food they were driven across the ice in a sleigh powered by huskies but when they arrived at Blanc Sablon all communication links were out of commission. After a wait the Baron managed to get two messages through to Henry Schuengal, general manager of the North German Lloyd, in New York. His first message read: "Made safe intermediate landing on Greenly Island, Straits of Belle Isle, necessitated by lack of fuel caused by strong winds and fog. Inform press." A

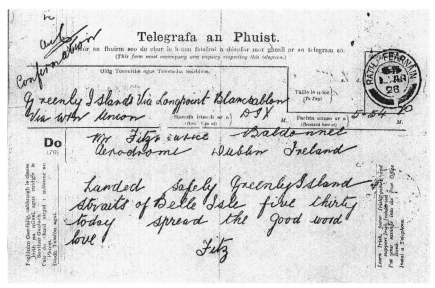

Copy of the telegram Fitz sent to his wife from Greenly Island.

later message asked that fuel be sent to the island and told of the damage to the machine.

Fitz sent the following message to his wife: "Landed safely Greenly Island Straits of Belle Isle five thirty today. Spread the good word, love - Fitz". The telegram gave Greenly Island as the sending point via Long Point - Blanc Sablon and was cabled through by Western Union. He also sent the following brief communique to his fellow-airmen at Baldonnel: "Air Corps, Ireland. - Landed on an iceberg - Fitz".

President Cosgrave sent a telegram to Fitz in his remote refuge. "To the crew of the *Bremen* and particularly to yourself as an officer of the Irish Air Force, I tender my heartiest congratulations on sharing the first flight from Europe to America. Your achievement will be notable in history. Ireland is proud of your gallant part in this great advance towards the conquest of the air. Please convey to Baron Von Huenefeld and Capt. Koehl my admiration and congratulations."

The Irish Minister for Defence, Mr. Fitzgerald, announced immediately that the Commandant had been promoted to Major and sent confirmation of his promotion in a congratulatory telegram on the Saturday.

Mrs. Fitzmaurice spent the weekend with close friends, the Meyers family, at Springvale, Rathfarnham, in the south Dublin suburbs. On Saturday night she was guest of honour at the dance in the city's most famous night spot of the period, the Metropole. When she arrived the lights were put out and spotlights were focused on her as she sat at her table. Vincent Rogers, the band leader, announced her presence and then the band played both the Irish and German national anthems. It was a night of rare celebration in Dublin.

"I cannot tell you how happy I am that my brave husband is safe," was how Mrs. Koehl responded to the news at her home in Germany. "It is a fine achievement and I am proud of him. I always knew he would make it and never lost courage." Both wives exchanged congratulations by telegram and awaited further developments from America.

Young Pat Fitzmaurice was left in the care of the Sheil family at Castlewarden, on the borders of counties Kildare and Dublin, only a short distance from Baldonnel. Mr. Sheil, like Fitz, was a veteran of WW1, and was a well-known veterinary surgeon. He was one of the early graduates from the Irish Veterinary College at Ballsbridge and was friendly with both Fitzmaurice and Col. Russell. The Sheil children, Mary (later Mrs. McNally) and Eamon (later a leading Dublin solicitor) were young playmates of Pat, who regularly stayed with the family when they lived at Somerton, Lucan, and at Castlewarden, to where they moved in November 1927. Both children had been in the *Princess Xenia* the day before her transatlantic attempt in 1927. They carried fond memories throughout their lives of these exciting days from their childhood, and especially the memory of the great relief felt by everyone when news was received of the safe landing of the *Bremen*.

Fitzmaurice's parents were overcome with emotion on hearing the news at their home, 113 Richmond Road, Drumcondra. His mother could not restrain her tears. "Thank God they have arrived," she said. "He was always a brave lad. Thank God, my poor boy is safe." Fitz's brother, Louis, manager at a large department store in Dublin and, as a newspaper noted, Scoutmaster of the Fairview Catholic Boy Scouts, expressed his "unbounded satisfaction" and said it came as no surprise at all "that the flight had become a 'fait accompli'".

In the US and Canada the big cities came to a standstill after hearing of the safe landing of the *Bremen*. A holiday like atmosphere prevailed as thousands of people danced in the streets and the merrymaking continued well into the night.

US President, Calvin Coolidge, sent the following message to the Governor-General of the Saorstat (Irish Free State): "I wish to express to you as well as to the people of the Irish Free State the great admiration of myself and the people of the USA for Comdt. Fitzmaurice's share in the magnificent flight and to rejoice for a safe arrival."

Canadian Premier, Mackenzie King, joined in the congratulations and told the aviators that "your achievement marks a distinct and notable advance in the development of aviation as a means of bridging the oceans and of making possible closer relations and friendships among the nations of the world".

The British Secretary of State for Air, Sir Samuel Hoare, and the Secretary for War, Mr. Davis, sent their congratulations to President Cosgrave and to the German Ambassador in London. Sir Samuel's message to the President read: "The Air Council send warm congratulations on part of an officer of the Irish Free State Air Force on first successful (east/west) flight of the Atlantic". Reporting on the message to the Irish President the London *Times* of 16 April commented: "Sir Samuel's congratulations will tighten the bond of brotherhood. Today the Free State Air Force takes pride in the feeling that the RAF is proud of it". I doubt if "it" felt flattered with such condescension.

Leader of the Opposition in the Dail (Irish Parliament), Eamon de Valera, not one of Fitz's most admired figures, sent a congratulatory cablegram to William Lyndon, Secretary of the American Association for the Recognition of the Irish Republic in Chicago. He wrote: "All Irishmen rejoice at Ireland's association with first crossing of Atlantic east to west (by plane). Admiration for courage is above party."

The British Press praised the achievers and the achievement - with certain reservations. The *Evening News* read: "It seems odd to those who during the war had no reason to rejoice over German flying to be now congratulating a couple of Germans. But there are no territorial boundaries in bravery; and none of us need be ashamed of applauding Capt. Koehl and Baron von Huenefeld. They and Comdt. Fitzmaurice, of the Irish Free State Air Force, rank now with Alcock and Whitten Brown."

The Observer stated that the Germans' distinction was "more than earned by their national cultivation of 'air sense', their intelligent appreciation of the functions of flying and their persevering efforts to perfect the technique". The *Morning Post* stated that it was "brave to attempt once but foolish to repeat", a comment that overlooked the fact that the success came to the trio on the repeat exercise. The *Daily Mail* had a similar comment and added that "the German machine was equal to any but the best British designs".

Having congratulated the airmen the *Daily Telegraph* advised that "now that the Atlantic has been flown both ways it would be wise to leave the ocean alone and devote themselves to the more serious problem of long distance flying overland". The *Times* commented: "So precarious a success is no guarantee that the feat can be repeated at will". The *Sunday Express* predicted the way forward for Atlantic crossings was by seaplane. "The trail has been blazed. It now remains to make it safe. Land aeroplanes can never be satisfactory Atlantic ferries. The future is with the flying boat."

Mrs. Fitzmaurice received messages from the Royal Aeronautical Society, the Limerick Steamship Co., agents in Ireland for the North German Lloyd, and from the British Legion congratulating "our comrade ex-Serviceman". She also received another communication from her husband requesting her to rejoin him in New York and to bring his military decorations with her.

The Baron's mother was ill and was not told of the flight until its safe completion. His brother told of the family's joy at the news: "We thank God with all our heart that He has preserved my brother and his companions," he said.

Commander Richard E. Byrd, highly acclaimed polar aviator, and one who knew the hazards of the Belle Isle coastal area better than anyone, was full of praise for the flyers. "This is great for Germany and Ireland. I felt sure that they could do it. The distance from east to west is equivalent to 600 miles more than from west to east because of adverse winds. This, therefore, was a most remarkable feat and shows the great courage and skill of the flyers. Their landing must have been hazardous because I know good landing places up there are scarce. It's a rough desolate coast."

Despite the strong reservations expressed in Germany to the flight before departure, the news of the safe landing was greeted with unrestrained euphoria there.

In the days that followed the safe arrival of the *Bremen*, President Field-Marshal Paul Von Hindenburg sent his congratulations to "the daring ocean flyers". Chancellor Marx was delighted because "this triumph is due to German technique and German daring". The ex-Kaiser sent a message from his exile in Doorn.

It is said that the exception proves the rule. One of the most outspoken critics of the transatlantic adventure, Herr Brandenburg, Director of the German Air Ministry, in a skilful usage of words reiterated his opposition to such flights by pointing to the exception, Capt. Koehl, who was now a national hero. "We warned against the flight, and we still believe that a flyer less daring and less skilful that Capt. Koehl, who is our finest aviator, would have failed in the attempt," he said.

Equally skilful were the script writers at Lufthansa, the company with whom Koehl had worked prior to his dismissal, a decision which caused him (and the Baron) much anguish in the days prior to the flight. "The whole German people rejoice over their heroes, especially Capt. Koehl," declared their statement. "The Luft Hansa joins in the rejoicing because it formerly employed Capt. Koehl and has always recognised his high flying qualifications. The prospects of the flight being successful were so small that the Luft Hansa opposed Capt. Koehl in order to save him from the fate of the other 29 victims of the Atlantic. Now we are delighted he has been saved for Germany."

Despite this spontaneous outburst of national pride in Germany, an undercurrent of discontent emerged in certain places in the days that followed regarding the flag carried on the *Bremen*.   It had been reported that the Baron had opted for the old Imperial colours rather than the black, red and gold of the Republic.   This dampened the ardour of the anti-imperialists to the achievement. Ironically the city of Bremen, after which the aircraft had been given its name and the citizens of which had largely financed the flight, voted down a motion to send a congratulatory message because of the colours carried.

But in America it was all unreserved praise for the aviators and their achievement.   In a leading article in the *New York Times* the writer said that "they had done all that careful preparation, prudent waiting for favourable weather signs, skill, stout hearts and daring could do to command success.   We cannot fail to recognise and reciprocate the international goodwill which animated them in their bold undertaking."

The New York *American* called Fitzmaurice "the Irish Ace" in its lead story.   It also had a dramatic sketch showing the wrecks of aircraft that had failed in previous attempts, with a sea monster rising from the deep, and above, flying triumphantly towards America, the *Bremen*, its German-Irish crew waving defiantly at the horrible creature below.   The caption read: "Three brave men, two from Germany, one from Ireland, escaped the fate of the equally brave men in the *White Bird*, the *Endeavour* and the *St Raphael*.   The wishes, hopes and prayers of the world were with the flyers."

The *New York Herald Tribune* under the banner headline "Victory!" commented: "These brave airmen took a desperate chance and won by the narrowest of margins.   Their victory may well stand for the victory of man."

The *Boston Globe* zoned in on the Irishman.   "The laughing face of this rollicking young Irish aviator, who brought the tricolor of the Free State, seemed to have added romance to the adventure. His youth, his daring, his courage, his devil-may-care spirit brought to the minds of Americans another Lindbergh and with the same confidence that the world had in Lindbergh people seemed to feel that 'Fitz' would bring the plane through."

Mayor Walker of New York was thrilled that his hunch had paid off. "I was convinced they would succeed. That's why I stayed until I got the cheerful report. It's a great victory for the science of aviation and a heroic achievement for that brave trio."

There was cutthroat competition between the major newspapers on the east coast of the US in the days that followed to be first with a scoop on some aspect of the story. There were planes held on stand-by in New York and Boston. No expense was to be spared in the effort to get to Greenly Island and arrange interviews with the main players in the drama. Money was no problem but accessibility to the marooned aviators certainly was.

While Herta Junkers and others in New York were devising plans for a rescue operation, frantic efforts were being made in the east maritime provinces of Canada to charter a plane to Greenly. Flying had been carried out with ski-fitted planes through the winter months but charter companies feared that there would be no snow-covered territory in the Belle Isle straits area at that time of year. There was also the risk in takeoff from ice-covered lakes due to the imminence of break-up. Similarly a seaplane was useless because there were no water areas suitable for takeoff. Adequate supply of fuel was another consideration for flyers because of the remoteness of Greenly. New York was more than a thousand miles from the island and Montreal was almost 900 miles distant. There was no known fuel cache in the Belle Isle area which more or less ruled out long distance flights.

The airmen had a good night's sleep and they awoke to a clear morning with the coast of Newfoundland plainly visible on the south side of the narrow strait with Labrador visible to the north. Had they had such clear visibility on the *Bremen's* arrival, they could have easily located their position, refuelled at St. Johns in Newfoundland, and pushed on to New York, Fitz felt. But he consoled himself that he and his comrades were on terra firma and remembered the old saying: "He who is down need fear no fall".

Chapter 17

The Rescue

R escuing the airmen stranded on Greenly Island, getting the *Bremen* airworthy again and being first with the news were the prime objectives, but not necessarily in that order, of the numerous newspaper groups vying for a piece of the *Bremen* action. There were few aircraft operators working in the eastern seaboard area with machines suitable for a dash to Greenly under the conditions then prevailing. It was not long, however, before a company was located that was prepared to "have a go". This was a small operator with the fanciful title of Canadian Transcontinental Airways Limited. It was a recently formed company that flew mails to isolated communities along the Quebec North Shore as far east as Sept Iles (Seven Islands). It boasted of two Fairchild FC-2W monoplanes and two experienced pilots, Romeo Vachon and C.A. "Duke" Schiller. Their winter base was located at Lac Ste. Agnes, 16 miles north of the popular summer resort of La Malbaie (Murray Bay) and 80 miles east of Quebec City where company president, Louis Couture, had his home. The town was serviced by the Canadian National Railway, which linked it with the big cities to the west.

The relief plane arrives at La Malbaie (Murray Bay) where spare parts and supplies were picked up for Greenly Island. Herta Junkers and Fitz are in foreground.

Couture was contacted by a number of prospective clients and seizing the opportunity he booked four places for the press on one of his machines to be piloted by Vachon, a native of Quebec who, coincidentally like Fitzmaurice, was born in 1898, had attended a Christian Brothers' school, had commenced his flying training in 1918 and had considerable flying experience to his credit. Among the passengers booked was a reporter for the *Toronto Daily Star*.

There was an electrifying air of excitement at the Lac Ste. Agnes base on that Friday evening as preparations were being made for the dash to Greenly, a round trip of 1,350 miles. "Duke" Schiller, an adventurous character, enjoyed being in the public spotlight. He had basked briefly in the international headlines the previous

Autumn, when as pilot of the *Royal Windsor*, he was on the point of a west-east Atlantic attempt which was called off at the last minute when the sponsors pulled the plug due to the risks and bad publicity involved. He felt he had been denied his chance of transatlantic glory then but now he was fully determined to make amends, if only in a secondary role. If he could not claim all the media attention for himself he saw a good opening here to, at least, share in this latest, and perhaps greatest, Atlantic drama.

A consignment of mail was due to go the following morning to Sept Iles, a small community 260 miles to the northeast and on the direct flight route to Greenly, over 400 miles further afield. But his plane, the second Fairchild, was undergoing a service and was not ready for the flight. It simply had to be made airworthy and in quick time. It had no compass and he had no maps at his disposal of the Greenly area but these things did not cause him concern. His main worry was the availability of his machine. Could it be made airworthy by the morning? If so, he would run the mails and Vachon would wait to take the passengers, when they arrived, in his machine which was at the ready. Mechanics worked all night and the Fairchild was ready for takeoff in the morning. Accompanying him on the flight were Dr. Louis Cuisinier, technical director at CTAL, and their chief mechanic, Eugéne "Ami" Thibeault.

Schiller had hoped to reach Greenly in daylight but poor conditions forced him to stop overnight at Sept Iles. The *Toronto Daily Star* editor was surprised to hear that a plane had already left the CTAL base without their staff man but brilliantly improvised a plan to ensure they would get their scoop, nevertheless, by sending a message to Sept Iles telling Schiller that he had been appointed their reporter on the mission. "Duke" enthusiastically embraced his new appointment and hastily despatched his first report from Sept Iles.

The weather had not improved by Sunday morning but the three men braved the driving snow and headed for Greenly. They made a brief stop at Havre Ste. Pierre and again 75 miles further on at Natashquan where they refuelled with the aid of a dog team. Guided only by a pocket compass which was of little help, Schiller depended on visual observation which was difficult in the conditions. Flying low over Greenly they observed the plane and the men waving at them. "Duke" took this as a sign to set down in the direction of Blanc Sablon but after landing there he knew he had misread the signal and within minutes was on Greenly and in the midst of the relieved flyers.

A nurse stationed at the Forteau hospital on the Labrador coast, Gretta Ferris, had just finished tending to the slight injuries incurred by Capt. Koehl and the Baron in the impact of the *Bremen* landing. Gretta was a correspondent filing local news with a small newspaper in the region and she used the occasion to get first-hand interviews with the aviators. These were later reported widely in the national and international press, which proved a nice windfall for the enterprising nurse.

The relief plane landed at 5.30 on the Sunday afternoon. It was Koehl's 40th birthday and this was the best possible present he could get. Cuisinier produced a crate of beer and the party was only starting as Gretta took her leave. Koehl was not to know that, as he was quietly celebrating a notable milestone in his life by drinking a beer with some companions thrown together by fate in one of the most remote locations on earth, there were huge celebrations honouring the aviators' feat taking place coincidentally in many cities in Europe and America. Nor was he aware that Lufthansa had named their newest aircraft the *Hermann Koehl* in his honour.

On closer examination it had been discovered that the damage to the plane was worse than expected but Koehl and Huenefeld would not consider leaving it. Neither did Fitzmaurice want to leave it but his German comrades decided he should fly out with the "Duke" and seek help from Herta Junkers and the North German Lloyd at Lac Ste. Agnes. As the Baron explained: "It was only natural that Fitz should be chosen. He was the only one of us who could really talk English." Dr. Cuisinier also stayed on Greenly awaiting Fitz's return with the spare parts and more provisions.

Fitz later explained that an examination of the undercarriage revealed that a main member had been fractured. He trembled when he contemplated that this must have happened on takeoff at Baldonnel after dropping back heavily on the ground having cleared the sheep. It had miraculously held together on getting airborne and during the flight but then collapsed in the drop landing on the ice at Greenly. "Our guardian angels must have been working overtime that morning at Baldonnel," Fitzmaurice reckoned.

Wearing his reporter's hat "Duke" provided the *Star* with the scoop of the year and perhaps the decade. The report was telegraphed on the Monday from Natashquan, where they were forced down in a blinding blizzard and decided to stay overnight. "What does a rescue plane look like to a couple of Germans and an Irishman who have just come down safely from a 36 hours' transatlantic flight and landed on a strip of rock and ice in a barren land a thousand miles from nowhere?," was the teasing question he posed readers in his opening paragraph. "Like a million dollars," he answered. "They were delighted to have help dropping in on them out of the skies like that and affording them a chance to get through to civilisation and their goal - namely New York."

"Duke" told readers of the *Star* the flyers' latest plans. "The idea is now that we shall fly in as soon as possible with skis and landing gear. After repairing the shaft we'll get the *Bremen* to Murray Bay where we can change her back to wheels and give them the start off for New York. The flyers are determined to conclude their flight," he wrote.

Fitz records that he "spent a most enjoyable evening with the traders and the local parish priest" at Natashquan. The following day they flew to Sept Iles where the first battery of reporters and photographers were laying in wait.   Fitz was happy to discover that the only newsreel cameraman to get through was an Irishman, Tom Hogan, who with the help of an American, Robert Fogg, managed to get the first pictures back to New York.   The Irishman had sold an exclusive story to the *New York Times* and he had also with him an exclusive from the Baron and Capt. Koehl for the Hearst press group.

The Duke and Fitz were met and entertained by the Mayor, C.J. Romeril, and Irishman, Pat Collier, the manager of a large pulp mill.   Fitz presented the mayor with a copy of *The Irish Times*, dated 12 April.   He had given other copies to reporters a little earlier.   They had been given to him by R. M. Smyllie, *The Irish Times* Editor, just before takeoff at Baldonnel.   Having refuelled, the Fairchild made the short hop to Clarke City, a small pulp mill community west of Sept Iles. It was here that Fitz enjoyed his first shave and bath since leaving Ireland.   They were given a huge Irish welcome of *ceol agus craic* (music and merrymaking) and the party continued well into the night.

The following day (Wednesday) the "Duke" and Fitz pressed on to Lac Ste. Agnes, 250 miles away.   Here an even bigger battery of media people, including many of America's best known reporters, used their brawn as well as their brains in the effort to outdo their rivals.   More importantly for Fitz, however, Herta Junkers and Freddy Melchior, of the Junkers Corporation of America, were there to meet them.   Melchior had received details of the spare parts needed by telegraph and had flown up from New York with them.   They were stuck at Lac Ste. Agnes, however, because they could not locate a set of skis for the undercarriage of the aircraft, and it would be futile returning to Greenly Island without them.

Meanwhile other rescue moves were being made elsewhere. The Canadian Government owned icebreaker, *Montcalm*, was dispatched to Greenly but was held up by heavy ice and, still over 50 miles from the island, called off its attempt to force a passage through on Wednesday, 18 April. In another part of the continent the *New York World* approached Commander Richard E. Byrd for the use of the Ford Trimotor. The aircraft was being prepared for his South Pole attempt and was being worked upon in Detroit. Edsel Ford, the Ford Corporation chief, realised the potential for a publicity coup for the company by its involvement in a rescue operation and soon found an alternative to the polar aircraft. This was the 4AT Trimotor, which was sitting in a hangar at the big Ford automobile manufacturing plant at Dearborn, Michigan.

Byrd's pilots, Floyd Bennett and Bernt Balchen, both recovering from colds contracted on a recent trip to Northern Canada, flew from New York to Detroit on the Wednesday. Bennett and Balchen were two of America's most experienced and accomplished flyers. Both had played prominent parts in Byrd's North Pole adventures and Balchen, a Norwegian and now a test pilot with the Fokker Aircraft Company in the US, had played a key role in Byrd's Atlantic crossing in the Fokker C-2 trimotor *America* the previous year. Bennett had missed out on that flight because of a bad injury sustained during the landing of the *America* at the end of a test flight earlier that year with Tony Fokker as pilot and Byrd, who was also injured, a passenger. Bennett, who had been a healthy robust individual up to that time, never recovered fully from the experience. When Commander Byrd called him on the *Bremen* recovery project he had been confined to bed with a fever since the end of March and was feeling far from well. Yet he jumped into action and without hesitation agreed to join Balchen on the mission.

The two pilots left Dearborn on Friday, 20 April, in a direct flight to Lac Ste. Agnes. Accompanying them were Charles Murphy, reporter with the *New York World*, Thomas Mulroy, the fuel engineer with Byrd's Antarctic team and Carl Wenzel of the Ford work crew who was to supervise the changeover from wheels to skis. It was an uncomfortable flight for Bennett, and when they arrived at their destination in the mid-afternoon he was put

Fitz (left) and 'Duke' Schiller (second from right) greet Floyd Bennett and Bernt Balchen on their arrival at Lac Ste. Agnes on 20 April 1928 in their 4AT Trimotor. They had come on a *Bremen* rescue mission - but within days Bennett was dead.

straight to bed in a local farmhouse. Dr. J.A. LaPointe, from nearby La Malbaie, was called and gave him medication. The doctor called again the following morning and seeing that Bennett's condition had continued to deteriorate he recommended immediate hospitalisation. Herta Junkers, who was in charge of rescue operations, arranged for Bennett to be flown to Quebec City, 75 miles away, where he was immediately taken by ambulance to the Jeffrey Hale Hospital under the care of Dr. W.H. Delaney. He was diagnosed as having pneumonia

Charles Lindbergh arrives at Quebec from New York with the special serum for the critically ill, Floyd Bennett.

and was in great discomfort.   Mrs. Bennett left her home in Brooklyn and took the train on the Monday morning for Quebec. With her was a specialist in respiratory diseases who brought with him oxygen and breathing equipment.

Balchen, bade his farewell to his sick friend and, with Fitzmaurice as his copilot, took off early on Tuesday morning for Greenly with a planned stop at Sept Iles on the way.   After refuelling Balchen had difficulty in getting airborne again and the final leg was delayed until Wednesday.   After 6 hours 30 minutes of flying time the trimotor was landed on the ice near Greenly shortly before midday and the spare parts and fuel was quickly unloaded.   The big trimotor had lots of goodies for the marooned airmen.   There was food and drink aplenty and also a supply of chicken aboard which was requested by the Germans in their messages to the outside world.   Herta Junkers had also purchased items of clothing for them in La Malbaie.

While Fitz had been away Cuisinier and Thibeault had the reservoir drained and the *Bremen* placed safely on oil drums. They had removed the propeller and readied the machine for the repairs to be carried out by mechanics flown in on the trimotor. It was all systems go as the mechanics went about their job of getting the *Bremen* flying again.

Floyd Bennett had appeared to be making progress in hospital but on the Tuesday (24 April) his condition became critical.   His doctor decided that an immediate supply of special serum, available only at the Rockefeller Institute in New York, was the one hope of saving his life.   John D. Rockefeller and Harry F. Guggenheim quickly obtained the serum and Charles Lindbergh, who had just arrived in New York to greet the *Bremen* heroes, straight away volunteered to fly it to Quebec.   The US Army Air Corps put a Curtiss 01-B-5 Falcon at his disposal for a direct flight and the famous airman arrived in Quebec that evening to a welter of excitement at the surprise visit of the Atlantic hero.   Commander Byrd had arrived earlier by train and prepared the way for the ace pilot so that no time was lost in getting the serum from the airport to the hospital. But it was all to no avail. Floyd Bennett died the following day. Having delivered the serum Lindbergh returned to New York and it was there that he was informed of his fellow aviator's death.

Meanwhile on Greenly the mechanics had completed their repairs on the *Bremen* on the Wednesday and it was fuelled up and moved onto the smooth ice of the Gulf of St. Lawrence ready for takeoff the following morning. Everything was checked and rechecked and all seemed fine. But, horror of all horrors, on Thursday morning the engine would not start. Frenzied efforts to get it purring again failed time and time again. More checks and rechecks were made and the considerable combined ingenuity of all those present was employed; but sadly in vain. It was as if the *Bremen* had made its own mind up that it had had enough.

To make matters worse news of the death of Floyd Bennett had filtered through and this cast a gloom over everything. Balchen was particularly upset at the news of his dear friend's death. He and the American had pioneered together in so many aviation escapades. The plan had been that the *Bremen* was to follow the Ford to Ste. Agnes where hordes of reporters and photographers were waiting in anticipation to get a glimpse of the now famous aircraft and to talk to the equally famous airmen. Failure to get the engine started and Floyd Bennett's untimely death forced a new course of action. It was decided to get to the funeral and plans to fly the *Bremen* from Greenly were reluctantly abandoned. With a storm threatening the plane was hauled to the mainland for safety reasons and secured. The flyers boarded the Ford and bade a sad farewell to Greenly. Balchen was at the wheel and Junkers mechanic, Ernest Koeppen, and reporter, Charles Murphy, both of whom had come to Greenly on the trimotor, were also on board. The *Bremen* was left in the care of Dr. Cuisinier.

Chapter 18

A Royal Reception

When the flyers arrived at Lac Ste. Agnes there was another unseemly scramble among reporters and camera personnel for "exclusives". There they were congratulated by Clarence Chamberlin, who had flown up from Hartford, Conn., to congratulate his fellow flyers. They were told that the whole of the US was waiting to welcome them and that the cities were awash with German and Irish flags. The flyers stressed to reporters that the celebrations would have to wait. Their first priority was to get to Floyd Bennett's funeral which was to take place in Washington the following day. Because of the circumstances they refused to give interviews and after relaying their copy to the newspapers that had commissioned their stories they headed for nearby La Malbaie. The 16 mile journey by huskies and sleigh was, as always, a very tiring trip and because of an early start for Washington on the following morning they retired early at a local hostelry.

Herta Junkers joined the party on the Ford trimotor and the group took off for the US capital early on Friday morning. They had planned to fly direct to Washington although they knew that they would be late for the funeral which was to take place to Arlington Cemetery on that afternoon. Instead they would lay a wreath on the aviator's grave. Bad weather forced them to land, however, at Curtiss Field, Long Island, and from there they were whisked by police car to Pennsylvania Railway Station in the heart of downtown Manhattan, where they caught the first train to Washington D.C.

New Yorkers had been preparing to give the airmen the most spectacular welcome ever given by their city. The Municipal Authorities had authorised the expenditure of $60,000 (£12,000) for the welcome, one-fifth more than had been spent on the reception given to Lindbergh the previous year. But the heroes' first entry to the mighty metropolis caught everyone by surprise and only a few New Yorkers got even a glimpse of them as they sped their way through the city to Penn Station. Their next entry

At Arlington Cemetery, Fitz visits the grave of a dear dead comrade, Floyd Bennett. He placed the Irish flag (bottom left hand corner), that he had carried on the *Bremen* flight, on the grave.

Fitz (with the 'Duke' beside him on the right) meets the assembled press for the first time after the flight at Sept Iles. The town's mayor, C.J. Romeril, is on extreme left.

would be a much different affair!

The city of Quebec went into mourning when news broke of Floyd Bennett's death. After a poignant Anglican funeral service in the small chapel at Jeffrey Hale Hospital, the coffin was placed on a gun carriage of the Royal Canadian Horse Artillery and was led through the crowded silent streets to the railway station by a guard of honour of the Royal 22nd Regiment. There it was loaded onto a special carriage on the Montreal Express for transfer to a train to New York and Washington.

A huge throng of people were present at Grand Central Station on the train's arrival in New York and from there the body was taken to the Seventy-First Regiment Armory where it lay in state. An escort of mounted policemen led the way and, with drums muffled, a naval band played Chopin's *Funeral March*. Many thousands filed by the coffin to pay their last respects to a man of rare ability, compassion and courage.

Although Bennett had held the relatively junior rank of chief warrant officer, President Coolidge, with the approval of the US Navy, accorded the dead airman an "admiral's funeral" and he was buried with full military honours at Arlington Cemetery on the Friday afternoon.   The aviator's wife was supported by Commander Byrd at the graveside.   Among the 3,000 mourners present were Secretary for Commerce (and next President of the US) Herbert Hoover, Rear Admiral W.A. Moffett, Herr Von Prittwitz, German Ambassador, and Professor Smiddy, Minister of the Irish Free State.

The transatlantic aviators and Miss Junkers spent the night at Bolling Field in Washington and the following morning they went to Arlington Cemetery to visit the grave of their dear dead comrade. Fitz placed on the grave the flag of the Irish Free State that he had carried on the Bremen and the Baron followed with a similar gesture with the controversial German flag he had carried with him.   Capt. Koehl and Miss Junkers laid wreaths on the grave. They remained at the graveside in silent prayer for some time. Outside the cemetery big crowds had assembled and cheered the flyers who refused to give interviews to press or radio.

They returned to Bolling Field where they boarded a plane for New York piloted by Bernt Balchen.   But bad weather forced the machine back to Washington and they took a train to the "Big Apple" instead.

This time New York was ready for them.   The newspapers reported their welcome as the greatest in the history of the city. "Even the reception given to Lindbergh, America's own hero, did not quite equal it," stated the *Irish Independent*.   "Extraordinary scenes of enthusiasm were witnessed, and at times the cheering of the people was on a scale never before experienced in this city, in which spectacular events are not altogether unusual."

Thousands of policemen guarded the three men as they were escorted to one of New York's most exclusive hotels, the Ritz

Carlton. Here they shaved and showered in luxurious and expansive surroundings, in stark contrast to the facilities that had been at their disposal at Greenly. Fitz still wore the red "windbreaker" which he had borrowed from the "Duke" in Canada. In typical lavish New York style Mayor Walker sent in seven of the city's top tailors to make new uniforms and outfits for the Irishman and his German colleagues.

The big function that night was in the hotel and the speeches were broadcast on all networks, countrywide and worldwide. Among the speakers were Mayor Walker, Admiral Byrd, Clarence Chamberlin and the flyers themselves. Fitz's ever present smile and quick wit made him the people's hero. In his speech he spoke of the many islands he had visited in recent days. He said he had left the Green Isle of Erin on Thursday, the twelfth, and landed on Greenly Island on Friday, the thirteenth. Fate had brought him to Seven Islands (Sept Iles), to Long Island and finally to Manhattan Island, he explained to a rapturous audience. If the function at the Ritz Carlton, at which everyone who was anyone in New York was present, was a breathtaking affair, it was but a prelude to the city's official welcome for the flyers staged the following day (Monday, 30 April).

Fitz led his comrades to the decision to wear their old uniforms for the ceremonies on the Monday. The flyers were driven from the hotel to Pier 68 at 10.30 in the morning amid ringing cheers from the vast crowds where they met Grover Whalen, chairman of the Lord Mayor's reception committee, and other city dignitaries. There they boarded the steamer, *Macon*, and escorted by very colourful police harbour boats, and with every type of craft for miles around sounding their foghorns and myriads of planes in the skies noisily zooming overhead, they made a triumphal tour of New York Harbour, around the Statue of Liberty and back to Battery Point at the southern tip of Manhattan Island. From there the parade began and, showered with ticker tape that fell like snow along the ten mile route, the flying heroes from the

Mrs. Fitzmaurice and her daughter, Patricia, pictured with Mrs. Koehl on their arrival in New York.

New York's Queen of the May for 1928. Here young Pat is seen wearing her father's Medal of Valour presented to him by Mayor Jimmy Walker.

On board the *Macon* approaching the Battery at the south tip of Manhattan prior to the start of the big parade in New York.

The parade makes its way up Broadway.

A city official whispers in Major Fitzmaurice's ear as the Baron holds Fitz's daughter aloft while Mayor Jimmy Walker has a firm grip on Robert E. Lee 4th - great great grandson of the famous Civil War General at City Hall.

other side of the Atlantic were deliriously lauded by more than two million people who jammed the sidewalks along Broadway. Ten thousand soldiers from renowned US Army and Navy Divisions, marched to the tunes of a profusion of bands playing stirring Irish, German and American music. It was a most fantastic sight.

The airmen's wives, Mrs. Fitzmaurice and Mrs. Koehl, along with the younger Fitzmaurice, Patricia, had arrived from Europe a few hours earlier on board the North German Lloyd liner Dresden just in time for the big celebrations. They were rushed to City Hall where it had been planned that the happy women would be reunited with their husbands during a break in the huge parade.

Mrs. Fitzmaurice had been ticked off by the Irish Legation in Washington because of remarks alleged to have been made by her that were published in the *New York World* attacking Mayor Thompson of Chicago for comments attributed to him in the press that were not complimentary to her husband. In a cablegram from Prof. Smiddy on 18 April the Irish Government was advised to "ask Mrs. Fitzmaurice to refrain from such statements as calculated to have unfortunate results." Irish National Archives record that the Department of Defence was asked to handle the controversy and on 20 April Mrs. Fitzmaurice sent a telegram to Smiddy emphatically denying that she had uttered any criticism of Mayor Thompson.

The planned reunion of the Fitzmaurices and the Koehls was delayed for a short time and *The Irish Times* informed its readers the following day the reason why. "At City Hall ... the crush was so great when the flyers arrived that they (the airmen's wives) could only stand on a table and wave and throw kisses to their husbands. Patricia, grasping a teddy bear, was much perplexed at the separation, and once during the speeches she broke away from her mother, climbed over two tables, and was within reach of her father when she was caught and held until the ceremony had concluded."

Mayor Walker presented the flyers with Medals of Valour from the State and parchment scrolls of Honorary Freemen of the City. "New York," he said, "joins in the rejoicing of Germany and the Irish Free State in your accomplishment and hails the symbol of the tie binding the countries. The flight will not soon be forgotten, and will intensify the affection for your countries in New York."

Fitzmaurice replied: "Your welcome is absolutely overwhelming, and I am sure that since the days of the Romans there has been nothing like it witnessed. ... Wireless and aviation are two important parts of communications, and we are thankful to contribute a little to the progress of aviation."

At the conclusion of the ceremony the national anthems of Germany and Ireland were played. The crowd broke through the police cordon in the crush and delayed the parade for half an hour. After the joyful reunions with their dear ones, the heroes of the day were on the move again. Fitz and Koehl were with Mayor Walker and Grover Whalen in the lead car. The Baron and Professor Smiddy were in Car No. 2 and Herta Junkers was in the next one. They drove triumphantly along Fifth Avenue stopping to deposit a wreath in the German and Irish colours at the foot of the Eternal Light, the city war memorial at Madison Square. Twenty thousand schoolchildren massed the steps of the New York Public Library to cheer on the heroes. Enterprising New Yorkers made a financial "killing" by selling window seats along the route for $10 a time and demand far exceeded supply. The towering avenues of the metropolis were awash with colour with flowers everywhere and flags and buntings dancing in the wind. Broadcasts of the celebrations were carried live by all the radio networks and some Dubliners picked up direct links from Station 2 XAF, New York, while others listened to reports of the historic day's proceedings, including Fitz's speech, relayed from Germany.

The flyers rounded off a memorable day with a visit that evening to the big heavyweight fight between Jack Sharkey and Jack

Delaney at Madison Square Garden on the invitation of Mayor Walker. The newspapers reported that it appeared that the 12,000 crowd at the fight had turned up to see the aviators rather than the boxers. The airmen got a huge ovation on arrival while the two principals climbed into the ring almost unnoticed. The big fight did not last long. Sharkey won on a first round knockout but the loudest cheers were reserved for the Irish aviator. "Fitz", "Fitz", "Fitz", chanted the fans. In response to clamours from the crowd the airmen climbed into the ring after the fight and were presented one by one to the crowd to further rousing ovations.

Fitz was left bewildered by events of the day. "I am still in a flat spin and every airman will know that that is about as hopeless a situation in which a man can get. This welcome of ours has been so overwhelming, and so significant in its suggestion of international friendship, that I cannot do it justice. All I can say for my two comrades and myself is that we are grateful, very grateful, and that we will carry the memory of it as long as we live."

But, as always, there were a few who did not fully enjoy the New York welcome. If the flying of the old imperial flag on the *Bremen* caused some eyebrows to be raised in Germany, the manifestation of Irish tricolour flags on the streets of American cities and, more especially, the absence of Union Jacks, caused offence to some Britons. Sir Charles Highan sent a telegram to the *New York Times* on the subject. "Can you explain please why as Fitzmaurice is a loyal British subject and Southern Ireland is part of the British Empire no British flags were displayed in New York or other US cities? If when Lindbergh was received in Europe we had displays of the state flag of Michigan and no US flag what would be said in America." Mayor Walker was dismissive in his reply to Sir Charles: "It is absurd. Major Fitzmaurice is an officer of the Irish Free State and as such was honoured with the flag of the Irish Free State."

Manhattan that night appeared as if it had been hit by a tornado.

One transatlantic hero salutes another. When the *Bremen* crew arrived at Washington, Col. Charles Lindbergh was there to greet them. The "Lone Eagle" is seen here congratulating Fitz.

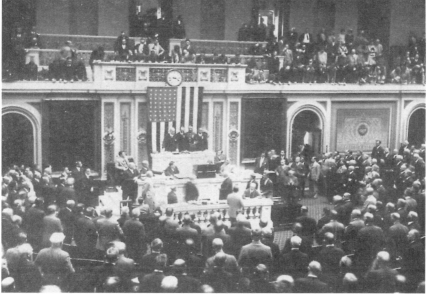

The airmen being introduced to Congress by the speaker, Nicholas Longworth.

U.S. President Calvin Coolidge pictured on the lawn of the White House with the airmen after he had presented them with the Distinguished Flying Cross, the first non-Americans to receive the honour. Irish Minister, Professor Smiddy, is on the left.

At Bolling Field aerodrome, Washington: Capt. Koehl, Fitz, the Baron, Frank Kellogg (U.S. Secretary of State), Col. Charles Lindbergh and Prof. Smiddy, Irish Minister.

It was a mess. There was litter everywhere. A massive clean-up operation was undertaken at an extra cost of $16,000.

Invitations poured in from cities all over the US and Canada inviting the aviators to celebrations in their honour, but for the next week the hectic schedule in New York kept them extremely busy. The numerous Irish and German societies all wanted a piece of the action, so too did the business institutions and leading American societies. It was one hectic round of dinners, luncheons, handshakes, interviews and speeches as the festivities continued for over a week in the city that never sleeps. Fitz threw the first ball at an afternoon baseball game between the New York Yankees and the Boston Red Sox and he met the famed Babe Ruth. It was a nonstop schedule for the airmen and by the end of the week they were exhausted.

It was a hectic time too for the airmen's wives, and for young Patricia, who was crowned "Queen of the May" at a special party in her honour on May 1st. She was adopted for the week as the darling of New York. The wives attended many of the functions with the airmen and were also invited to parties hosted by a committee of the city's leading ladies, headed by Mrs. Chamberlin.

There was a brief relief from the unremitting New York festivities circuit to fit in a date with a very important person - the President of the US, Calvin Coolidge. On Wednesday the group took the Junkers F13, now fitted with the repaired propeller of the *Bremen,* to Washington where they were cheered by large crowds. Fred Melchior, of the Junkers rescue team, had tried everywhere unsuccessfully to find a replacement for the *Bremen's* damaged propeller. To expedite matters he had taken the one from the F13 and brought it with other spare parts to Greenly. In the meantime the damaged *Bremen* propeller was repaired at the Junkers plant and fitted on the F13. At Bolling Field aerodrome the fliers were received by Col. Lindbergh and Frank Kellogg, the Secretary of State. Addressing the three airmen Mr. Kellogg warmly welcomed them "with feelings of admiration on your magnificent exploit". He told them: "Your task was indeed one to test the powers of human endurance. Its successful accomplishment has stirred the entire nation."

The group was escorted to The White House by a troop of cavalry and there further tributes were paid to the flyers by the President. The three men were presented with the US Distinguished Flying Cross, the first foreigners ever to receive the award. A special bill had to be rushed through Congress to allow this to happen. The citation declared: "For exceptional skill in making the first westward nonstop transatlantic flight in an aeroplane from Europe to North America."

The presentation was followed by lunch on the lawn hosted by the President and Mrs. Coolidge. The President had a reputation as a somewhat distant man of few words but Fitz found him to be a friendly host who was very knowledgeable about Ireland and its history. Fitz recalled him paying "great tributes to the Irish people and referred in glowing terms to what they had done in the opening up and development of the United States."

Fitz also had animated conversations with Herbert Hoover, then Secretary for Commerce and the man who was to replace Coolidge as President later that year. Hoover, whom he found to be "erudite and warm-hearted", was at the time the most popular man in America. When he became President the economy was booming and Americans had confidently expected a continuation of conservative Republican laisser-faire policies. But in October 1929 his whole political and private world was to collapse around him with the Wall Street Crash, the greatest disaster ever to strike the financial world. With the value of some leading stocks slashed by over two-thirds, thousands of Americans had seen their entire life-savings wiped out in a matter of days. The panic and crash in the New York Stock Exchange came at a very bad time for Fitz, who was just about to capitalise on his fame when the bubble burst.

Following a visit to the Tomb of the Unknown Soldier at

Arlington, where the flyers placed wreaths, they visited Capitol Hill.   Here Senators and Congressmen were anxious to talk to them and they were loudly cheered as they were being introduced to members of both Houses.   They later attended a press conference at the National Press Club. Fitz told reporters that he and his German comrades, intended to fly the *Bremen* back to Europe emphasising that "we will do it if it is possible".   The group were entertained that night at a Government banquet in their honour at the Mayflower Hotel, hosted by Speaker of the House of Representatives, Nicholas Longworth.

They took off the following morning for New York to more celebrations.   The flyers continued to make the headlines and extensive coverage was given to their every move and word. The *New York Evening Post* of Saturday, 5 May, published a special souvenir supplement with a huge pictorial spread on the story.

Details of the US tour itinerary were completed by the following weekend.   First stop was Philadelphia on Wednesday, May 9th, where they paid tribute at the statue of Commodore Barry, an Irishman from County Wexford, founder of the US Navy.   At the civic banquet Fitz was seen scribbling some notes on the beautiful expensive damask tablecloth, in preparation for his speech, by the president of the hotel group that owned the hotel in which the function was being held.   The hotel chief approached the top table with a pair of scissors and, having asked Fitz to sign the tablecloth, he proceeded to cut the piece out of it and sent it off to be framed to the Irishman's great amusement.

Next day it was Cleveland, Ohio, and on Friday and Saturday the flyers were given a huge welcome in the Windy City.   Here they met up with Hugo Junkers and his wife, who had arrived from Europe to join in the celebrations.   Like in New York the Irish and Germans are strongly represented in Chicago but if the 'Big Apple' has a definite Irish appeal, the 'Windy City' has more of a German flavour.   The scale and extravagance of the New York reception could not possibly be matched anywhere else,

The "Three Mustketeers of the Air" were big news on their visit to Chicago.

240

but Chicago has an inimitable style all its own and gave its guests a memorable time.

The reception by their countrymen and women of the midwest, many of who came hundreds of miles afield to acclaim their achievement, made Koehl and the Baron feel exceedingly proud.

On Friday the flyers were guests of Mayor "Big Bill" Thompson at the South Shore Country Club and then they toured downtown Chicago in an open car, through streets bulging with excited humanity, stopping for a moment of reflection at the Washington monument. Koehl and

The airmen flanking Mayor "Big Bill" Thompson in Chicago.

the Baron were delighted to chance upon some friends and relatives along the route.

Fitz remembered the Mayor as a "most flamboyant and eccentric character who administered the city's affairs at times wearing a 'Ten Gallon' hat and carrying a pair of pearl-handled revolvers".   He had earned a dubious international reputation for his personal attacks on King George V of England.   In public he hated England and everything it stood for but privately it was a different story.   He confided in Fitz that he had, in fact, the greatest respect for His Majesty and the English people.   It was simply the logic of politics he explained to a keen if somewhat confused listener.   "Son", he said, " in a place like Chicago, municipal politics are international politics in a very real sense.   Why this man's town is just bung full of Irishmen and Germans."

The Mayor, who made no reference whatever to the controversy evoked by the report in the *New York World* attributed to Mrs. Fitzmaurice, presented his guests with the Freedom of the City and had them enrolled as Chiefs of an Indian tribe.   That evening they were entertained at the home of the German Consul, Dr. Hugo Simon.   Next day came the big parade along Michigan Avenue and on to Soldier's Field, where the two hours spectacle of spirited dance and song was punctuated by congratulatory speeches.   Later there was a banquet for 4,500 people at the Stephens Hotel.   *The Chicago Daily News* of the Saturday gave the visit the royal treatment with a huge glossy picture of the three men adorning half the broadsheet front page of its magnificent photogravure souvenir pull-out section.

On Sunday, May 13, Koehl attended Mass in St, Patrick's Catholic Church and then it was on to Milwaukee, an almost one hundred per cent German city, where they were received by Mayor Hoan and Governor Fred R. Zimmermann.

Next came St. Louis, where Lindbergh's famous plane had been built and from where he had flown to New York before making his epic flight to Paris.   Rain did not dampen the public's enthusiasm and the visitors were given a regal time. The Baron, taking part in the opening ceremony of a German community sponsored home for the aged, spoke on his favourite theme, peace among nations. "May all national discord be buried in this earth we break today," he said in his speech to his countryfolk.

On Tuesday the flyers were in Detroit. Here they were shown around the big Ford plant at Dearborn by Edsel Ford and later had lunch with Edsel's father and founder of the automobile empire, Henry Ford. For Fitz this was the highlight of the entire US tour. He later spoke in awe of the great Irish-American genius who had played such a major part in shaping human destiny.

"He was the least ruffled and most calm individual in the whole works. A man of great charm he showed us the social club where both he and his wife supported cultural folk dances of the various nationalities to be found amongst his workers. He talked much of Ireland in which his father, William Ford, was born and from where he had set out as a penniless emigrant to seek a living in America.

"Never have I been so deeply impressed as I was with the simple charm of this amazing man. In his own private shop in the engineering laboratory he showed us the first car he had built. He was then employed as an engineer in the powerhouse of the Edison Illuminating Company of Detroit and had taken seven years, working through the nights, to complete the job. His huge industrial empire was the outcome of an unbridled imagination. He was the supreme practitioner and champion of free enterprise. Had other industrial magnates shown but a modicum of the crystal clear logic and practical common sense of Henry Ford the economic depression of the early 1930s would never have arisen and World War 11 might never have become a reality."

Edsel Ford informed his visitors that as the Detroit factory was going through a period of transition - they had only commenced producing the new model after years of churning out the old Model T - money was being lost on every car rolling off the assembly

In Detroit in the office of the City Mayor - L to R: Capt. Koehl, Fitz, Mrs. Evangeline Lindbergh (mother of Col. Charles Lindbergh), the Baron, the Mayor and Edsel Ford.

The three airmen descussing their future plans with Herta Junkers, daughter of Prof. Junkers, before their return to Europe.

line.   So soon as the human element became proficient in the new job it had to perform they could speed up every other department of production proportionately and enormous profits would commence to roll in.

The visit to the Ford plant left the Irishman bewildered and bemused. "For the first time I was most forcefully struck by the extraordinary advance of the scientific and mechanical age, to which, even if only in a minor fashion, I was actually related and belonged."

Later, in the early 1950s Fitz, contemplating the genius of Henry Ford, penned these prophetic words: "The genius of man is beyond belief.   It evolves through different phases, eternally seeking perfection, towards the millennium.   Today we can see the advent of the electronically controlled factory in the operation of which the human element will practically disappear.   They will be replaced by the new science of electronics which will automatically handle everything from the raw material stage to final assembly and packing.   The work so produced will be of a higher precision than anything ever previously achieved."

Henry Ford had just come back from a visit to Europe where he had examined the potential there for expanding his growing automobile empire.   He was keen to set up a major motor manufacturing plant in County Cork, the home of his ancestors, but he objected strongly to the restrictive Free State tariffs on cars imported from Britain.   Ford was a firm believer in the merits of free trade and he lobbied strongly to have the tariffs dropped for car imports in both countries.   He reckoned the Free State would be the main beneficiaries in such an arrangement with the massive increase in car exports to Britain from a big new Cork manufacturing operation.   But the Irish Government stood to lose £250,000 if the levies were dropped and it was felt that this would be too much of a sacrifice on a cash starved exchequer.   This difference led to a standoff between the Irish Government and Mr. Ford and he cancelled his intended visit to Cork to mark his protest. The Detroit automobile magnate apparently did not vent his anger at the Irish Government in his talks with Fitz. Had Ford made a forceful point of the issue Fitz would most likely have recorded some note on the subject.

The visit to Detroit had started on an uncertain note. The Junkers plane had been badly damaged when it landed in a "dead stick" as it came down on a muddy field at the Ford airport. But the flyers were uninjured and were given a tumultuous reception by the city officials. They met Charles Lindbergh's mother as well as some of the best known names in American aviation including Brock and Schlee, Stinson, Haldemann and Eddie Rickenbacker, the top-scoring American ace in WW1, with 26 hits to his credit during the last eight months of the war.

With their plane under repairs the group took the train to Boston, their next port of call. Here the welcome was again unrestrained. They were accorded the Freedom of the City by Mayor Malcolm Nickols and received the Medal of the State of Massachusetts from Governor Alvin T. Fuller.

Canada beckoned next. This was the country from where they had begun their American odyssey. The flyers felt that it was only fitting, out of courtesy if not obligation, that they should take in some Canadian cities on their tour before returning to Europe.

Taking a break in their train journey to Montreal, they paid a day visit to New York State capital, Albany, on Monday, 21 May. Here they were congratulated by Governor Al Smith as ten thousand people lined the streets to greet them. One of the first things the flyers did on their arrival in Albany was to send a message to Col. Charles Lindbergh on the first anniversary of his Atlantic flight wishing him "many happy landings".

Their base for the day was the DeWitt Clinton Hotel. Here the Baron got a chance to clear up confusion surrounding the handgun he carried with him on the flight. There were reports doing the rounds that he had carried the gun to kill the others and then himself as a quick and clean escape route if faced by a gruesome death situation on their adventure.   He denied such rumours flatly to reporters at Albany.   "That is not so", he declared.   "I did take a revolver but only for our protection in case of accident. Suppose we had dropped into the ocean in our plane and had to fight off sharks.   It would have come in handy then, you bet."

While relaxing in the hotel lobby in the afternoon the Baron received a telegram informing him that the *Bremen* was damaged beyond repair.   That meant an end to the airmen's hopes of flying back to Europe in her.   The Baron appeared crestfallen having read the message.

Late that night the group rejoined the train for Montreal.   They were met the following morning at Windsor Station by Mayor Camillien Houde.   German and Irish clubs had helped the city fathers prepare a warm Canadian welcome.   That evening they attended a banquet and later went to the theatre.   Fitz met up with some of his old RFC friends during the day including his one time flight instructor Alex "Noisy" Knight, a native of Owen Sound, Ontario, who now worked as an auto salesman in Toronto.

There had been speculation in recent days that the Baron was organising the shipping of a replacement Junkers plane (the Europa was mentioned in despatches) to fly the airmen back to Europe. But these stories were knocked on the head when he received a phonecall during their stop in Montreal informing him that North German Lloyd in New York had booked their passage to Germany on the liner, *Columbus*, for 9 June.

In Montreal Fitz denied a report that he intended to become a US citizen.   "I intend returning home to Ireland where there is much work to be done," he told reporters.   "We have an aerodrome at Baldonnel that can be improved and I propose to assist in the development of Irish aviation to the fullest extent." The last city on their tour was Quebec.   This was where Floyd Bennett had died and the visit conjured up poignant memories of the US flying ace's bid, heroic in the circumstances, to rescue the *Bremen* crew on Greenly.   Mayor Auger and Hector Laferte,

In Quebec on the last day of the tour of American cities - Fitz planting a tree at St. Sacrament Parish to mark Arbour Day.

Speaker of the Legislature representing the Government, greeted them on arrival. The three aviators along with Mrs. Cuisinier, wife of Dr. Louis Cuisinier, who was still on Greenly, each planted trees at St. Sacrament Parish on St. Foy Road, to mark Arbour Day celebrations. Tea was served at the home of Lieutenant Governor Narcisse Peridue and a banquet later in the evening was hosted by Premier L.A. Taschereau.

On Friday, 25 May, the flyers were back in New York. Their agent, Harry A. Bruno, who handled the grand tour of the nine American cities, made arrangements for them to spend the next two weeks in seclusion. The group had finally got a well-earned rest in the run-up to their trip back to Europe by sea. This period of seclusion gave the flyers the opportunity to work on a new book based on their recent experiences being published by G.P. Putnam & Sons.

The Baron, who had felt quite ill in Chicago, disguised much inward physical suffering during the tour with a warm smile for the public's benefit. He knew his health was in decline but instead of opting for a more relaxed lifestyle, which might ease his suffering and extend his life-span, he was determined to get the most out of the time he had left. After the hectic US tour he was particularly in need of a break and time to recuperate.

On their last day in New York they all spent a quiet morning in their hotel getting ready for the long sea voyage. Koehl was guest of honour at a luncheon in the Patchogue Elks Club, Long Island, in the afternoon fulfilling a promise to his uncle, Professor John Koehl, who had a summer home there. Fitz and the Baron had tea with Professor Junkers and his daughter, Herta, at the Sherry Netherland. Early next morning they all said goodbye to America as the *Columbus* set sail for Europe.

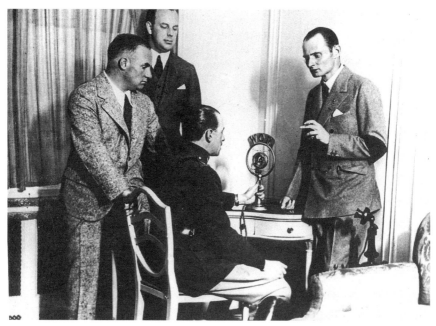

Major Fitzmaurice broadcasting on World Overseas Radio from New York.

Above and below - scenes from the big parade in New York.

Ten thousand soldiers from renowned U.S. Army and Navy Divisions marched in the New York parade.

Major Fitzmaurice lays a wreath at the War Memorial in New York.

Ticker tape fell like snow along the ten mile route in New York.

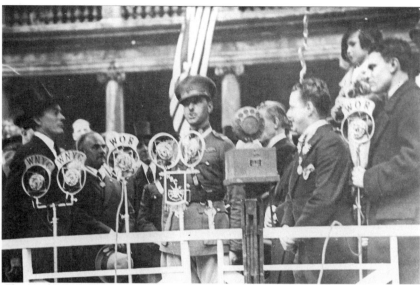

Fitz speaking at City Hall as Mayor Jimmy Walker (on left) listens attentively. "Your welcome is absolutely overwhelming and I am sure that since the days of the Romans there has been nothing like it witnessed."

The airmen in jubilant mood as they acknowledge the adulation of the New York crowds.

Everyone wanted to catch a glimpse of the intrepid aviators.

The picture tells it all - scenes of euphoria in New York for the airmen's visit.

Chapter 19

Back in Europe

After a brief stopover at Plymouth, where they were greeted by the mayor and a welcoming party, the airmen arrived in Bremerhaven on 18 June, coincidentally the first anniversary of the Germans earlier attempt to fly the Atlantic. The liner *Columbus* was met by a squadron of Udet "Flamingos", a light aircraft designed by Col. Gen. Ernst Udet, whom Fitz came to know well and respect greatly. The entire route from Bremerhaven into Bremen was lined with people in festive array and indulging in the traditional German greeting to its military warriors of showering their heroes with flowers and loudly shouting out each of their names.

The reception in Bremen was warm and touching. Fitz could see that the success of the flight had given the German nation, whose confidence had been undermined by the Treaty of Versailles, a rare cause to celebrate. They were honoured with the Freedom of the City and the parchment scrolls were presented to them by the Mayor. They also received beautiful silver trays of the most exquisite workmanship. They were later entertained at a lavish banquet. The City Fathers had apparently abandoned their earlier prejudices in respect of the flag carried on the flight in view of the magnitude of the achievement and what it had done for the self-esteem of the nation and particularly its significance for the City of Bremen.

The following day the *Bremen's* sister ship, *Europa 11*, brought them to Berlin. Tempelhof aerodrome was a seething mass of humanity. They were cordially received by the directors and executives of Lufthansa and each was presented with a gold drinking goblet, a magnificent present. The goblets were filled with champagne and a toast was drunk with each presentation.

When it came to his turn the Baron refused the toast and banged the goblet on the table. Turning his back on his hosts he made, what Fitz described "a most uncomplimentary remark, the next thing to sacrilege in Germany, a country of sabre duels, where honour could only be restored in the gymnasium". You could hear a pin drop. Everyone was in a state of shock, not least the Irishman. He had not expected such uncharacteristic behaviour from his affable and cultured colleague. Fitz later found out that the Baron did it because of Lufthansa's summary sacking of his friend, the Captain, for having engaged in the *Bremen* undertaking. This had embittered him sorely and he could not forgive the people responsible. Lufthansa did everything they could to discourage the flight yet now they were sharing in the success. It was more than the frail Prussian aristocrat could swallow.

During the airmen's visit to Berlin the *Berliner Tageblatt* announced German preparations for transoceanic flights were further advanced than had been previously disclosed. The report stated that a start would be made with a new ten motor Dornier hydroplane and that the traffic would be under the control of Captain Koehl, "who becomes a high official of the Lufthansa company".

President Hindenburg received the airmen on Thursday, 21 June, and presented them with a signed photograph of himself in a silver frame. They were entertained to lunch by Berlin's

The liner, *Columbus*, is welcomed by a squadron of Udet "Flamingos" on its arrival at Bremerhaven on 18 June, 1928.

Smiles all round as the *S.S. Columbus* docks at Bremerhaven on the return of the airmen and their wives from the US.

Fitz emerges from the *Europa* at Tempelhof Aerodrome, Berlin, from where the fantastic journey had begun almost three months earlier.

The airmen cheered on by Berliners as they pass the Brandenburg Gate.

Meeting city dignitaries in Hamburg.

The hugh welcome in the City of Bremen.

The flyers being handed refreshments on their return to Berlin.

dignitaries at the Town Hall and their names were inscribed in the Golden Book of the city.

In Berlin Fitz had a visit from the British Air Attache, Group Captain Christie. After congratulating him, Christie told him that His Majesty's Government feared that the Germans would make the most of the occasion to reassert their past military honour and glory. He asked Fitz not to be associated with such behaviour. He also said that he had been instructed to pass on the word that he (Fitz) would be awarded an honour by the King on his arrival in London.

In the meanwhile the following despatch was received by the Irish Government via Downing Street from R.C. Lindsay, His Majesty's Ambassador in Berlin: "The celebrations have not been without a certain political meaning. Hermann Koehl, who appears to be a man of comparative simplicity and discretion, was somewhat overshadowed by the more dramatic and far more egotistical personality of Freiherr von Huenefeld. The latter, who is a violent adherent of the monarchist cause, was at one period adjutant to the ex-Crown Prince in Holland and makes no secret of his loyalty to the ex-Emperor and to nationalist ideal ... is not a man of any political acumen ... I consider it only right in the absence of a Free State Minister in Berlin to express appreciation of the modesty and tact displayed by Major Fitzmaurice in circumstances of very great difficulty ... i.e. that the Germans were in control of the festivities." (Source: Irish National Archives).

Despite the British Ambassador's appreciation and the Air Attache's revelations Fitz never saw the King and never heard any further news of the honour promised. The flyers' reception in England on the conclusion of a celebratory tour of German, Hungarian and Austrian cities was, not surprisingly, distinctly subdued. On their arrival at Croydon Airport the flyers were subjected to a Customs examination and were asked to produce their passports. Fitz was not at all impressed with having to go through these formalities. He had not got his passport with him but he happened to have his British war decoration medals which he produced. (Mrs. Fitzmaurice had brought Fitz's military decorations to America with her on the request of Prof. Smiddy). "Here is my passport," he told a startled official, showing him the medals. The secretary of the Royal Aero Club intervened and this prompted a speedy end to immigration procedures.

Many of Fitz's old flying friends were assembled for the function in their honour at the Savoy. It was an imposing gathering but the Irishman found it a frosty affair. The speeches were brief and to the point. Brigadier-General Lord Thompson, Secretary of State for Air in the Labour Government of the day, ruffled more than a few of Fitz's feathers with his insensitive asides aimed at generating a few laughs. After complimenting Fitz's companions, Lord Thompson said that the Germans (whom Fitz felt certain he loathed) were most fortunate in their choice of a "passenger".

He called Fitz the "good luck mascot" of the flight and added that it was "the desire and ambition of all Irishmen to go west, and I think we can say that Major Fitzmaurice went west quicker than any of his compatriots before him".

Fitz did not think these put-downs were at all funny. When called to respond and having spoken of the flight and his experiences, to the delight of his many fellow flyers around the room, he took issue with the noble Lord on his offending remarks. He said that if the Germans had wanted a mascot one could have been purchased in Woolworths for the sum of sixpence and weighing but an ounce. It hardly made good sense to bring along an Irishman in full flying kit weighing nearly two hundred pounds on such a long and hazardous undertaking. Fitz felt a lot better having got that off his chest.

The airmen arrive at Croydon for a short stopover in London.

Having spent the night at the Savoy the flyers were seen off at Croydon the following morning, Tuesday, 3 July, by a small crowd that included Capt. McIntosh, Fitz's Atlantic partner of the previous year. The return to Dublin was a triumphant one. Fifteen Air Corps planes took to the air at 5.30pm and provided an escort for the *Europa*. The *Irish Independent* had the story. "Remarkable scenes were witnessed at Baldonnel Aerodrome and in the city. When the *Europa* landed at Baldonnel, the people broke through the cordon of troops and rushed wildly to the machine. For a time the three airmen were unable to leave the plane. Capt. Koehl appealed in vain to the people to keep back. Finally troops succeeded in clearing a space for the visitors. They were carried shoulder high to one of the hangars."

The report told of the scene on the Naas Road out of Dublin. "Every kind of vehicle - motor cars, motor cycles, buses, jaunting cars, bicycles - moved towards the aerodrome."

President and Mrs. Cosgrave, accompanied by the full Government Cabinet, greeted the flyers on their arrival at Baldonnel. They were cheered along the ten mile route into the city by wildly excited crowds, taking up every vantage point. The addresses of welcome were delivered on a specially erected platform outside the GPO in O'Connell Street. The gathering in the city centre was, according to one source, "unquestionably the largest ever seen in the metropolis". The *Independent* reported that an unprecedented number of people fainted in the crush, and twenty people were treated at Jervis Street hospital nearby. Luckily no one was seriously injured and the St. John Ambulance detachment, who were on hand to deliver first aid, were complimented on having done a wonderful job.

Later that night the Freedom of the City of Dublin was conferred on the three aviators, who entered the banqueting hall at Clerys to the strain of "See the Conquering Hero Comes". For Fitz this was a very special occasion. This, after all, was the city of his birth and here he was being honoured by his own people amongst

The streets of Dublin were lined with admirers to welcome Fitz home after the flight.

The three airmen stand to attention for the German and Irish National Anthems at Leeson Street Bridge during the big parade in Dublin.

Section of the crowd in Dublin city centre.

Fitz comes home - the scene at O'Connell Street, Dublin.

family and friends.   He was now to join such eminent Irishmen as Charles Stewart Parnell and George Bernard Shaw as a Freeman of the City.   The previous recipient of the award was, coincidentally, a man who had helped him to finance an all-Irish attempt, the tenor, John Count McCormack.   In later years he was to be joined in this highly exclusive club by, among others, US Presidents, John F. Kennedy and Bill Clinton, Pope John Paul 11, Mother Teresa of Calcutta and Nelson Mandela.

Over 650 people, representing every strand of political, business and cultural life in the country, were present at the function.   The attendance list was a veritable Who's Who of the Ireland of the late 1920s.   Chairman of the organising committee was Garda Commissioner, Seamus Murphy, while it is interesting to note that Fitz's longtime admirer, Sean Lemass, was a member of the executive committee.   So too was prominent Labour T.D., Bill Davin, who represented Laois in the Dail (Parliament), the county in which Fitz grew up.   John A. Costello, later leader of Fine Gael, and twice Taoiseach, was also on the broadly based committee. Fitz's dear friend and loyal supporter, Senator Gogarty, delivered the keynote speech putting the magnificent feat in context and forecasting a leading role for Ireland in the development of commercial aviation.

The following day (Wednesday, 4 July) was again a busy one. The airmen visited the President in the morning, had lunch with the German Consul General, then attended a lavish garden party at the residence of the American Minister and were guests of honour at a state reception hosted by the President at the Metropole.

The Irish Army, at a function at McKee Barracks, conferred the Sword of Honour on the three flyers and for Fitz, next to the Freedom of the City of Dublin, this was his most treasured prize.

Another highlight for Fitz was the warm welcome given him on the Thursday on a visit to Limerick, the ancient stomping ground of many generations of both his paternal and maternal ancestors.

The city of Limerick accorded him a civic reception and finished off a real Irish Fáilte (welcome) with a lavish banquet and entertainment.

Next morning it was off to Holland on an invitation from the former Kaiser, who was in exile at Doorn Castle. The flyers landed at Soesterberg aerodrome, near Utrecht, and were taken in the "Imperial" car through flag bedecked streets to the village of Doorn, where a festival in their honour was taking place.

Having read and heard so much about the overwhelming pride of the man in the heyday of his power and glory, Fitz had expected to meet a "vainglorious fallen idol". The man he met was very different to the one he had visualised.

"I immediately recognised the handsome well-chiselled features with the pointed and well-trimmed beard and upward pointed moustache of the ill-fated monarch who had benevolently ruled seventy odd million of his subjects in a country, once the most powerful nation in Europe. His hair was a silvery grey and he stood in a stiff military fashion with head proudly upheld. He showed no signs of bitterness or humiliation. Here was a heartily effusive, charming country squire welcoming his guests to a weekend house party. His left arm was stunted and withered. He gripped a walking stick in fingers covered in diamond, ruby and sapphire rings. He sparkled with wit and humour and introduced us to family and staff.

At dinner Fitz was seated on the right hand side of the former Empress, Princess Hermine. She asked him if they had been received by the King on their visit to London.

Fitz said they had not met the King.

"Oh! then they must still be cross with us", joked her Majesty.

"I'm afraid, ma'am, they're seemingly more cross with us," he replied. This greatly amused the ex-Kaiser and his wife.

Koehl and the Baron were conferred with the Order of the House of Hohenzollern by the ex-Kaiser who presented Fitz with a beautifully framed autographed photograph of himself and a set

of diamond and gold cuff-links.
The flyers spent the weekend
at Doorn after which Fitz returned
to Ireland and Koehl and the
Baron flew to Cologne. There
the reception for the German
aviators was decidedly chilly.
The visit to the ex-Kaiser had
stirred the political flames again
and the ever-present undercurrent
of unease for carrying the Imperial
flag on the *Bremen* now became
an overt show of resentment. The

At the City of Limerick banquet (l to r):
Desmond Fitzgerald T.D., Minister for
Defence, the Lady Mayoress, the Baron,
the Mayor, "Tiger" O'Brien, and Fitz.

official reception that had been arranged was cancelled. Koehl
explained the visit to Doorn as a private one and a few days later
as he flew over Heidelberg he dropped a wreath on the grave of
the late President Ebert to demonstrate that his motives in visiting
the ex-Kaiser were not political. The Baron explained himself in
similar terms and said that as a free man he must be allowed to do
as he saw fit. The political controversy that surrounded the visit

At Government buildings in Dublin (l to r): Gen. Richard Mulcahy, Eamon Duggan, Herr
Von Dehn, German Minister, Fionan Lynch, Desmond Fitzgerald T.D., Minister for
Defence, Paddy Hogan T.D., Minister for Agriculture, the Baron, John Costello S.C.,
T.D., William T. Cosgrave, President Executive Council of Irish Free State, Fitz, Prof.
O'Sullivan and Capt. Koehl.

to Doorn even divided the city of Dessau, where the *Bremen* was built. But when the two men returned there they were warmly welcomed by Professor Junkers and church bells peeled and crowds cheered.   Capt. Koehl was soon back in his old job at Lufthansa while the Baron returned to doing the things he liked best - and soon was busy preparing for a new flying adventure.

Meanwhile at Greenly attempts to rescue the *Bremen* were turning into a fiasco. Cuisinier and Thibeault had worked lovingly on the engine to get the *Bremen* ticking over again and had overseen its laborious relocation to the highest point in the vicinity behind Blanc Sablon (Long Point). Canadian Transcontinental Airways had provided almost the only link with the island in the rescue operations but now the US Army decided to get into the act.   This was a high level decision and two amphibians were

The airmen met the former Kaiser, Wilhelm II, at Doorn.

despatched from Bolling Field, Washington, to Greenly on 12 May. They picked up the Junkers pilot, Fred Melchior, at New York. Robert Cannon, CTA chief, strongly objected to the US Army involvement and wrote a letter to Canadian Prime Minister, Mackenzie King, complaining that his company had spent over $25,000 already on the operation and asking him to protect their interest in the rescue bid.

When the amphibians reached St. Johns, Newfoundland, one of the pilots, Lieut. Fairchild, was stricken with appendicitis and had to be replaced. A litany of other mishaps delayed the high-powered operation along the way. A week later the planes finally arrived at Greenly but because of the breaking ice there was no suitable landing area. Melchior, who had come prepared for such an eventuality, strapped on two parachutes and jumped. He landed safely and was soon joined by Cuisinier and Thibeault with whom he immediately discussed the next move. The two amphibians headed for St. George's Bay, Newfoundland, and then on to Pictou, Nova Scotia, where the plan was that they await the arrival of the *Bremen*.

Melchior, climbed aboard the *Bremen* and settled himself in the pilot's seat, with Thibeault next to him and Dr. Cuisinier as passenger. The aircraft gathered speed in its downhill run over rough terrain but Melchior failed to get the plane airborne and, almost inevitably, disaster struck. One of her wings hit some shrubbery and the plane went out of control and crashed. This mishap ended hopes of getting her airworthy again. It seemed once more as if the *Bremen* was telling the world that she was refusing to be forced back into the air. The three men emerged from the wreck badly shaken, physically and mentally. Their valiant efforts to get the *Bremen* airborne again had come to an inglorious end. Melchior sent out the message that the plane had crashed, that plans to fly her out from Greenly had been abandoned and that she would have to be shipped out instead.

The US Army Air Force involvement in the botched rescue

attempt came under critical scrutiny in aviation circles, especially the part played by Chief-of-Staff, Major Gen. James E. Fechet, who became personally involved. *Aviation*, an influential periodical, sought an explanation. "To lend assistance in getting the *Bremen* out of Greenly Island is a worthy undertaking for the US Air Corps, yet at the same time it is a bit mystifying that the *Bremen's* crew should carry on touring the country and leave it to the officers of rank in the Air Corps to head the rescue operation," it commented.

The extent of the flyers' triumphal tour in America was also testing the patience of Irish officials, but for a different reason. Ireland was waiting to greet them. The Irish Minister, Prof. Smiddy, reported to the Minister for External Affairs in Dublin on 22 May indicating "some impatience that the aviators were spending too much time in America before returning home".

The flyers were coming to the end of their triumphant tour of American cities and were on a short stopover at Albany, N.Y., when they received the shattering news from Melchior that the *Bremen* had crashed.

As the warmer weather made Greenly more accessible, many visitors came to see the famous machine. It also attracted the souvenir hunters. Thibeault had to use his gun to chase looters away on the night of 8 July and sought police protection. A detail from the Quebec Provincial Police was sent to Greenly on 12 July. It had been reported that the *Bremen* had been stripped of costly equipment but Dr. Cuisinier confirmed a few days later that the plane was intact and nothing had been taken.

It took some time to locate a suitable ship servicing the region to convey the plane back to Quebec. The machine was dismantled under Dr. Cuisinier's direction awaiting removal. On 25 July the steamer, *North Shore*, set sail for Blanc Sablon from Quebec and on 4 August, the ship was back at Quebec docks with its precious cargo, with the wings on the main deck and the fuselage on the upper deck. It was quickly reassembled by Cuisinier and was the main attraction at the Quebec Provincial

Exposition during the first week of September.

In the meantime the Baron had decided where the *Bremen's* new permanent home should be - the projected municipal museum of the City of New York. On 13 August, Germany's Ambassador to America, Jacob Gould Schurman, announced that he had received a letter from the Baron offering the plane as a gift to the city of New York. In his letter the Baron indicated that he had put all his earthly possessions into the *Bremen* and its sister plane the *Europa*. The

Cover of *Dublin Opinion* for May 1928.

munificence of friends, he explained, had permitted him to sacrifice the *Bremen*, as a slight return for the warm and sincere friendship and confidence which Americans of all classes had freely granted him and his companions. "A bridge has been built across the ocean that never can be destroyed," he wrote.

After the big show in Quebec the plane was dismantled again and was shipped on the North German Lloyd steamer, *Krefeld*, for Germany on 17 September for the International Aviation Exposition in Berlin. Ten days later the ship arrived in Bremerhaven and the plane was immediately loaded on a railroad car, to the loud cheers of a big crowd of spectators. It was showing all the signs of the hard times it had experienced and its fuselage and wings were badly rusted. After the big event in Berlin the plane was transported to the Junkers factory at Dessau where it was completely overhauled before its return to New York the following May.

To the Bremen

Ah! let it rest forever where it lies,
Great wearied bird, who bore across the sea
Leaving behind what lesser spirits prize -
The undaunted Three.

'Twere sacrilege to move thee from that spot
Thy destiny accomplished, here we'll raise
Thy mausoleum, so ne'er be forgot
Thine and their praise.

Others, as greatly daring, may arise
Thy deed may emulate, but ne'er surpass
Thy chivalrous-wise challenge to the skies,
The storm's fierce blast.

Be thou an emblem of sweet peace and then
Of manful striving, striving ever on,
No coward peace, but such as by brave men
Only is won.

Eugene MacSweeney

MacSweeney, the artist, is here seen in his workshop. He was uncle of Lil Fitzmaurice, who was married to Fitz's elder brother, Louis.

Chapter 20

The Wall Street Crash

On his return to Ireland from Doorn, Fitz was still in demand and invitations came rolling in from cities, towns and organisations all over the country. The Sunday following his return (15 July) he made a brief stop at Maryborough (now Portlaoise), where he grew up. There had been great jubilation in the town at the success of the *Bremen* flight, according to the report in the *Leinster Express*, which had, and still has, its base in the town. In the company of General Eoin O'Duffy, Commissioner of the Garda Siochana (police), and Major Heimburg, the Hamburg police chief, he broke a flight from Thurles, in County Tipperary, to have tea with some old friends. They were met by W.P. Aird, the local T.D. (M.P.), and were entertained at the home of a well-known and long established family in the area, the Meehans, on whose property at the Kennels' Field the plane landed.

Fitz's visits to the town were rare since he had left it as a schoolboy. He had made a short visit with his wife to see his parents on his return to Ireland after WW1. During the Civil War he had landed there with mechanical trouble on a flight from Fermoy to Dublin. A few years later he and another Air Corps

Fitz bidding farewell to some of his old comrades outside the cookhouse at Baldonnel in 1929 just after his resignation from the Irish Air Corps.

At the launch of the book *The Three Musketeers of the Air* in August 1928.

officer had broken their flight to the south at Portlaoise, landing at Togher, two miles from the town.

As the weeks slipped by life gradually eased back to normality for Fitz.   But he found it difficult to adjust to the humdrum pace of ordinary life after his experiences of the previous three months. "I began now to be filled with a most uneasy restlessness as to the boring routine of peacetime soldiering.   It proved too much of a strain on my somewhat temperamental disposition."

He had to find fresh fields to conquer.   It was not the best of times for innovative thinking in Ireland.   The country was paying the price for the Civil War and most of the energy and finances of Government were being applied to economic and infrastructural rehabilitation.   The policy of financial stringency applied particularly to military expenditure and this had a stultifying effect on Air Corps activities.

Fitz had the ideas, which were followed with keen interest in America and elsewhere, but little notice was taken of them in his own country.   One proposal was to develop Galway as a major Atlantic port of call.   Two German Shipping Lines were researching the viability of having their liners stopping there instead of Southampton and transhipping their passengers and freight by air to their destinations.   It was estimated that this could save between 24 and 36 hours on a journey which could give the companies concerned a decided edge on the North Atlantic route.   Nothing ever became of the idea.

The book, *The Three Musketeers of the Air*, which the airmen had been working on in conjunction with Putnams, the publishers, was launched on August 8.   It was published in both English and German languages and proved a best-seller.   Fitz received widespread exposure for his prediction in it that "within fifty years transatlantic flights will constitute a public utility service, engines and route organisation having been perfected".   In fact a regular transatlantic service was established in a much shorter time span than he had anticipated in 1928.   He had not reckoned on a second world war, far more devastating that WW1, in which aerial warfare played a central role and which led to the rapid development in aircraft speed, reliability, durability and versatility.

During this time, while Fitz was pondering his future, he was summoned to a meeting by the Minister for Defence, Desmond Fitzgerald. He did not count the Minister among his close friends and wondered what was bothering him. He soon found out. The Minister asked him bluntly how much money he had made out of the endeavour. Fitz felt this was an insult and told his inquisitor so. He said that he had been paid $22,000 for a radio interview and had received a cheque for $25,000 from the *New York Times*. He explained that all the money had been paid into a common pool to defray the costs of the undertaking. He also told him of the $12,000 they had received from the Electrolux Company for carrying the miniature model of their new vacuum cleaner on the *Bremen* flight. That had been handed over to Professor Junkers to help defray some of the expenses. He also told him of the tempting contracts (one worth $300,000 for a lecture tour of the States) he had turned down to preserve the honour of the Irish Army officer's uniform and the dignity of the State. The Minister noted every detail of Fitz's response.

While in America Fitz had been impressed upon by Professor Smiddy, the Irish Minister, that on no account was he to engage in contract activities and that he would be adequately compensated in due time. On his return he remained optimistic because of all the glowing speeches he had heard from Government Ministers of the great glory he had achieved for his country.

His reward duly came in the course of time. The Official Gazette announced that he had been promoted to the rank of Colonel and that the appointment was backdated one year. Fitz's alert brain did not take long to convert this into money terms. He was to get a little over £150 for his efforts. He also had the dignity and title of the rank of Colonel, the duties of which rank he had been carrying out for the previous three years. This was paltry compensation for what he had achieved, Fitz felt. He was left totally shattered.

His fellow officers had been more magnanimous. A collection was made among army officers and the fund came to £518-8-0. A total of 610 officers subscribed and the contributions were headed by subscriptions of five guineas (£5-5-0) from the aforementioned Minister for Defence and the Army Chief-of-Staff, Lieut. Gen. D. Hogan. Details of the presentation fund survive in the records of the Army Archives.

Despite the disappointment at the State's paltry monetary acknowledgment, Fitz remained determined to make his mark in his own country. His efforts became directed towards the establishment and development of a commercial service linking Ireland with Great Britain and the continent. His close friend, Col. Charles Russell, threw in his lot with him and they put together a comprehensive plan that seemed to them as having real promise and potential. Christmas came and went and still the Government, yet again, failed to show the slightest interest. A very frustrated Fitz decided that that was the last straw. He was now seriously considering his future in the Air Corps.

Meanwhile in Germany Baron Ehrenfried Guenther Von Huenefeld, who had been diagnosed some time previously as having a terminal stomach and intestinal cancer, finally succumbed to his illness on the night of 5 February, 1929. He died on the operating table in a Berlin hospital as surgeons sought for the umpteenth time to postpone the inevitable. He was in his 37th year. Less than a week before he died he telephoned Captain Koehl and told him that he was suffering excruciating pains in his stomach and that he "must submit to the knife again soon".

Fitz was on a short visit to London when he heard the news. It came as no shock to him. He felt a genuine loss with the passing of a close friend who had touched his own life in such a dramatic way in the not so distant past. He told reporters that the Baron was "one of the finest men I have ever met". He added: "His name will live in the history of aviation to which he rendered tremendous service."

The Baron remarkably, yet so typical of the man, had made one more famous flight in the months prior to his death. In the new *Europa*, now jointly owned by the Captain and himself, he had set out on the morning of 18 September 1928 from Berlin, destination Tokyo. He had planned to make a transpacific crossing but this did not materialise. He was accompanied by the Swedish pilot, Karl Lindner, and top Junker mechanic, Paul Lengerich, who had played a crucial part in the preflight preparations of the *Bremen* at Baldonnel, on a trip aimed at promoting better relations between Germany and the rest of the world.

First stop was Sofia, capital of Bulgaria, and two days later they were in Baghdad, capital of Persia (now Iran). They were held up by the authorities there while their credentials were being investigated. They arrived in Calcutta on 27 September and from there flew to Allahabad and on to Mandalay where heavy rain delayed their departure for a number of days. The Baron was fully aware of that city's association with the famous English poet, Rudyard Kipling, whose immortal lines,

"On the road to Mandalay
Where the flyin'-fishes play"

must have had a special significance on his visit there for the aviator poet.

On 14 October the *Europa* reached Canton and the following day they arrived in Shanghai. They flew overnight on the last leg of a fantastic adventure but a heavy rainstorm forced them down on waste ground, incredibly a mere 15 miles from their target, Tokyo, having missed the airport because of poor visibility. The plane was badly damaged and the flyers had a very lucky escape from serious injury. After presenting the plane to the Aero Club in Tokyo the Baron took the Trans-Siberian Express for Europe and was back in Berlin on 19 November. He contracted a fever from his arduous efforts and this signalled the beginning of the end for him.

Captain Koehl and Fitzmaurice led the pallbearers at the funeral on 9 February. The memorial service was held at the Evangelical Cathedral while a fleet of aeroplanes flew over the spires. Among those represented were President Hindenburg, the ex-Kaiser, the ex-Crown Prince and the ex-King of Bulgaria. Messages of sympathy poured in from all over the world, particularly from America. Chief mourners were his aged mother and his surviving brother. Pastor Bruno Doehring paid tribute to the Baron as "a man who gave his life for the Fatherland". He read two poems, one written by the Baron on the eve of his death which he titled *Bequest to the German Nation*, and the other by the ex-Crown Prince addressed to the Baron's mother. Four members of the Steel Helmet, who had kept a death watch at the bier, took their places in the guard of honour behind Koehl, in navy and blue aircraft uniform and Fitzmaurice, in his officer's uniform of the Irish Free State. As the flags were lowered on the coffin the choir sang the old German soldier's farewell anthem, *Ich Hatt Einen Kameraden*. Thousands lined the streets as the funeral cortege moved along the Unter den Linden through the Brandenburg Gate and on to his final resting place in the small cemetery at Steglitz, where the vault of the Von Huenefeld family is located.

Shortly before he had left for the funeral in Berlin, as Commanding Officer of the Air Corps Fitz had sent his Annual Report, as he was obliged to do, to GHQ. His covering memo reflected his frustration in his work. "As an example of the futility of compiling Annual Reports, I am attaching a copy of last year's. I am sure you will agree with me ... that nothing has been done (in the past year) to alleviate the impossible conditions under which I have been endeavouring to operate this highly technical Corps, in which men's lives are constantly in danger, even in times of peace. In the circumstances, I have the honour to inform you that I am forwarding the resignation of my commission under separate cover."

The die was cast. Fitz severed his links with the Irish Air Corps a mere week after attending the burial of his dear comrade, the Baron. He picked himself up quickly after these depressing days for him and he wasted no time in getting down to the business of making things happen again. It was high time to capitalise on his exploits and his talents, he reckoned. A few days after his resignation he unfolded plans for making Galway a major transatlantic port. The *New York Times* of 18 February told of his proposal to halve the journey time on the Chicago to Berlin route by setting up a new service from Halifax to Galway. Four days later the *New York Sun* reported that he and Koehl expected to demonstrate the practicality of refuelling aeroplanes in the air on their proposed transatlantic trip later that year.

He made plans for a visit to New York but before he went he dabbled briefly in Irish politics. Polls were taking place on 14 March and Fitz threw in his lot with President William Cosgrave and his Cumann na nGaedhal party. He dropped leaflets from an aeroplane over Dublin on the day of the election asking voters for their support. (A sample copy can be seen in Dublin's National Library. On one side was the President's appeal and his photograph captioned "Ireland's greatest statesman" and on the other was Fitz's appeal with his photograph titled "Ireland's greatest sportsman".)

On 24 March he boarded the North German Lloyd liner, *Dresden*, at the County Cork port of Cobh, and sailed for New York. He had a briefcase full of opportunities and he had names and addresses of many important contacts. He intended exploiting every last one of them. Lady luck, or "Old Mother Chance" as he liked to call it, had sided with Fitz at all the important moments of his life up to this, and now he wanted just one more lucky break to land himself a secure future. He found his new career invigorating and productive at the start but as time passed by so did the opportunities.

Fitz was in New York as guest of Brady, Cryan and Colleran Inc., a city real estate firm engaged in the development of an airport at Massapequa, Long Island. He was met at the pier by Grover Whalen, who was now the Police Commissioner. From there they went to City Hall where he renewed his acquaintance with Mayor Walker. He revealed his plan to make a round-trip flight over the Atlantic between Potsdam and New York in a tri-motored seaplane. The final details including the trifling matter of financing the expedition, had not been entirely settled, he told his eager listener.

The press latched on to his visit and gave it wide exposure. They particularly zoned in on the fact that he had brought back with him the text of the Baron's last poem. He circulated copies to reporters and paid a public tribute to his late comrade. He characterised the Baron as "the cleanest, finest, most wonderful gentleman it has ever been my privilege to know."

There was a reception for him at Mecca Temple, 135 West Fifty-fifth Street, at which he spoke of his plans for a two-way flight of the Atlantic and the airport project. He also told his audience of the importance of radio in long-distance flying. "If we had had radio, we would have landed right at Mitchel Field," he said. This was a line he had used so often and was to repeat time and time again ad nauseum. His talk was broadcast live on the radio station WMCA.

The Massapequa Park project was a big exclusive housing scheme aimed at wealthy clients and was billed as "the world's first development with its own airport". The promoters were Irish-American estate agents who saw aviation as the transport of the future for the upwardly mobile and well-heeled. In their promotional material they told prospective clients that airport facilities would, in the future, be as important to the development of communities as the railroad station and because of this they had donated a tract of land to property owners at the Park to be used as a private flying field. They had commissioned Fitz, because of his name and reputation, to help sell the project. The new 30 acre airport, which was owned by a well known figure in the world of aviation, Frank C. Ryan, was called the "Fitzmaurice Flying Field" and was formally dedicated on Sunday, 12 May, to a fanfare of publicity featuring Fitz in the lead role and with a glittering supporting cast.

Coincidentally on the same day at Lewisohn Stadium nearby in New York City a crowd of 10,000 people, mostly German, attended an athletics fixture in honour of the Baron. Mayor Walker and Senator Robert G. Wagner dedicated a plaque in honour of the aviator poet. Fitz sent a telegram which was read to the crowd. So too did Clarence Chamberlin, who regretted his inability to attend; but late in the day he flew to the venue and circled the stadium a number of times, a tribute which was loudly acknowledged by the fans. Another telegram was received from the German heavyweight boxer, Max Schmelling.

Four days later the *Bremen* was back in New York to be put on permanent display by the city's Museum of the Peaceful Arts, which had yet to be opened. While awaiting a permanent home the plane was put on public show as part of a transportation exhibition at Grand Central terminal. It was suspended as if in flight from the high roof on the east balcony of the station's main assembly hall. The unveiling ceremony was jointly performed by Mayor Walker and Fitzmaurice on 21 May before a crowd estimated at 17,000. The long white curtain veil was pulled aside to the strains of the British anthem *God Save the King* which the *New York Times* surmised was "in honour of Colonel Fitzmaurice". This must have been an embarrassing moment for all concerned.

The Massapequa project kept Fitz in the limelight and the money helped pay his living expenses. This, he knew, was only chicken-feed. He was at the same time pursuing the big payoff. He sought out an acquaintance, Charles Mitchell, a prominent Wall Street financier and President of the National City Bank, and discussed some projects with him. One of these was the selling of the Junkers rights in the United States.

When Professor Junkers visited the US in the wake of the successful flight he revealed that he had hoped to found a company in America that would manufacture planes for the entire country. Nothing had come of it, however, and Fitz was now trying to resurrect interest in the plan. Mitchell put him in contact with a financial house searching around for such projects and over lunch Fitz sold the client the idea. He felt sure he could clinch the deal by getting Professor Junkers' consent. Immediately after lunch he booked his passage back to Europe and within hours was on the *Mauritania* as it headed out on the Atlantic.

In Dessau he contacted the Professor who sent along Dr. Kaumann, whom Fitz had met in New York, and who had satisfactorily negotiated a Junkers rights contract in Japan. Fitz told Kaumann what was on offer. "How long do you propose to stay in Germany?", inquired the doctor. "I want to be back in New York by the end of the month", replied Fitz. "Frankly if I were you," retorted the doctor, "I would find myself a house here in Dessau and take out a twenty-one year lease. If you have concluded the deal by the time the lease expires you will have succeeded in doing an excellent job."

This was not a very encouraging response from one he had believed was a friendly intermediary. Fitz had been full of confidence that the Professor would jump at the offer he had brought with him. He soon found out that the doctor's judgement was sound. Talks with the Professor proved very difficult, indeed, and dragged on without result for some months.

Fitz got to meet many influential people during this time and he was invited to parties where he hobnobbed with socialites. But he kept his eye on the ball during his German visit and persisted in trying to convince the Professor the merits of his proposal. He had been authorised to offer the Professor $500,000 in cash for his aeroplane patents, with a first option on all his future developments. In addition he was empowered to go to a limit of

$500,000 and the customary royalties on the Junkers "Jumo" aero diesel engine, then the only one of it kind in the world but which after ten years of development work was still in its experimental stages.   After almost five months of tough talking the aging professor agreed to sign along the dotted line.

Fitz jumped on the first liner for the US.   This just happened to be the *Bremen* which left Bremerhaven on 14 October.   It docked at New York Harbour late on Tuesday, 22 October.

What was to take place within the next seven days was the most catastrophic financial disaster the world has ever known - and Fitz's budding business empire was to collapse with it.

On Wednesday morning he rang the president of the company for whom he had negotiated the deal.   He was away in Washington on business he was told and would not be back in his office until the following morning.   At 10am on Thursday, 24 October, he went into conference with the president and top executives and all the details were checked and double-checked.   Fitz was congratulated on the part he had played in putting the deal together.   He was to be rewarded with a vice-presidency on the Board of the American $5 million company with a salary of $25,000 per year plus expenses.   Everything was fine.

A condition of the agreement was that a cheque for $100,000 be paid immediately after Fitz's arrival in New York into the Professor's American bank account and that the contract be concluded within a period of 30 days.   The cheque was actually on the president's desk awaiting his signature when they broke for lunch.   The group adjourned to the Banker's Club to celebrate the clinching of the deal.   During lunch the company's representative on the floor of the Stock Exchange reported to the president that trading was slow there.   Within a half an hour all hell broke loose on the money markets as everyone made a scramble back to their offices.   The bottom had suddenly fallen out of the market.   Panic broke out on Wall Street when prices fell an average of 18 points.   More than 12 million transactions were recorded on 24 October alone. Ticker tape machines failed to keep up with the pace of trading as investors scrambled to sell before prices fell still further. A consortium of banks acted swiftly to contain the situation but it was only a temporary delay. Shares soon resumed their relentless fall, plummeting by an unprecedented average of 40 points on the day that became known as "Black Tuesday" - 29 October, 1929. Wealthy people became paupers overnight.

Fitz, as he finished lunch on the Thursday, found it difficult to grasp what was happening. He tried to talk to the company president, but was abruptly dismissed by him. He company chief him to go away and come back on Monday morning when things had settled.

When Fitz came back on Monday morning he found the whole district completely cordoned off by police, as thousands of frenzied citizens, who had got their fingers burnt in the crash, tried to force their way through. He managed to get to the offices of his client and what he witnessed there was quite bizarre.

"The offices were an absolute shambles. Men, almost hysterical, with bloodshot eyes, stubble beards and shaky hands were struggling to bring order out of chaos. The floors were littered with half-eaten sandwiches and empty coffee cups. These men had not seen their homes since I last saw them on the previous Thursday.

"The world seemed to be falling apart. Suicides, by shooting or jumping from the windows of tall skyscrapers, were commonplace, as men and women found their life's work suddenly obliterated. Lost and forlorn I could only look on in wonder," Fitz recalled.

New York was turned into a graveyard in a matter of days. The liveliest city on earth less than one week before was now an eerie place. The night clubs and other places of entertainment were deserted. The grim spectre of fear stalked the byways, the laneways and main thoroughfares.

Fitz had seen his many months of hard work and his secure future vanish in a matter of minutes. To add to his pain all the money he had made to date had been invested in shares. He was now stony broke in a strange city. His former financial friends did not want to know about him. They had enough worries of their own. They advised him "to go fishing, go jump in the lake, go do anything but simply go away".

The *New York Times* of 15 October told of Fitz's plans to go away - but not precisely what his former business friends had in mind. It reported that plans were

Pandemonium erupts on Wall Street.

at an advanced stage for the first missionary air expedition - to an almost inaccessible region in southwest Africa - and that Col. James Fitzmaurice and Captain Hermann Koehl would participate. Father Paul Schulte of the Oblate Brotherhood in Cologne had come to New York to enlist the interest of American Catholics in the project for which, he stated, $100,000 had already been collected in Europe. He said he had discussed the matter with the aviators and it was planned to launch the expedition in the early spring of 1931. It would have been another aviation first for both Fitzmaurice and Koehl but, while Koehl got personally involved in Catholic missionary work, Fitzmaurice had other things on his mind.

Koehl and his wife visited New York in December 1929 on a Christmas vacation. He jokingly told reporters that the main purpose of the visit was "to spend Christmas for the first time in America; to fondle my machine, the Bremen, in the Grand Central

Terminal; to see my comrade, Fitzmaurice, and to view America for the first time from an angle other than from the shoulders of two husky Irish policemen who accompanied me wherever I went during my first stay in New York".

While in the US, Koehl studied technical improvements connected with aviation, including new instruments for use in fog, a new apparatus for measuring altitude and especially the work of the Daniel Guggenheim Fund for the Promotion of Aeronautics. Two days before Christmas the two aviators met at the Ritz-Carlton. They told reporters that they had not given up their plans "for flying the ocean from west to east. We want to finish the job we started when we flew to Greenly Island, but we will wait until we get the equipment which we believe is fast being developed in Europe." The pair had another reunion in Indianapolis and Charles Lindbergh flew specially from Colombo to meet them there. On his return to Germany, Koehl said he had seen many interesting things on his trip but he believed that his country was abreast of America. "America is wonderful," he said. "But Germany is more wonderful. I am glad to be on German soil again."

The Baron's Last Poem

Ere that the silence which I oft have known
Clutches my throat with final grip of death'
My soul is conjuring up once more
The picture of the land that gave me birth.
Thou soil, whose womb brought forth my mortal self,
To you - the alm and essence of the fight -
I send my greetings when our Lord ordains
That suddenly the bond which ties my life
To earth shall break and night envelop me,
My German land, dying, I think of thee.
I see thy royal cloak of ermine
Ere the eternal slumber breaks my eyes;
I see the crown which once adorned thy head;
The sword thou once drewst in battle.
The healthful fragrance of thy soil,
Succours my heart as evening draws nigh.
My voiceless prayer ascends through space and time:
"Protect, oh Lord, my country's glorious might!"
But if the veil that now obscures my vision
Lifts once again, because a morning new
Is granted me, I'll bow my head
And be again thy faithful champion.

(Loosely translated from German)

Chapter 21

Meeting with Hitler

By January 1930 Fitz was facing a very uncertain future. He was on a constant lookout for new opportunities. One came his way at what he termed a "modest" cocktail party in New York when he chanced to meet two interesting individuals from Kansas City. One was Chairman of the Chamber of Commerce there and the other the City Manager. They were involved in attracting new industry to the city. He discussed the Junkers project with them briefly and they invited him to Kansas for further discussions.

At a luncheon party in a country club there, at which many of the city's leading business people were present, Fitz outlined the proposal which he had been certain was dead and buried. He came away with a promise of half of the capital needed for the $5 million project and a factory site on the edge of the municipal airport at a nominal fee, free of rates and taxes for twenty years. He was jubilant at what he had just negotiated during the greatest financial slump in American history. He now was left to raise $2,500,000 to bring the project to fruition.

He hurried back to New York and put the proposal to his bankers, the Guarantee Trust Company, whose President lined up a prospective client in Baltimore, aviation company chief, Glen L. Martin. Fitz went to Baltimore and discussed the project with Martin. A few days later he received a letter confirming Martin's interest in the proposal. In the meantime he had sent word to Professor Junkers advising him of the development. He received a reply telling him to hold fire until the arrival of the Professor's representative, Dr. Hagermann, in New York.

Deutsche Lufthansa postcard - showing the Junkers G31 which was named the *Hermann Koehl (see page 218).*

Martin came up to New York on Hagermann's arrival and the three men discussed the details of the plan. It seemed to be going fine when Fitz was called away briefly on another business matter leaving Martin and Hagermann alone together. When Fitz returned Martin was in a hurry to leave saying he had a few other calls to make. He said he would write on his return to Baltimore after giving the matter further consideration. Fitz duly received a brief letter which stated Mr. Martin's regret that he could not support the project. Once again the Junkers' deal had collapsed at the last moment. Fitz blamed it on the intervention of Hagermann but could never find out what exactly had been discussed during his brief absence from the New York meeting.

The following days were devoted to the completion of another project at Port Washington, Long Island. He tested and proved the merits of a small amphibian aircraft, after many trials and difficulties. It showed loads of promise but he could not secure any financial backing. America was definitely in the financial doldrums he realised and capital for any new enterprise, irrespective of how attractive it seemed, was not be found.

Fitz was feeling desperate and badly in need of a lucky break for a change. He devoted his energies to writing and radio talks to keep the wolf from the door but the studio armchair and the writing desk did not suit his restless disposition.

He now turned his attentions to the vast land tract of Labrador and wondered what great mineral wealth could be under that barren landscape. He researched the geological formation of the area and that of eastern Quebec with the full cooperation of the Canadian Minister in Washington. He put together a business plan to set up an exploration company but this never materialised.

The second anniversary of the flight of the *Bremen* was marked in New York by ceremonies at Grand Central Station organised by the Newspaper Club of New York. Fitz was the main celebrity. He was still a popular figure but one without a steady job.

Two months later the media focus was again on the Atlantic with the much publicised east-west attempt by the celebrated long-distance flyer, Air Commodore Sir Charles Kingsford Smith, who was known as the Australian Lindbergh. With three others, including the Irishman, Capt. Paddy Saul as navigator, he set out from Portmarnock Strand, Dublin, in his famous plane, the three-engined 675 h.p. *The Southern Cross*, on 24 June and $31\frac{1}{2}$ hours later landed successfully at Harbour Grace. They had compass problems nearing American landfall and flew around in circles in foggy weather for many hours over the vicinity of Cape Race. As with the *Bremen* the plan had been to fly directly to New York. A few days later they took off for Oakland, California, to complete an around the world flight which received international acclaim and vast media coverage.

With Kingsford Smith and crew continuing on their journey almost straight away it left little time for them to talk to the press. This opened the door for Fitz who was on hand to provide the expert analysis of the flight and of the hazards of flying the Atlantic.

He told reporters that *The Southern Cross* had encountered similar compass problems as had the *Bremen* because of the big changes in magnetic variations over short distances in the Newfoundland area.   One reason why compasses go wrong around Newfoundland and Labrador, he said, was because of large deposits of magnetic ore there.   He did not tell the press that he had done extensive geological research in the region, but he obviously remained convinced of the vast riches of natural resources to be found there.

Since the *Bremen* had landed on Greenly over two years previously, Fitz's lifestyle had changed radically. Despite his restless spirit he had, nevertheless, conformed admirably to the sedate Irish family way of life expected of an army officer in the Dublin of the period.   He had been keenly interested in his job and had been a devoted husband and loving father. His genuine care and concern for his family comes across clearly in the reports and correspondence of the day.   His record of loyalty to whatever cause he espoused was second-to-none.

But he was not an easy man to get on with.   He was a straight-talker, who did not suffer fools gladly. He had a sharp caustic wit, he liked to impress people and he was inclined to be pompous in manner.   His penchant for persisting with the mannerisms and accent of a British officer annoyed a lot of people.   You simply loved him or you hated him.   Over the years he cultivated many close friends and probably just as many bitter enemies.   Fitz yearned for the good life but seldom could afford it on his army salary in a cash-starved country.

New York changed all that.   Here he had the rich and famous fawning around him, seeking out his company and regaling him at lavish restaurants and on the hectic social round.   Here he could shake off the inhibitions of a sedentary home life in a small and highly conservative community and let himself go with the flow in a land of liberalism and opportunity.

Since the landing of the *Bremen* in Greenly he had spent little time with his wife and daughter. His family had gradually drifted out of his life. Having evaded the clutches of many zealous and passionate American female admirers, who wooed him with their charms and their opulence, he was finally overwhelmed by the attractions of a pretty German sculptress, Baroness Barbara Von Kalckruth. She fell in love with him and was intent on marrying the buccaneer Irishman at the first opportunity. There was one problem. He was already married.

While getting a divorce in America was not unusual and did not present a major obstacle, it was simply unheard of in the Ireland of the time. There was no divorce there. The Catholic Church was a dominant force in the infant Irish Free State and since divorce was banned by the Church it was also banned by the State.

Fitz travelled to Ireland in mid-1930 to see if he could sort something out. Although Bill was English and a Protestant she was one of the few officers' wives who got involved in the cleaning of the little chapel at Baldonnel and in tending the flowers there. After a long, happy and stable relationship reports of her husband's philandering abroad shocked her deeply. By early 1930 she had come to terms with her new situation. Her husband had effectively deserted herself and Pat. Fitz's growing reputation as a socialiser, gambler and womaniser was a scandal waiting to break in Ireland. The scandal was more than Bill could take. Her marriage was dead and she wanted out - out of her marriage and out of the country.

The divorce proceedings and the custody case in relation to their daughter, Pat, was arranged for Belfast, in Northern Ireland, which was, and still is, under the jurisdiction of London and British law. Because Fitz was an Irish Catholic, with a very high profile at home and internationally, the Church authorities went into a damage limitation exercise. The ultra Catholic society, the Knights of Columbanus, offered their services to Fitz. His case was prepared by two prominent members of the society, leading Dublin solicitor, John Sheil, uncle of Eamon and Mary Sheil, Pat's childhood pals, and top Dublin barrister, Cecil Lavery.

While awaiting the divorce hearing Fitz returned to America, where he was immediately plunged into the news again. The liner *Reliance* berthed in New York on 18 September, but he was told his passport was not in order and was not allowed ashore. His authorisation to stay in America had been cancelled because of his trip to Ireland and it had not been renewed. While awaiting clearance he was entertained aboard the ship by its captain, Conrad Luck. After examining his case for three hours immigration officials decided to allow him a time extension and he was released in his own custody.

The Philadelphia *Bulletin* announced on 8 November, 1930, that the Irishman had bought an estate near Koenigsberg, in Germany. It revealed that he intended settling in Germany for a while and planned to build a summer house there. A week later the public found out why. The *Newark Star-Eagle* of 17 November ran a double column photograph of the German beauty who had won his heart stating that the Baroness had told reporters that as soon as Fitz had obtained a divorce she would marry him.

Just before Christmas Fitz made plans to go to Europe to "settle up his affairs before returning to America to join the staff of a large airplane manufacturer", according to the *New York Times* of 20 December. The report gave no further details of the nature of his new job. Some of his friends in New York arranged a goodbye party at the Park Central Hotel. The party-goers included his flyer friend, Bernt Balchen, Kermit Roosevelt, and former heavyweight boxing champion, Gene Tunney.

The divorce duly came through and Bill was given custody of their daughter, Patricia. Fitz's romance with the Baroness was to fizzle out soon afterwards.

He was back in the U.S. in the spring of 1931 and was soon busy testing planes, trying out new ideas and planning new adventures. In May it was announced that he was planning a round trip flight to Europe later in the summer and had selected as his copilot and navigator a former officer of the U.S. Navy, A.S. Stanford. They set 15 June as the date of departure from Harbour Grace, Newfoundland, in a direct flight to Dublin. From there they would head south for Africa and return via South America. The Sikorsky S.38 amphibian would be equipped with two-way radio.

By mid-June, though, Fitz had a different project occupying his mind. In an interview with his fellow Irish transatlantic aviator, Capt. Paddy Saul, which was published in *Flight* magazine, Fitz gave details of a new flyingboat he had designed. It was a two-seater aimed specially at flying clubs, with component parts easily and cheaply available. A monoplane with twin water-cooled engines of 45 h.p. designed by William Harpur it would have a cruising speed of 90 to 95 mph and the estimated cost he put at £250.

In late 1931 Fitz still entertained plans for an Atlantic crossing which he would follow with a trade tour of European capitals with Capt. Saul, but this was put in abeyance while he pursued yet another brainwave. This time he came up with the idea of flying mail from New York to European cities. He sought an aircraft that would enable him carry a ton cargo of air mail covers and a sufficient fuel range for a flight from St. John's, Newfoundland to Dublin, the longest leg of the journey. He felt the Bellanca Aerobus was ideally suited for the job. He located a suitable engine in the US Naval Service Research Department, a new 1000 hp Rolls-Royce machine. He wrote to the Irish Minister in Washington outlining the benefits of his project for Ireland and asked him to use his influence in getting the Irish Government to issue a special issue Air Mail stamp which would be franked in the Irish Office in Washington. Fitz proposed purchasing the whole issue and selling the stamps on to the numerous philatelic organisations around the world. This would have financed the undertaking and shown a profit of between £60,000 and £100,000, he estimated.

The Minister in Washington, Mr. McWhite, who had served with distinction in the French Foreign Legion during WW1, told him he felt it was a good idea and said that he would take up the matter with the President of the Executive Council in Dublin. Fitz was upbeat about the likelihood of backing from the Irish Government. He would surely get their support because of the attractiveness of the proposal and the great honour he had achieved for the country, he assured himself.   But after some time he was told it was a non-runner.   The Irish Free State had already plans to bring out a special stamp to mark the Eucharistic Congress which was taking place in Ireland in 1932.

This news left him in a frenzy of rage and utterly frustrated. What was to stop the Irish Government issuing two special stamps in the one year, he wondered?   The reply, he knew, could well have been influenced by his divorce in 1930. The Catholic Church has never recognised civil divorce and, indeed, it is in only very recent years that the Irish Republic has legalised it.   The Irish Government of the period and successive ones in the decades that were to follow danced to the tune of the Catholic hierarchy. Although Fitz still claimed to be a Catholic he was enraged at the notion of his country being run by the bishops.

Still desperately seeking the break he felt he was entitled to, he decided that he would have to seek his fortune elsewhere.   He was getting more and more frustrated with America now in the throes of a great depression.   In the better days he had travelled leisurely down the east coast in a Lockheed Vega as far as Buenos Aires, across South America to Valpariso and back via Mexico City and San Francisco.   During this trip he had met many Irish-Americans and gained a lot of knowledge about South America. In Mexico City he had had discussions with some business acquaintances.   This would be the perfect base for an operation requiring access to the South American markets, he felt.   He decided to go to Germany to negotiate the South American rights of the Junkers contract with the Professor.

Germany was in a state of political turmoil when Fitz arrived there. His visit coincided with the Nazis rise to power. On 30 January, 1933, Adolf Hitler became Chancellor. The position was offered to him by the aging President, Paul Von Hindenburg, who had denied him Chancellorship two months earlier in favour of General Kurt Von Schleicher. The Nazis were already the largest party in the Reichstag. Hitler moved immediately to consolidate his power. Within days he had given the government unlimited power to ban all public meetings and control the press.

Fitz watched the Brown Shirts marching by in a torchlight procession from his room in the Adlon Hotel on the Unter den Linden. Later that night he was a guest at the German Aero Club Ball in the Kroll Opera House. At midnight Hermann Goering, who had become Secretary of State for Air, made a grandiose entrance to thunderous applause. He delivered a most warlike speech before breezing out again. Hitler's reign of terror was about to get under way.

Fitz, did not know it at the time, but he was witnessing first-hand the beginnings of the darkest days in the world's history. He was passing the Reichstag building on the way to a party the night it was burned down, 27 February. With the driver he alighted and mingled with the crowd watching the conflagration. The building was a mass of flames but there was no sight of a fire brigade. Fitz thought that this was most unusual in such a highly organised country as Germany!

Within days the Nazis began making arrests of political enemies. On 20 March the first concentration camp was opened at Dachau and three days later an enabling law was introduced giving Hitler dictatorial powers. The customary German salutation of "Guten Tag" was changed by decree to "Heil Hitler".

He also saw the start of the Jewish pogroms. The expressions of apprehension and bewilderment on the faces of Jews as they waited in fear and trembling for what was to come, was etched indelibly on his mind and was to haunt him for a long time to come.

Not one executive of the German aircraft industry was available to talk to Fitz in the days and weeks that followed. They were all commandeered to lay the foundations for the Luftwaffe, which was to become such a mighty aerial force and was to wreak such havoc in WW2. The Junkers plant at Dessau was taken over by the Government and the old Professor was placed under house arrest at a castle near Munich. What a time to come to Germany to do business! Fitz's luck was certainly on a losing streak.

The Irish aviator had many contacts - he invariably called them "close friends" - in the aristocratic class including the ex-Crown Prince. Most of them saw in Hitler a means for re-establishing national pride and they cooperated with him, getting army commissions in return. Through such contacts a meeting with Hitler was arranged.

His appointment was for 2pm in the Reich Chancellery. On the dot of 2pm the massive double doors of the dictator's office opened and standing in the middle of the room, wearing his familiar riding boots, was the man himself. He clicked his heels and raised his hand to the shout of "Heil Hitler". He clasped Fitz's right hand in his, pressing his left hand on top of both, the old double handshake which the Irishman later discovered was the prerogative of royalty. Fitz was led by his host to a round table and entertained to a nice treat of coffee and pastries. He found it difficult to follow Hitler's German although he had become quite good at understanding the language. The discussion was pleasant and Hitler

Adolf Hitler

showed a keen interest in Fitz's aerial exploits and ideas. He made a forceful case for his vision of Germany obviously aimed at sending his guest away with the 'right' message. Little did Fitz know of the demonic power that was to be unleashed in the years ahead by this gentle and pleasant sounding individual.

Because of his friendship with the ex-Crown Prince, Wilhelm, Fitz was invited to parties in the beautiful Potsdam Palace, Cecillianhoff. At these functions the guests were seated at round tables at one of which the ex-Crown Prince presided and his wife and sons presided at other tables. These were regal affairs and his host always appeared meticulously attired in the mess uniform of his regiment, the Death's Head Hussars, wearing all his Orders and Decorations.

Among the other interesting individuals he met on his German visit were fellow aviator, Ernst Udet, and Cardinal Von Faulhaber, both of whom detested the dictator. Udet was a brilliant flyer and became a Colonel-General in the Luftwaffe. He carried his hatred for Hitler and all he stood for until his death by suicide during the war. Cardinal Von Faulhaber, whom Fitz met on several occasions, denounced the Nazis fiercely in the years that led up to the outbreak of war. He escaped arrest only because they feared the power of the Catholic Church. Fitz admired him greatly. "He was not only a Prince of the Church but a Prince of men", he declared.

Fitz left the Nazi scene with confused impressions of what he had witnessed. Without any contracts and with little cash he returned to London. There he joined a Flying Pageant which toured England, Scotland and Wales. He enjoyed the experience and the cash came in handy. "This had all the glamour of the old barnstorming days of flying, and it enabled me to resume my old associations in English aviation circles and with the aircraft industry there."

Chapter 22

The Melbourne Air Race

In 1932 a Century Celebrations Committee was set up in Melbourne to examine ways in which the city's centennial year of 1934 could best be marked. The following year it was decided that the main event would be an international air race from England to Australia. As well as Government sponsorship down under, a wealthy Australian sweet manufacturer, Sir MacPherson Robertson, promised major financial support. The race was divided into two categories. There was a prize of £10,000 and a gold cup on offer to the winner of the speed event and a prize of £2,000 for the winner of the handicap event. Mildenhall, Suffolk, 12 miles from Bury St. Edmunds, was chosen as the starting point for the 11,000 miles marathon, or "Air Grand National" as it became known. The starting date was fixed for 20 October 1934. There were six compulsory intermediary landing places on the route: Baghdad (2553 miles), Allahabad (2,300 miles), Singapore (2,210 miles), Darwin (2,084 miles) and Charleville (1,389 miles) with the last leg to Melbourne a mere 787 mile hop.

This was the biggest competitive event ever in the history of aviation. Many of the world's best-known aviators had their eyes on the first prize which offered fame and fortune.   Fitz was determined to give it his best shot.   First he needed a generous sponsor which he quickly secured.   The wealthy Irish businessman, Joe McGrath, who was head of the Irish Hospitals Trust which ran the world's biggest lottery, agreed to support him.   McGrath was keen to have an Irish interest in this most prestigious international event.   It would be good publicity for the infant Irish Free State and also for his lottery company, which sold sweepstake tickets all around the world.

Fitz immediately set about securing the best plane for the job. He contacted all the British manufacturers explaining to them what he required.   British standards of design had dragged behind developments in other countries he believed, but he was anxious, nevertheless, and so was Joe McGrath, as an exercise in good public relations with the neighbouring country that British manufacturers be given the first option.   McGrath had promised the full prize money to British charities if his entry won the race with an all-British plane.   If the machine was made in some other country the money would be divided between charities in that country and Britain.

Fitz sought a machine allowing a range of 3,000 miles in "still air", with a cruising speed of not less than 230 mph, incorporating a retractable undercarriage and a controllable-pitch propeller conforming to International Convention for the Regulation of Air Navigation (I.C.A.N.) standards.   A few British companies, including Handley Page and Vickers, had initially shown some interest but he was not surprised to find that, from his own knowledge of the engines then available and of the low international status of aircraft design then in Britain, no manufacturer there was prepared to take a serious look at the project.

He felt his best chance to get what he wanted was in America and he hastily left for New York.   From there he flew down to Wilmington, Delaware, to see an old aviation acquaintance, Guiseppe Bellanca, who operated a small company producing civil aeroplanes.   He had sold a number of his planes to the US Army Air Corps and Navy.

Fitz was quite familiar with Bellanca's brilliant work and lofty reputation.   Charles Lindbergh had sought a Bellanca for his Atlantic solo flight but the asking price was out of his reach.   After Lindbergh had procured the sponsorship in St. Louis he went back with the money but Bellanca's new partner, Charles Levine, told him that they would sell him the machine only on condition that they reserved the right to say who would fly it.   Lindbergh went to the Ryan company in San Diego and the rest is history.

Two weeks after Lindbergh's historic transatlantic flight Levine, with Chamberlin as pilot, flew the Bellanca plane *Columbia* nonstop from New York to Germany to break the world long distance record.   Three years later the *Columbia* flew the Atlantic again, the first plane to fly the Atlantic twice.

Upon his arrival in Wilmington Fitz outlined his requirements and sketched out the airplane he had in mind to Bellanca, asking him for a quick reply.   He wanted to know if Bellanca could get what he required off the drawing board and into the air in just over a year.   The American designer quickly assessed the situation and felt confident that he could deliver the goods in time.   He assured Fitz that he would meet the deadline if the Irishman was willing to accept full responsibility for any teething problems that might arise after the initial test flight.

Fitz had one further consideration.   He had recently read an article written by the then editor of *The Aeroplane*, C.G. Grey, pointing out that the main object of the marathon air race was to "improve the breed" by producing an air mail machine that could be used to speed up British Imperial communications.   The Irishman reckoned aircraft specially designed for the carriage of mail over such routes as the one to Australia should be equipped with jettison devices which would enable the pilot to drop the mail in an emergency and it could later be picked up and flown to its destination.   Fitz adapted the idea to suit his present purpose.

The Irish Swoop

He instructed Bellanca to provide a dump valve in the bottom of the main fuel tank which would enable him jettison that portion of his load in a matter of seconds. Bellanca had no problem with this request and Fitz gave him the order to go ahead with the project. The Irishman felt that the contingency modification to the fuel tank was a good idea. Little did he think that it was the one part of his plan that was to backfire with disastrous results in the run-up to the big race. Fully satisfied with the progress he had made in the US he returned to London to work on the preparation of route maps and the navigational problems involved in the venture.

Fitz was guest of honour at a luncheon in the Savoy Hotel, London, in late April, 1934, at which it was announced that McGrath was financing the Irish entry in the race and that the Colonel would be the pilot. The luncheon was hosted by John Dulanty, High Commissioner for the Irish Free State. The guests sat at tables forming the outline of a huge monoplane. Among those present were Sir Hal Colebatch, Agent-General for Western Australia, the artists, Paul Henry and Sir John Lavery, Capt. Spencer Freeman, representing the sponsors, Maurice Healy K.C., and Fitz's close ally of many years, Senator Oliver St. John Gogarty.

Joe McGrath was unable to attend but in his letter read at the function he described Fitz as "an old friend". "While there are, I am glad to say, many Irishmen with excellent records in aviation, I could think of none better than he to fly this plane", he stated. McGrath revealed that more than a year previously his organisation had approved of a scheme for an international air race sponsored by Hospitals Trust similar to the London to Melbourne Race, but on seeing that the two schemes might clash, which would be hurtful to both of them, he decided on sporting grounds to cancel their own plans and enter a machine in the Robertson Race instead. He stated that he was leaving the choice of machine to the pilot. "I have every confidence in leaving the selection to Fitzmaurice. Where or how he shall select his machine is a matter for himself; what he decides I shall stand by, as I know that in coming to his decision he will be animated by the one motive alone, that is, to select the plane that he thinks will give him the best chance of winning". It was not disclosed that Fitz had been selected as pilot a long time previously or that he was already advanced in his plans to use an American plane.

While in London Fitz received a letter from Bellanca stating he would have to use a Curtis Wright engine as the new Double Row Pratt and Whitney Wasp Junior, upon which they had decided, was still on the Army's secret list. Bellanca had failed in his efforts to get it delisted. Fitz was not prepared to leave it at that. He set out for America again, this time to a fanfare of Irish music provided by pipers at Waterloo Station. He met the Irish Minister, Michael McWhite, in Washington and he arranged a meeting with Mr. Dern, an Irish-American from the Mormon State of Utah, then Secretary of State for War. Fitz told Dern his problem and the Minister, after listening attentively, pressed a bell on his desk. A door opened and in walked the then Chief-of-Staff, General Douglas MacArthur, later to become renowned allied commander in WW2 who recaptured the southwest Pacific and was in charge of the occupation of Japan. They were introduced. Dern asked MacArthur the reason why the engine had been retained on the secret list. Fitz was amazed at MacArthur's intimate knowledge of such a relatively minor detail in view of the immensity of the organisation over which he presided. The Chief-of-Staff explained that all that was required to release the engine was the Minister's signature. Fitz's trip had been justified.

After a party in his honour organised by officials of the Bureau of Aeronautics in Washington, at which many members of the House of Representatives and the Senate also attended, Fitz, accompanied by Mr. Dern, was flown back to New York by another of his "old friends", Major Jimmy Doolittle. The Major was later to distinguish himself as Commander-in-Chief of the Eight American Air Force with the rank of Lieut. General. In New York, Mayor La Guardia laid on a banquet for him that night at which Dern, McWhite and many other high profile politicians, airmen, bankers, industrialists and journalists were present to bid the Irishman farewell, after his short but successful visit. He was given a police motorcycle escort with screaming sirens to a waiting liner due to sail for Southampton.

Fitz chose an ex-RAF Flight Sergeant, Eric "Jock" Bonar, as his copilot. He had served in the Irishman's squadron in the RAF. He was an experienced mechanic and had also trained as a pilot. They would alternate at the controls with Fitz looking after the navigation and Bonar attending to engine maintenance during stops for refuelling. It was the ideal combination, Fitz felt. The Irishman was confident that nothing could stop them from winning. Every detail of the trip was examined minutely and to make doubly sure of the facilities along the route Bonar was sent to Singapore to study the aerodrome layouts up to that point.

As soon as Fitz got word that his plane was approaching completion, he and his copilot left for Wilmington. Men were working double shifts, day and night, at the Bellanca plant struggling to get the job finished. The intense heat and humidity in Delaware made conditions in the factory almost intolerable. It was touch and go, but the deadline was met and, after a series of tests, the plane and crew caught the last liner that would get them to England in time for the race. There was no opportunity for a final airworthiness test due to the tight sailing schedule but Fitz was sure that this detail could be overcome on his arrival in England. It was not a problem, he felt. How wrong he was!

He was delighted with his modified Bellanca "Skyrocket" type 28-70 machine, featuring a Twin Wasp Junior engine capable of developing 700 hp and fitted with an ultramodern radio direction finder developed by the US Navy. The only defect he could detect lay in the engine cowling which was splitting, owing to the tremendous air pressures built up inside it, as the metal was not of a sufficiently heavy gauge. He arranged to have a heavier one built and shipped over on the next boat.

Bigger trouble lay in store on arrival at Southampton. Windy conditions there prevented any cargo being transferred to the waiting tender and the ship continued on to Bremerhaven where the plane was deposited on the quayside almost two miles from the aerodrome. With the help of as many hands as Fitz and Bonar could find the machine was pushed along roads and through fields, ditches and fences, all of which had to be made good again. This aeroplane push through the countryside must have presented an unusual and amusing sight to passers-by but for Fitz and his comrade it was a painstaking and tricky operation. They finally made it to the airfield from where they flew the Bellanca to Eastleigh Aerodrome where the final touches were added to its appearance. The plane and her crew arrived at Mildenhall on Tuesday, 16 October. A Pratt and Whitney engineer fitted the new cowling and in the process introduced his own system of engine cooling baffle plates. Fitz was delighted with this work and with the entire operation. It was the first time in aviation history, he congratulated himself, that an aeroplane had come off the drawing-board and had flown, "actually above the demanded performance", in just one year.   It was a remarkable feat by any standards.

The razzmatazz surrounding this major international aviation event was reaching a climax as the Irish entry settled in at Mildenhall, four days before the race was due to start.   By Wednesday twenty-one speed planes had gathered for the greatest race in history.   They were made up as follows: Britain (9), America (3), Australia (2), Holland (2), New Zealand (2) and one each from Denmark, New Guinea and Ireland.   The schedule of departure times was distributed.   First off would be the world's most famous husband/wife duo, Jim and Amy Mollison, in their De Havilland Comet and one of Britain's favourites.   This was one of three DH Comets in the line-up for Britain.   O.C. Jones and K.F.H. Waller were in another due off fourth and C.W.A. Scott and T.C. Black, the eventual winners, due off seventh, were in the third one.   Scott had previously set a record for the flight from England to Australia.   His entry was well fancied by the bookies. So also was another British entry, an Airspeed piloted by Capt. Neville Stack, whose family came from County Kerry, and which was entered by Sir John Siddeley.

The American challenge was led by the colourful character, Roscoe Turner, and his copilot, Clyde Pangbourne, in a Boeing Transport.   Turner, who was a lion-tamer in his spare time, held US coast to coast records in both directions.   Pangbourne was the first to fly over both oceans and later earned a living as chief pilot of a travelling circus in which he carried 125,000 people without a single mishap.   The youngest pilot in the field was a twenty one year old Australian, C.J. Melrose, who had flown his Puss Moth the month previously from Australia to England in eight days.

There was disappointment with the news of the late defection of Sir Charles Kingsford Smith because of an accident to his plane. Another late cancellation was that of the irrepressible American, Wiley Post.   He was to fly in his famous plane, *Winnie Mae,* named after the daughter of the sponsor of his record round the world flight in 1933. Another American who did not make it was Jimmy Weddell, who was killed while testing out his machine in New York a short time earlier. A French entry faltered because of a crash at Le Bourget airport as it set out for Mildenhall.

There was enormous public interest in the huge array of aircraft on display. Apart from the DH Comets, the Boeing and the Airspeed there was an unprecedented collection of makes and models including a Douglas DC2, a Northrop 2 PLCM, a Monocoupe, a Fairey 111, two Fairey Fox Mark 1s, a Lockheed Vega, a DH Dragon, a Desoutter Mark 2, a Miles Falcon M.3, a Miles Hawk and a DH Leopard Moth.

But the plane that commanded the most attention was the Irish entry. This was considered the "dark horse" in the field and leaks on its capabilities had helped to instal it firmly as the pre-race favourite. On the Wednesday, three days before the off, it was put on display for the press and public. It was christened *The Irish Swoop* by Mrs. Joe McGrath. "I pray you may have the power which is the symbol of the bold Irish spirit of adventure that has scattered the sons of the Gael all over the world," she said as she smashed a bottle of Irish whiskey with a mallet made of Irish bogwood. "I pray that you may soar over the oceans and continents, and swoop to victory with the swiftness and precision of a swallow flying to its winter home."

Two of Britain's top jockeys were there for the christening. Steve Donoghue and Michael Beary, who were riding in the Cesarewitch later in the day, came up from Newmarket. "If I were only on the Bellanca this afternoon, I should be on a dead cert and you could put your shirt on me," said Steve to reporters with a smile.

Bernard J.W. Hughes was one of *The Irish Swoop's* greatest admirers. In a delightful first-hand account of the happenings at Mildenhall in the days before the flight, which he submitted to Irish Army Archives, he tells of a 14 year old aviation fanatic schoolboy's memories of the scene. He remembers the treatment of the Irish entry by the English press.

"Both the English popular and aviation press featured Col. Fitzmaurice and the Bellanca as somewhere between an intrusion and a joke ... the general tone was acid, unkind and partisan. The atmosphere was not improved by the support given to Col. Fitzmaurice by the Nazi newspaper, *Der Angriff*."

Bernard found lodgings for the week near the aerodrome and remembered the arrival of the Bellanca.

"I woke up ... and pulled the bedroom curtains to see directly across the road a bell-tent, and the Bellanca with its tail almost in the hedge. So the Bellanca was not using the hangars and not parking on the concrete apron to be at the mercy of the crowds, but a good five minutes walk from the other aircraft."

Bernard recognised Fitzmaurice from photographs he had seen in *Flight* and *The Aeroplane* magazines. From behind the hedge he heard the Bellanca people talk of the need for a cup of tea and toilets. He intervened and told Fitz and his entourage that he could arrange these things for them at the guest house where he stopped just across the road. This was run by two kindly brothers he nicknamed the Marx Brothers because of their uncanny likeness to two members of the famous movie family of comedians. Over the next three days "Tea with the Marx Brothers" became the password and to the delight of the young aviation enthusiast he was rewarded with an honorary job on the ground-staff of the Bellanca.

On the Wednesday Fitz had handed the Clerk of Scales at Mildenhall a certificate of airworthiness for his machine which was weighed for the full load of 8,350 lbs., and gave notice that he intended to fly it with this gross weight. The certificate had a note on the bottom which read: "Total fuel capacity is 600 gallons, which corresponds to a gross weight of 8,350 pounds. Airplane was investigated and tested for this higher gross weight, and conforms substantially with all international requirements, except length of landing run."

Fitz pointed out the words "except length of landing run" to the officials concerned, and explained that as he had had less than two hours to catch his boat from New York to England with the machine, there had not been time to complete the landing run test with full load. He had, therefore, informed the American Government that he would complete this test in England. He told the officials that he was now prepared to complete this test before them on the Mildenhall ground, if they so wished, but was informed that it was considered unnecessary.

Earlier in the day Fitz had phoned an official of the Air Ministry relating the circumstances. The official had stated that he did not consider a test necessary in view of the wording of the rest of the certificate.

The next day, Thursday, an official came to Fitz and said all was in order except for three things still required to complete the formalities for the race, namely, pilots' licences, lifebelts and Very lights. Fitz said that these would be produced the next day and this was duly done. No reference whatsoever was made to the airworthiness certificate and there was a witness from the Irish Hospitals Trust present to confirm what had happened.

At lunchtime on the Friday the bombshell dropped. Fitz was informed by one of the staff assisting in the preparations that he had heard it from a member of the Race Committee that he (Fitz) was to be disqualified from competing in the race on the grounds that his certificate of airworthiness was not in order as he had not done a full load landing. The irate Irishman made frantic efforts to see the Race Committee but was informed that as most of its members were occupied in receiving visitors they could not see him until 5pm. Among the visitors to Mildenhall that day were King George V, Queen Mary and the Prince of Wales. Fitz was introduced to the Prince, Edward David, later King Edward V111 who abdicated in 1936, by his Air Equerry, Wing Commander Fielden, later Captain of the Queen's Flight with the rank of Air Commodore, whom Fitz had known in his RAF days. Fitz had high regard for the Royalty and was impressed by the Prince's knowledge of aircraft, but at that particular time he had other matters on his mind.

He did not get a hearing until nearly 6pm. The Chairman handed him a memorandum with the following message: "Competitor No. 29 - The USA certificate of worthiness in respect of the aircraft entered by this competitor states that the aircraft complies with the I.C.A.N. requirements at a gross weight of 5,458 lbs, and adds a note that at a gross weight of 8,350 lbs the aircraft complies with the I.C.A.N. requirements except in respect of length of landing run.

"The committee are prepared to allow the competitor to start at the lower limit or at a weight not exceeding the higher limit provided that he notifies in writing to the Committee at which level he elects to fly. If he elects to fly at any weight exceeding the lower figure he will be subject to disqualification unless a reply is received to the cable dispatched to the USA Department of Commerce on 18/10/34 certifying that the aircraft complies substantially with all I.C.A.N. requirements at a load not less than the load at which the competitor elects to fly."

Fitz was livid at this late, late, decision by the Race Committee. Joe McGrath had visited Mildenhall earlier in the day and had left unaware that there were any difficulties. Having consulted with Capt. Spencer Freeman and Jack O'Sheehan, representing the sponsors, the following reply was drafted:

"I elect to fly at a gross weight of 8,350 lbs, and sign this document reserving my right to appeal in the event of my being disqualified.

"I would point out also that upon referring this question of landing run with gross weight of 8,350 lbs to the A.I.D. (Aeronautical Inspection Directorate) officials and later to the Clerk of the Scales, I expressed my willingness to demonstrate this test, and was informed that it was considered unnecessary.

"I respectfully protest most strongly against the lateness of the

Race Committee's objections."
  Fitz signed the memo:
  "J.M.C. Fitzmaurice, Colonel,
    Chief Pilot,
    Entry No. 29,
    7.35pm, 19th October 1934."
Just as he was completing and signing this acceptance an official came along with a cabled reply from the Department of Commerce, Washington.   It read as follows:
  "Bellanca plane C of A for 5,458 lbs. Owner prevented further tests. Stated he would adjust weights with you."
The Race Committee went into conference again and after the meeting had concluded they told Fitz that they could not allow the machine to rise with a greater weight than that of 5,458 lbs. Fitz told them that he was in the race as a sporting event and not for the prize money. He said that he was still willing to fly under the disqualification terms offered to him earlier in the evening. He laboured the point that although the machine had an all-up weight of 8,350 lbs, and had satisfied I.C.A.N. requirements for a takeoff at that weight, it would never be called upon, on account of the dump valve in the main 480 gallon tank, even in the event of complete power failure on takeoff, to touch down with a greater load than 5,470 lbs.   The officials pointed out that the use of a jettisoning device such as a dump valve was not included in I.C.A.N. regulations. Fitz countered by directing their attention to wheel-brakes or flaps (a device which considerably reduces the speed of approach in landing while enabling the pilot to have complete control of the machine) with which many of the planes were equipped. Where in the I.C.A.N. regulations were these covered he asked, knowing that they were not covered. But the Race Committee refused to accept his line of argument. He gave notice of appeal to the stewards.   At 11pm, seven and a half hours before the race was due to start, he was told his appeal had been dismissed.

Accepting the lesser load meant that instead of having a radius of 3,000 miles he could only carry sufficient petrol to fly from six to seven hundred miles, thus making it impossible for him to travel from one checking station to another. He would, therefore, have been forced to take another route entirely for which he had no charts. The Aero Club were asked if they could supply the charts but they replied that they could not. There was no other choice but to withdraw from the race.

The news of the withdrawal caused a sensation. The media had whipped up interest in the race to a frenzy with readers and listeners avid for any snippet of news from Mildenhall. The Irish entry had established itself as a likely winner and it was the bookies' favourite. Even the British press was now coming around to taking the Irish entry seriously. The *Daily Express* assessed *The Irish Swoop* as follows: "Bellanca American six-seater, low-winged monoplane. Secret engine. Might be in Melbourne before others are at Singapore. Speed, unverified, 275 mph. Range 3,000 miles. Irish dark horse." The *Daily Sketch* conceded that Col. Fitzmaurice was "the hottest favourite in the England-Melbourne race".

But now for some vague technicality, from the public perspective, the favourite was forced out of the race. Fitzmaurice's withdrawal was the big story on the morning of 20 October. The race itself became almost something of an anticlimax.

Irish Hospitals Trust, the owners of the plane, complained that they had not been treated in a reasonable manner by the Race Committee. They put forward the same points that Fitz had already made to the officials. Guiseppe Bellanca was furious when he heard the news. As far as he was concerned the plane conformed to all load factor requirements. "It is to be regretted", he said, "that this unfortunate incident occurred, savouring somewhat of lack of sportsmanship, and at the same time defeating the high purpose for which the race was initiated."

The Royal Aero Club responded telling the Press Association

that they were in possession of the US certificate of airworthiness and that it certified the plane for 5,458 lbs only. They had been informed that Fitz had refused any further tests in the US and that he had said he would adjust weights with the Royal Aero Club. This, they pointed out, was tantamount to a jockey saying before a race that he would "adjust weights" with the stewards of a race meeting. The RAC regulations for the race were perfectly clear, they stated, and had been fulfilled by the other machines in the race.

Fitz and his copilot were anxious to start half an hour after the other competitors and fly to Australia outside the race but were advised against it by the sponsors because it was now into the early hours of the morning and Freeman and O'Sheehan felt that it would be unwise to let the airmen go on such a long and testing mission with such little rest. But irrespective of the sponsors concerns for the safety of the airmen, the Aero Club ensured that *The Irish Swoop* did not leave Mildenhall on the following day with a full load. When Fitz returned to the plane on the Saturday morning he found two policemen there whose duty it was to ensure that the petrol was unloaded. His guns were well and truly spiked. Fitz was left an embittered man. This had been a wonderful opportunity to clinch a secure future and re-establish himself as an aviation icon. It was to be his last.

The feeling of being wronged, instead of diminishing with the years, continued to fester within him. His side of the story was certainly well publicised at the time and there was widespread sympathy for the manner in which he was treated. But after the Melbourne race he gradually receded from the public stage except for the occasional guest appearance at an event, article in a newspaper or mention on radio. Other events, and especially the rise of Nazism and the talk of war, pushed his achievements into the background. Mentions of Fitz became rarer and rarer and even then when his name was mentioned, it was almost invariably in relation to the flight of the *Bremen*. Such reports usually appeared around the time of the anniversaries of the flight. Such was the case in April 1963 when a letter to the Dublin daily, *Evening Herald*, recalled the famous flight. But it also referred to the Mildenhall incident. The writer posed the question: "Were the Irish robbed?" His own view was that they were not.

This evoked a lengthy and hard-hitting response a few evenings later from Fitz, now in failing health, almost forgotten and living in relatively poor circumstances in a bed-sit in Richmond, London. "Actually," he wrote, "it was barefaced robbery of the meanest description on a flimsy technicality". He went on to restate his case and concluded by pointing out "that all long-range aircraft of today are compelled to fit such a dump valve to jettison the bulk of their fuel in the event of an emergency landing ... so my entrance to the race was a valuable contribution to aeronautical progress". This underlines the fact that almost thirty years after the traumatic event at Mildenhall Fitz remained bitter about his shoddy treatment by race officials. He was obviously still a man proud of what he had achieved, though, even if by that time his feats were all but forgotten.

With all the activity of Irish interest centred on the stewards room on the Friday evening as the public flocked to the main aircraft parking area some distance away trying to get glimpse of the Royal party, the subject matter at the heart of the controversy, *The Irish Swoop*, was left deserted - except for its avid teenage fan, who remained loyal to the cause. Bernard Hughes recalls his boyhood memories of that fateful day.

"I wasn't fighting back a crowd. If anyone approached I polished a bit of Bellanca with a duster and tried to look as if I belonged ... Here was the most promising aeroplane entered in the race, with a very experienced pilot, the hopes and backing of the Irish Free State, being guarded by a schoolboy with a cardboard badge and two yellow dusters ... As dusk fell I expected someone would come to cover up the engine and cockpit glazing, but no one came, and I wanted to be up at 3 am on Saturday to see the start of the race."

The machine was taken to Croydon Aerodrome on the Monday, 22 October, for fully loaded landing run tests the following day. The American Embassy sent along representatives to inspect the test but just as the pilots were ready to take off, an official of the aerodrome approached them telling them that the authorities did not consider Croydon suitable for the test. It was on to Lympne Aerodrome, near Portsmouth, but here they had not sufficient weights to weigh the plane. On the Thursday the plane finally underwent the test with the full load and was passed as airworthy.

Word had come through on the previous Tuesday that Scott and Black in the British Comet had won the race and the £10,000 first prize by completing the course in 2 days, 22 hours and 59 minutes. All but seven hours and 24 minutes had been spent in flight. The Dutch entry of Parmentier and Moll in the Douglas finished second and the US entry of Turner and Pangbourne in the Boeing was third.

Fitz and Bonar set out from Lympne Aerodrome on Friday morning, 26 October, to tackle the new record set by Scott and Black. With a following wind of 40 mph smack in her tail giving her a ground speed of 270 mph *The Irish Swoop* was making excellent progress. But dead on track just over Liege in Belgium the most curious vibrations began to develop in the machine. They throttled back to 120mph but the weird vibrations continued so they decided to turn back.

Over Lympne they jettisoned the contents of the main tank and effected a safe landing. On examination Fitz discovered that, so far as he could see, the full load landing of the previous day had not damaged any stress member of the machine, but to his horror he found that it had caused the tyres to spread to an extent which would not permit them to go completely home in the recesses into which they folded when retracted. This was the cause of the terrific turbulence they had encountered which threatened the complete destruction of the tail unit and the subsequent disintegration of the machine in the air. Fitz had been foiled again. His worst fears had been realised. The machine's undercarriage was never designed to cope with full load landing and he believed it would never have to, because of the dump valve precaution. He had not provided, however, for what he termed the "asinine wisdom" of the Race Committee.

The plane was returned to America for a complete overhaul. It was later acquired by Jim Mollison who flew it from New York to London in record time which, Fitz was happy to note, proved the worth of the machine.

Chapter 23

"Begrudging Thanks They Only Gave"

A fter the disqualification of the Irish entry in the London/ Melbourne race Fitz almost vanished from the scene. He spent a lot of his time in the US working on a variety of projects, mostly on aircraft design. For a while he took a deep interest in the development of the engine-less plane, the glider. He also did some research, design and promotional work in Europe. In September 1936 he was featured in *Flight* magazine, introducing a new French designed two-seater monoplane to the British market. It was the small Bassou F.B. 30 with its snappy little Mengin power unit which he flew from Paris to London in three hours. Two weeks later *The Aeroplane* magazine put him and the Bassou under the spotlight again intimating that the little monoplane was arousing much interest in flying clubs at an asking price of about £300.

In 1938 Fitz wrote to the Air Ministry in London informing them that he planned to live in England and asked for permission to wear the DFC, conferred on him by US President Coolidge, while there. The Air Ministry asked the Department of External Affairs in Dublin for their comments. National Archives records note that there was some sensitivity within the Department about being asked to report back to the British on the issue.   On 20 December the Irish replied that there was "no objection to the wearing of the decoration by Mr. Fitzmaurice here".

The clouds of war were gathering menacingly through the 1930s and in 1939 they unleashed their venom that engulfed the world in a barbaric conflagration.   Fitz returned to England for the war years where he managed a serviceman's club in London.

Similar to Fitzmaurice, who was conferred with the Freedom of Dublin, the city of his birth, Capt. Koehl became an Honorary Citizen of the city of his birth, Neu-Ulm, as a result of the flight.

In August 1931 he and his wife accompanied the Mayor of New York, Jimmy Walker, and top aviator, Bernt Balchen, on a courtesy visit to Baroness Von Huenefeld, the late Baron's mother in Berlin.   Back with his old company, Lufthansa, he got involved in aircraft design and gave lectures.   One of Koehl's creations was a most unusual looking tailless plane, like a gigantic bat, which had its first public trial over Tempelhof Aerodrome in Berlin in late September of the same year.   A book on his experiences, *Airman's Escape*, was published in 1933.

Koehl became increasingly distressed at the course of events in the Third Reich and with the rise of Hitler.   Due to an ongoing difference of opinion between Secretary of State for Air, Hermann Goering, and himself on the development of new aircraft, the aviator was pushed into the background.   He died in Munich on 7 October, 1938, from kidney failure at the relatively young age of 50.   Despite his uneasy relationship with Goering, who had served in his command during WW1, he was given a full military funeral and buried in Pfaffenhofen Cemetery near his native Neu-Ulm.   Amongst the attendance was Rudolf Hess.

Fitz was back in Ireland in the late 1940s, looking for work, and while there he tracked down many of his old contacts and comrades.   He found some good friends in Aer Lingus where his achievements and valuable contribution to the development of aviation was still remembered.

Fitz revisits Baldonnel in September 1962 - a sad and lonely figure 34 years after the famous flight.

He revisited the scenes of his youth in Portlaoise, where he met a few old acquaintances, including the Aldritt brothers, Joseph and his dear friend of yesteryear, Louis.   He was shown around the town and introduced to townspeople by Joseph's son, Donie.

The Aldritts were still busy in their garage workshop, which had been opened by Donie's grandfather, Frank, in 1897.   There Fitz saw the remains of the little aircraft he had helped to build with the Aldritts and master carpenter, Johnny Conroy, during his school days.   It was perched safely and unobtrusively on a large cross-member high above the workshop floor, forgotten and forlorn.   It was a poignant moment for Fitz because he knew that it was this unpretentious little contraption that had sparked his

Fitz recalls old times at Baldonnel with George Barton and flight-sergrant, Leo Canavan, on his visit there in 1962.

initial interest in aviation so many years before. Did he remember the local clergymen telling old Mr. Aldritt and his sons that they should be ashamed of themselves for trying to invent such a machine because "it was unnatural for man to fly"? It had had its passing moment of glory before fading into obscurity. Its story, in a way, resembled Fitz's own. Like Fitz, too, it would never again to able to recapture old glories for now it was without its engine, which had been disposed of by some inexplicable oversight on somebody's part during the post-war years.

He lived with his companion Josephine Russell in a house owned by Eileen O'Halloran at 34 Belmont Avenue, Donnybrook. It was during this time he dictated his memoirs to Josephine and she and Eileen helped him with its composition. Parts of the script relating to his flying days were published in a book published for the silver jubilee of the transatlantic flight in 1953 titled, *Bremen Ireland-America 1928*.   Much of the contents had been already published in a series of articles for *The Irish Times* in 1951. He supplemented his small Air Corps pension by submitting articles to the newspapers on his own experiences and on aviation matters but these appeared only on an occasional basis and merely served to keep the wolf from the door.

Fitz briefly emerged from the shadows of anonymity with the approach of the Silver Jubilee of the flight of the *Bremen* in 1953. Herr Wuril, of Bremen Airport, wrote telling him of plans for the ceremony being organised by the local government and Bremen Flying Club and offering him the place of honour at the event. The organisers did not know where Fitz was now living and the envelope containing the invitation was addressed merely, "Mr. James C. Fitzmaurice, Ireland".   How Fitz was located by the postal authorities is a little story worth telling.

Dublin man, Sean Roycroft, recalled for me this incident which pleased Fitz considerably.   Sean was in charge of the training of new staff in Dublin Postal District in early 1953.   As part of the programme he led a team of newcomers at what was known as the "Blind Desk" at Pearse Street Sorting Office, where insufficiently addressed letters were dealt with.   He noticed a letter addressed "Mr. James C. Fitzmaurice, Ireland". By sheer coincidence he knew that Fitz now lived in a flat at Garville Avenue, Rathgar, only a short distance from where he himself resided.   Had he not known Fitz's address it is certain that the letter would have been returned to sender "address unknown".

Sean was surprised to see the envelope reproduced in an issue of the *Times Pictorial*, a weekly publication, a few weeks later along with Fitz's own comments.   Fitz by that time was very much the "forgotten hero" but this showed that he still retained a degree of fame seeing that he could be located with such a skimpy address.   He was so pleased some people still remembered him that he decided to share the good news with others. Fitz accepted the German invitation and with both Koehl and the Baron long since dead, he was given VIP treatment on his visit to Bremen. But for coincidence and the watchful eye of Sean Roycroft he would have missed the big German event.

Fitz had hoped that the anniversary would have been marked in Ireland. A new national festival, "An Tóstal", was being organised for April and Fitz had proposed to the authorities that the *Bremen* anniversary celebrations could be tied in with the other events. He had suggested that the *Bremen* could be brought to Ireland on loan from the Ford Museum in Dearborn, Michigan, where it was on permanent display, for the occasion. He was disgusted when no interest whatsoever was shown in his suggestions.

"It would have been an excellent opportunity for reminding the world that Ireland had a share in one of the important events of aviation history," he told the *Sunday People*. It seems strange to me that the Germans should attach more importance to this occasion than the Irish, who have, after all, many fewer flying achievements."

Perhaps the reasons for the neglect of the Irish Government to mark Ireland's significant contribution to one of the outstanding achievements in the history of aviation can be encapsulated in officialdom's response to requests to mark the Silver Jubilee by issuing a special stamp. On 26 November 1952 the Secretary to the Department of Posts and Telegraphs, Dr. McDonald, made this response: "I feel that the issue of an official Irish stamp to commemorate the event would be out of place and would be regarded as over emphasizing Irish participation in what was essentially a German undertaking".

In the epilogue to his book published in 1953 he wrote:

"We, who comprised the crew of the Bremen were, of course, adventurers just as was Columbus when he set forth to prove the earth was round - and, incidentally, collided with the American continent. All great developments on the road of man's conquest of a hostile environment have small and risky beginnings, inspired by large and perhaps over-optimistic visions of what those beginnings may ultimately portend.

"Tennyson in 'Locksley Hall' written 100 years ago, was seeing in the regions of his mind something not greatly different from that which we saw:

For I dipt into the future, far as human eye could see,
Saw the vision of the world, and all the wonder that would be;
Saw the heavens fill with commerce, argosies of magic sails,
Pilots of the purple twilight, dropping down with costly bales."

That same year, 1953, was also the 50th anniversary of Powered Flight. Fitz had hoped to make some useful cash by giving television talks and doing some newspaper work in the US. He wrote to a good aviation contact of his in New York, J.H. Doolittle, asking him if he could organise a working visit. Doolittle, who had been pilot on the flight from Washington to New York on his visit to US Secretary of State for War, Mr. Dern, in 1934, wrote back stating that he had been in contact with Harry Bruno (who had organised the grand victory tour of US cities after the transatlantic flight in 1928) and his thinking was that "it would be very difficult to make satisfactory arrangements to cover expenses". This was another slap in the face for Fitz, now down in the dumps. His star had waned in America. The newsworthiness of his achievements had been long since overtaken by other events.

Through all the years since he and his wife had divorced, Fitz and his daughter, Pat, had very little contact with each other. Mrs. Fitzmaurice, after winning custody of Pat, returned to England. She remarried some years later. She wrote Fitz completely out of her life and discouraged any communication between him and his daughter.

Pat remembers her father visiting her at boarding school and also of one meeting between Fitz and her mother which developed into a running row. Mrs. Fitzmaurice persuaded him to put £1,000 in a trust fund for his daughter which she could redeem when she reached twenty-one.

Pat was married at 18 and was a widow before she was 21. Her husband, Haydn Mortimer Jones, was a fighter pilot with the RAF and was killed in action during WW2. They had one son, Terence. When she came of age she received the proceeds of the trust. Fitz wrote to his daughter commiserating with her on the loss of her husband. Not knowing his address she wrote back through the bank in which her trust had been kept, thanking her father for the money. She would much preferred to have spoken to him face to face.

Pat married Michael Selwyn Jones, brother of her first husband, who also saw service with the RAF in WW2 and there was a son, Haydn, and a daughter, Edwina (Ashby), in their family. They enjoyed a very happy marriage for over forty years until Michael died some years ago.

In the early 1960s Pat's eldest son, Terence, was watching the television programme, "This is Your Life", hosted by Eamon Andrews. The person featured was Capt. R.H. McIntosh, otherwise "All-Weather Mac", Fitz's companion on the attempted transatlantic crossing in the *Princess Xenia* in 1927. One of the guests was Fitz. Terence rang the show producers but they would not give him his grandfather's address or phone number. They did, however, agree to pass on any correspondence they might receive for him. .

In May 1962 James King, a reporter with the *Sunday Express*, tracked down the forgotten hero to his single-roomed bed-sitter in Richmond.

Under the banner headline "Forget me, pleads Atlantic air hero" with a smaller heading announcing "The Irishman who blazed the trail for today's jets misses the golden rewards", King told of his meeting with Fitz, now partially blind and in failing health.

"He was wearing striped flannel pyjamas ... Tall and of military bearing, he looked older than his 64 years. His eyes blinked behind horn-rimmed spectacles. To neighbours and the occasional visitor he seems a typical old soldier living out his pension alone in a single room ... A forgotten hero. A man whose exploits, 34 years ago, won worldwide acclaim ... Yet today this sole survivor of that epic flight is a sick lonely man, who pleaded: 'Please don't say where I am. I want to be left alone. I am finished with aeroplanes and public life. I want to be forgotten.' "

After telling him the story of the flight Fitz was asked by King if he felt cast by the wayside and if he was bitter. "No, I feel no bitterness," replied Fitz. "I don't think about the past any more. I no longer have an interest in anything. All my time is spent in being ill. All I think of now is getting better. I have no pension. As you can see I live modestly ... "

Later that year, in September, Fitz was guest of honour at the International Air Transport Association conference in Dublin. During his stay in Ireland he revisited Baldonnel for the first time in many years. It was an occasion full of nostalgia for him.

"It's great to be back again", he said, "and to meet some of my old friends - but there are so few of them left. I only wish I was still able to fly and I would have a try at one of the new aircraft here."

At the aerodrome he met Flight-Sergeant, Leo Canavan and George Barton, both of whom were present at Baldonnel on the morning of the historic flight. He was most delighted to meet and have a chat with his old and trusted colleague, Johnny Maher. He later lunched with Officer-in-Command of the Air Corps, Col. Willie Keane, a cadet in 1928 and a great admirer of his, along with other officers including the US Military Attache to Ireland, Col. F. O'Brien.

Some time after the "This is Your Life" show on "All-Weather Mac", Pat managed to make contact with her father and they arranged a meeting. She and some of her family had lunch with him and he promised to come stay with them at their home in

Aylesbury when the children were on their school holidays. He never came but returned to Ireland to pursue an improved pension. He lived in Flat "A", 64 Grosvenor Road, Dublin, where he was tenderly minded by his long-time partner and closest friend, Josephine Russell. Although helped out by the occasional old acquaintance who visited him, he could not secure the acknowledgement or the pension he felt he was due in his own country. Around this time a frail, almost blind and totally disillusioned Fitz, scribbled the following lines on the inside cover of a book:

Was it for this the wild geese spread
The grey wing upon everytide.
Was it for this the Bremen sped,
For this Fitzmaurice almost died.

Still fumbling in the grassy till
Begrudging thanks they only gave;
Romantic Ireland's dead and gone
It's with O'Leary in the grave.

Despite his failing health he took up an invitation to visit Munich in mid-1965 where he was presented with a medal for his services to aviation. On his return his condition worsened and on Sunday, 26 September 1965, he died in Baggot Street Hospital in Dublin.

Immediately on dying Fitz became a national hero again and received the official acclaim of his country, something he had failed to achieve in his lifetime after the euphoria of his victorious homecoming in 1928 had died down. He was given a State Funeral complete with full military honours. The coffin, draped with the Tricolour, Ireland's national flag, was borne on a gun-carriage from St. Mary's Church, Haddington Road, to Glasnevin Cemetery. On reaching the approaches to the cemetery a guard of honour of officers, NCOs and men of the Air Corps, under

The guard of honour takes up its position at the State Funeral.

Capt. Patrick Nugent, rendered their tribute.   The No. 1 Army
Band played the solemn music of the Requiem.   Ten pilots from
the Air Corps acted as pallbearers under Lt. Col. Malachi O'Higgins,
and Military Police formed the bearer party.   The firing squad
were drawn from the Second Motor Squadron.   Chief Marshal
was Comdt. P.M. Quinlan.

Among the mourners were former President William T.
Cosgrave, the man whose signature made it possible for Fitz to
take part in the *Bremen* flight.   Also there were high-ranking Army
officers, and representatives of the German Embassy and the
various civil airlines in Ireland.   Two of his former pupils, Lt. Col.
T.K. Curran and Lt. Col. Finbarr O Catháin, were there as was Col.
Delamere, who was now Manager of Dublin Airport.   The Army

The cortege makes its way through Glasnevin Cemetery to Fitz's final resting place.

was represented by the Adjutant-General, Major-General Sean Collins-Powell and the Air Corps by O/C, Col. Willie Keane. Aer Lingus was represented by its Chairman, Patrick Lynch, its General Manager, Dr. J.F. Dempsey, and its Chief Pilot, Capt. Aidan Quigley,

who has written at length about
the aviator's exploits in
newspaper and magazine articles
and in his excellent book, *Green
is My Sky.*

Pat's first visit to Ireland since
her childhood on the occasion of
her father's funeral was a
traumatic experience for her.
She was accompanied by her
eldest son, Terry, and other
mourners included Fitz's only
sister, May, his partner, Josephine
Russell, and cousins, Bill and
Eileen Linnane, and Thomas
Drumgoole, his nearest living

William T. and Mrs. Cosgrave were
among the mourners.

A volley is fired over the grave as the famous aviator is about to be interred.

relations in Ireland.

Three volleys were fired and the Last Post and Reveille were played as Ireland's most famous aviator was laid to rest in his family grave.

Liam Byrne in his highly commendable *History of Aviation in Ireland* wrote a superb chapter on "The Forgotten Hero". This is the way he ended his story: "His funeral to the cemetery at Glasnevin was that of a national figure and as the Tricolour-draped coffin reached its resting place, ambassadors, representatives of the government and dignitaries from every corner of the country looked on. For the first time since 1928 the forgotten hero was remembered."

Epilogue

Ayear after Fitz's death a golden opportunity was missed to adequately honour the man and his achievements. It was the 50th anniversary of the Easter Rising of 1916 and in a fever of Republicanism that swept the Irish Republic in 1966, a number of prominent public buildings and locations, such as big railway stations and military barracks', were named after the leaders of the rebellion. Baldonnel became Casement Aerodrome in memory of Sir Roger Casement who was executed in London for gun-running aimed at arming the rebels. Casement had no connection whatsoever with aviation. His name could have been associated more appropriately with some other installation or edifice. Fitzmaurice, even in death, was snubbed by the authorities.

But while Fitz's fame had diminished with the passing years, the plane he had flown with Capt. Koehl, into the history books was turned, as the decades rolled by, into something of an icon from the pioneer days of aviation. The *Bremen* had been suspended high above the main hall in New York's Grand Central Station in 1929 as a temporary measure until the beneficiaries, the Museum of the Peaceful Arts, could find a permanent home for it in the city. Fearful that they could not get the finances they needed for their undertaking, the group disbanded in 1931 during the Great Depression, and the plane was moved to the Smithsonian Institute in Washington D.C. In 1936 it was acquired by the Henry Ford Museum at Dearborn, Michigan, just outside Detroit. Numerous requests from Germany and Ireland over the years to procure it on loan were turned down. It had become too significant a treasure to risk parting with, even for a short time.

There was huge disappointment in Germany in 1968 when the Museum refused a request by Mr. K. B. Kindermann, then President of Hugo Junkers-Geselschaft E.V., for the loan of the plane for a function honouring Prof. Junkers' elevation to the Hall of Fame of the Deutsches Museum. (Mr. Kindermann visited Dublin 10 years later to speak at a 50th anniversary Commemorative Lecture). In his reply the Curator of Transportation at the Ford Museum, Leslie R. Henry, wrote:

"The Bremen is displayed in conjunction with two airplanes used by Admiral Byrd in his polar expeditions, the Fokker Arctic airplane and the Ford Antarctic airplane. These three airplanes,

The *Bremen* had been on permanent display at the Henry Ford Museum at Dearborn, Michigan, for over 60 years until its temporary loan in 1997 to the City of Bremen for the 70th and 75th anniversary of the flight.

grouped together, are particularly important to us technically because they illustrate how Mr. Henry Ford combined the configuration of the Fokker and the aluminium construction of the Junkers to produce America's first and significant all-metal, multi-engine, multi-passenger airplane, the Ford Tri-Motor.

"Because of the trust committed to us to preserve the Junkers Bremen, because of its tremendous historical significance in American history, and because of its technical contribution to the advancement of American aviation, we could not possibly remove the Junkers Bremen from our collection either permanently or temporarily. We are sure you will understand that the Bremen is an inseparable part of our unique collection of great and important civilian aircraft."

Ten years later the cities of Ulm and Hanover wished to borrow the *Bremen* for a seven month period around the time of the 50th anniversary. This time the request was made through the German Embassy in Washington DC. Requests from Ireland and the Deutsches Museum in Munich had already been turned down. Because the request had come through the Embassy it required some backstage diplomacy on the part of the Ford Museum to justify their refusal. The *New York Times* ran the story of the rift, not so much between the countries at a diplomatic level, but between Ireland and Germany and the Ford Museum. Under its heading "New Air War" the writer finished off the story on a compromising note: "As a kind of a peace offering Ford officials said they have granted the request of Irish television to film the Bremen in the newly rebuilt Transportation Section of the Museum."

Neu-Ulm laid on elaborate celebrations to mark the centenary of the birth of its most famous citizen, Capt. Hermann Koehl, on April 15 1988. Knowing that the Ford Museum would not part with the *Bremen* the organisers were prepared to settle for a part of it - the control stick - which they intended putting on temporary display in their shrine to Koehl in his home town. Randy Mason,

Curator of Transportation at the Museum, replied saying that it would be impractical to loan the control stick because of complications in disassembling the mechanism. He offered one of the two compasses in the cockpit, which were easily removable, instead. During the festivities a memorial tablet was mounted on the house where Koehl was born and a street was named after him.

After extensive discussions perseverance finally paid off when the Ford Museum agreed to release the plane on loan to Germany in early 1997. A group of Bremen businessmen, with the full backing of the Deutsche Lufthansa Berlin-Stiftung, negotiated the loan for a seven year period which would cover both the 70th and 75th anniversaries of the flight. The deal covered the safe transport and restoration of the plane that would go on display in a special pavilion at Bremen airport.

The *Detroit Free Press* carried an extensive feature on the lending of the famous aircraft to the land of its origin. In his article, columnist Neal Rublin wrote: "Clara Deck, the museum's intriguingly titled 'conservator of large objects', confesses that she never gave the Bremen much thought ... The airplane did not turn her propeller until last fall, when a delegation from Germany came to visit in Dearborn. They had petitioned the museum to loan the airplane to the city that shares its name, and 'they treated it like a sacred object. They all had to touch it, to lay hands on it."

The article told of how Clara had "cleaned grime from its crevices with a Q-tip, daubed paint on its tail, and fretted as it was taken apart and crated for its trip home on a Luftwaffe cargo jet". The article told of Clara's feelings at seeing the plane being taken away: " 'I'm sorry to see it leave,' she says. As museum carpenters finished packing the wings and tail two weeks ago, she felt like throwing herself across the ailerons: 'Can I just spend a few more minutes with it', she pleaded."

That, more so than anything else I have read, sums up the effect this hallowed hunk of metal that is the *Bremen* has on people who know its story.

A cairn marks the spot on Greenly Island where the *Bremen* landed. Antonio Cormier, whose grandfather, Joseph Alfred Cormier, sent out the first news of the landing from his little post office at Blanc Sablon, has put together a sizeable collection of photographs, newspaper cuttings, letters and other memorabilia, of the *Bremen* landing and eventual rescue. These are now housed in a museum, situated on the Quebecan mainland just across the straits from Greenly, dedicated to the *Bremen* and run by Brest Historical Society.

In the wave of enthusiasm that prevailed in America in the aftermath of the famous flight the three aviators central to the *Bremen* had their names perpetuated in a number of ways.   A street in Gander, Newfoundland, another one in Long Island, New York, and a small community in Saskatchewan, are named after Fitzmaurice while streets and monuments elsewhere commemorated his German comrades.   The newly independent Irish Free State, despite the enhanced prestige gained for it on the international stage because of Fitzmaurice's part in the adventure, did not lay down any permanent markers to honour the man or note the event.   He became the forgotten hero.   Nor did the country capitalise on its new found reputation in the world of aviation.

It was through no fault of Fitz that the Free State did not make the most of a golden opportunity presented to it to establish itself from the early stages as an important player in civil aviation.   On August 9, 1928, he chaired a meeting in the Hibernian Hotel, Dublin, with the aim of setting up an aero club to promote the development of civil aviation in Ireland.   Six days later the Irish Aero Club was formally inaugurated.   He was elected chairman and the first committee included Col. Charles Russell, Senator St. John Gogarty and Osmond Gratten Esmonde TD.   This was the birth of civil aviation in Ireland.

Because he was frustrated by the almost total lack of interest of the Irish Government in the development of a new and exciting aviation industry in the years that followed, Fitz decided to employ his energy and talents elsewhere. He had visualised the tremendous opportunities for Ireland. Its geographical position gave it a key edge in linking the two most lucrative markets in the world, America and Europe. He had the ideas and the technical know-how but he hadn't the money and a cash strapped government would not risk the investment needed in such uncharted waters.

While he was pursuing the golden fleece in England, France and Germany, and for the most part in America, modest moves were being made by others in Ireland to set up a viable commercial civil airline business. Col. Russell got seriously involved in plans to start a national airline. So too did another former Air Corps colleague, Capt. W.P. Delamere. Sean Lemass spared no effort in trying to tie the various strands together.

The Aero Club staged some air displays which whetted the public appetite. There was a bonus for enthusiasts on Sunday, 3 July 1932, when Scottish flyer, Jim Mollison, who was on a fact-finding mission to Ireland with his wife-to-be, Amy Johnson, took up an invitation from the club and gave a thrilling exhibition in his Puss Moth aircraft at Baldonnel. The following month Mollison took off from Portmarnock Strand on the start of the first successful east-west transatlantic solo flight.

In July 1933, Sir Alan Cobham's Air Circus came to Ireland and staged spectacular displays throughout the country. Cobham had made a historic flight to Australia in 1926 for which he received a knighthood. He, more than any other pioneer, helped foster air-mindedness among the public in Great Britain and Ireland in the twenties and thirties. Cobham completed another tour in Ireland later that year and in 1935 he was back again by public demand. At the end of that year he sold the circus to C.W.A. Scott, who with T. C. Black had won the London to Australia Race the previous year. The Scott Circus put on displays throughout

The granite marker at Baldonnel identifies the spot where the *Bremen* began her flight.

Ireland in May and June 1936. These displays helped keep public interest in aviation at a high.

Both Cobham and Scott were asked for an input into getting a civil airline off the ground. So too was Lady Mary Bailey, Irish aviation pioneer and the first woman to fly the Irish Sea. Cork County Surveyor, Richard F. O'Connor, also became closely involved. He was a man with a vision of Ireland's key position in international aviation. In May 1936 Aer Lingus was born. Dublin solicitor and Chairman of the Irish Aero Club, Seán O hUadhaigh, became its first chairman, with Johnny Maher, the Chief Engineer, and Eric Armstrong, the airline's first pilot. It had one small biplane, the *Iolar*. From that humble beginning grew a company that was to earn a respected place in international aviation and become a valuable asset for the Irish people.

Fitzmaurice had sparked the fire of public interest in the development of aviation in Ireland and had initiated the concept of a national airline but he had missed out on events leading to its creation. While Aer Lingus grew, Fitz's star shone for a while and then waned as he continued to follow one dead end idea after another. His valuable contribution in putting Ireland on the world aviation map was little acknowledged in his own country for the rest of his lifetime. Since his death, however, the *Bremen* achievement and his vital role in it has been saluted with increasing frequency.

On the occasion of the forty-fifth anniversary of the flight in 1973 a commemorative plaque, cast in bronze, was unveiled by the Taoiseach, Liam Cosgrave, son of William T. Cosgrave, in an impressive ceremony at Baldonnel. The inscription reads:

> The first non-stop East to West
> flight across the Atlantic by
> Captain Herman Kohl
> Colonel James C. Fitzmaurice
> Officer Commanding the Air Corps
> and Baron von Huenefeld
> in the Junkers W33 aircraft
> "BREMEN"
> Took off from Baldonnel on
> 12th April 1928.
> The beginning of the Take off run
> is marked by a stone 20 yards west.

The stone is a granite marker laid on the spot where the Bremen started the takeoff run. It shows the outline of the monoplane and the inscription: "BREMEN, 1928". The Ambassador of the Federal Republic of Germany, Dr. Horst Groepper, delivered the address to a distinguished gathering.

Five years later a number of events were organised in Ireland to mark the 50th anniversary of the *Bremen* flight. The centrepiece was the Royal Aeronautical Society (Dublin Branch) Commemorative Lecture and Dinner at the Burlington Hotel on Monday, 10 April.

This was chaired by Capt. J.C. Kelly-Rogers, President of the Dublin Branch and pilot of the first Aer Lingus commercial

Pat Selwyn Jones (centre front) on her visit to the Mansion House in Dublin where she met the Lord Mayor, Seán Dublin Bay Rockall Loftus (second from right at front).

At the opening of the new restaurant at Kingswood Country House, Clondalkin, Dublin named in honour of Col. James Fitzmaurice. Pat Selwyn Jones inspects the model of the *Bremen* built by Tim Costello (on left). Also in the picture are Brendan Ellis, Haydn Selwyn Jones and Tommy O'Byrne, owner of the Kingswood Country House.

transatlantic flight. He had a superb flying record and retained a keen interest in aviation matters all his life. His ambition was to establish an Air Museum in Ireland to match the best elsewhere. Among the exhibits he tried to obtain were the *Bremen* itself and also the old aircraft built at Aldritts. He failed on both accounts and although he collected a number of interesting artefacts and memorabilia his passing put an end to this superb project.

The speakers at the Lecture were Col. Willie Keane, Johnny Maher, Comdt. D.V. Horgan and Capt. Karlheinz Kindermann, ex-Chief Pilot of Junkers and President of the Hugo Junkers Society in Germany, who flew from Germany to read a paper from Capt. Loose, copilot on the 1927 German transatlantic attempt, who was unable to attend due to his age and ill-health.

Col. Keane spoke of meeting Fitzmaurice when the aviator returned to Ireland in the 1960s. He was a broken man who suspected he had made the wrong decision in not returning to take his place in civil aviation in the country of his origin, Keane said.

Comdt. Horgan, who was a lieutenant and PRO for the Air Corps at the time of the flight, in the course of his talk recalled Fitzmaurice inviting the Germans to lunch at Baldonnel on their first visit to Ireland. The lunch for eleven people cost £7-14-0 and it took him until 1929 to get the bill paid because a row broke out between the Departments of Defence and Foreign Affairs over who was responsible for it.

Other jubilee events included a special aeronautical exhibition at Dublin Airport, a flight by Aer Lingus Boeing Jet retracing the flight path of the *Bremen*, the unveiling of a 50th anniversary plaque and the opening of a new apprentice training school at Baldonnel.

The Irish Minister for Tourism and Trade, Bobby Molloy, visited the Ford Museum at Dearborn for celebrations there and presented the curator with the Aer Lingus Trophy to mark the visit. There were air displays, an air rally, exhibitions and a special *Bremen* commemorative stamp was issued in two denominations, 10p

The author pictured at the Ford Museum, Dearborn, Michigan, in March 1997. All that remained of the aircraft *Bremen* at that stage was the fuselage. The other parts had been shipped to Germany.

and 17p. A wreath-laying ceremony at the grave of Fitzmaurice was held on Tuesday, 26 September, the thirteenth anniversary of his death. There were also activities organised to coincide with the celebrations taking place in Germany that year.

Tim Costello, a producer with RTE, made a film on the *Bremen* flight and found the story so fascinating, and the part that Fitzmaurice had played in it so ignored, that he immediately became a "Fitzophile" and has embraced the cause of promoting the due recognition of the man and his feats ever since.

Tim has been working with Brendan Ellis, a retired architect, and a few other equally enthusiastic people for many years in doing everything possible to perpetuate in a fitting way the memory of Fitzmaurice. Brendan's enthusiasm for the cause is infectious. He was sad when the opportunity to name Baldonnel aerodrome in his honour was missed. But he has other ideas on what might be done to compensate for this lapse. Why not name Dublin Airport after him he wonders? If Sydney can name their airport after Australia's greatest aviator, Air Commodore Sir Charles Kingsford Smith, why cannot Dublin name its airport after Ireland's greatest aviator, Col. James Fitzmaurice? Or why not name the

Irish Government jet after him, he asks? If Germany can have a Government jet called the Hermann Koehl, why cannot Ireland name their's the Col. James Fitzmaurice?

On 9 February 1996 the Fitzmaurice Flying School was officially opened at Baldonnel by the then Minister for Defence, Sean Barrett. Two months later on 12 April, on the 68th anniversary of the flight, the main restaurant in the Kingswood Country House in Clondalkin, a stone's throw from Baldonnel, was named the Col. James Fitzmaurice Room. Tim and Brendan organised the event and Pat Selwyn Jones, accompanied by her son, Haydn, were there to mark the occasion. They were flown from England by Ryanair and when they arrived in Dublin they were given an official welcome by Aer Rianta, the Irish Airports Authority. During her visit Pat was shown around Baldonnel by Air Corps officers and was also entertained in the Mansion House by the Lord Mayor, Sean Dublin Bay Rockall Loftus, who pointed out the names of the three heroes of the Bremen including that of her father's, on the Freedom of the City scrolls.

The town of Fitz's youth, Portlaoise, is marking the centenary of the birth of Fitzmaurice, 6 January 1998, by naming a new recreation area in the town centre in his honour. A special committee in the town have also commissioned a bronze bust of the aviator which will be unveiled to mark the 70th anniversary of the flight on April 12, 1998. A number of other events are planned in Germany and Ireland to mark the anniversary and Col. Fitzmaurice is one of four famous Irish aviators being commemorated on postage stamps by An Post (Irish Post Office) in 1998.

Fitz wrote: "In Irish air transport much has been achieved and a great future develops, of which our people will be justly proud. I feel certain that in that pride of achievement, the adventure of the Bremen will be seen in all its full significance, and that my dead comrades and I, will therefore, not soon be forgotten."

He is no longer forgotten!

Acknowledgements

In my research for this book I trawled through various archives in Ireland, England and the U.S., commissioned help from German sources and met hundreds of people more than willing to fill in the gaps.   I am deeply indebted to those who gave me personal interviews, to those who made documentation and photographs available to me and to those who wrote or rang with information.

First and foremost my deepest appreciation goes to Pat Selwyn Jones who was so kind and understanding with me.   No one could have been more helpful.   She allowed me browse through her father's memorabilia and trusted me with all materials and photographs in her possession.   Pat's help was invaluable and I was so pleased to have made her acquaintance.

It was also my pleasure to meet on many occasions, and get to know very well, two men whose interest in Fitzmaurice and the flight of the Bremen is all-consuming.   Brendan Ellis and Tim Costello are dedicated to the cause of ensuring that Fitz's achievements are fittingly recognised in his own country.   They assisted me in every way possible.

Some other people deserve particular mention for their help:

Dan Loughrey, Director of Corporate Affairs, Aer Lingus; Bernie Kenny and Yvonne Bolger, Aer Lingus;

Bob Harris of FAS and formerly of Aer Lingus;

Comdt. Peter Young and Comdt. Victor Laing of Military Archives, Dublin; Col. Kevin Hogan, Officer-in-Command, Irish Air Corps, Baldonnel:

Captain Kevin Byrne and Sergeant Pat Dempsey, Irish Air Corps, Baldonnel;

Lt. Col. Michael O'Malley, Irish Air Corps;

Judith E. Endleman, Head of Historical Resources and Benson and Edith Ford Curator, Henry Ford Museum, Dearborn, Michigan, USA;

My good friends and fellow Laoismen, Jack Cowley and Mike McEvoy, and their wives, Marie and Kate, Detroit, Michigan.

Gúnter Strangemann who spearheaded a committee comprising of businessmen from the city of Bremen in acquiring the famous aircraft on loan for a seven year period from the Ford Museum in Dearborn, Michigan.

Antonio Cormier, Société Historique du Canton de Brest, Quebec, whose grandfather sent the first messages out of the Bremen's landing at Greenly Island.

My good friends, Bill and Lily McEvoy, Long Island, New York and Stephen and Mary Conroy, Roundwood, Mountrath, Co. Laois, for their encouragement and assistance;

Cait Kavanagh of Laois County Library, who spared no effort in locating useful material;

Edwin Phelan and staff at Laois County Library;

Anne Marie Heskin, Supervisor FAS-Leinster Express indexing project, and her staff;

Donie Aldritt and Frank Aldritt, Portlaoise;

Michael O'Brien, Philip Meagher and members of the Col. James Fitzmaurice Committee in Portlaoise;

John O'Brien, Portlaoise;

Gerry Meredith, Portlaoise;

Dr. Pat McCarthy of The Military History Society of Ireland.

Peter Simkins, Senior Historian, Imperial War Museum in London;

Jarlath Conerney and Lt. Col. John Moore of The Royal Aeronautical Society, Republic of Ireland Branch;

Peter Pletschacher, of Luftfahrt-Presse-Club, Frankfurt, Germany;

My good friend Michael O'Carroll, Tramore, Co. Waterford, for surfing the Internet on my behalf;

Mary McNally and Eamon Sheil of Dublin;

Bill Linnane and Eileen McCaffrey, Dublin;

A.P. Kearns, Dublin.

My special thanks also to the following: William O'Gorman, Dublin: Vincent Donnelly, Raheen, Limerick; Valentine McCarthy, Dublin; Sean Roycroft, Dublin; Tom Nisbet, RHA, Dublin; Mamie O'Halloran, Killaloe; Fr. Dermot McNiece, Marley Grange, Dublin; Michael Burgess, Sligo; B. Doorhey, Dublin; Ciarán Mac an Ailí, Dublin; Richard Redmond, Waterford; George Watson, Monaghan; Peter Deevy, Limerick; Sean Ryan, Dublin; John Conway, Limerick; Gearoid O'Sullivan, Dublin; William P. Ryan, Dublin; Seamus D. O'Hea, Dublin; Michael Barrett, Dublin; George Harvey, Waterford.

Sincere thanks too to the staff of the Leinster Express and Imperial Print, particularly Martin Connolly for his assistance in getting the book into print. Special mention too must go to journalist and writer, Seamus Dunne, for his professionalism and advice in reading my text.

A heartfelt appreciation to my wife, Carmel, and my son David, who both worked with me on the project, and to all my family and friends for their interest and encouragement.

Bibliography

For the readers convenience I have noted my sources, where I considered it feasible, throughout the text.
The account of Fitz's earlier years is based largely on his own memoirs (unpublished) kindly supplied by his daughter, Pat Selwyn Jones. This includes his schooldays, his war experiences, joining the RFC, his time in the Irish Army Air Corps, and his travels after the flight. Pat also allowed me access to other primary material in her collection.
Personal reminiscences and information were received from many individuals and sources listed in Acknowledgements.
Other primary sources included:
Irish National Archives
Military Archives, Dublin
National Library, Dublin
Irish Air Corps
The Public Record Office, Kew
Henry Ford Museum, Dearborn, Michigan, US
The Smithsonian Institute, Washington
National Library, London
Imperial War Museum
Aer Lingus
The Royal Air Force Museum, Hendon
The Royal Air Force Personnel Management Centre, Gloucester.

Much of Fitz's own writings concerning the flight have been published and used by others in their writings on the flight. Apart from his own work and other published sources, for verification and additional information I found the contemporaneous accounts of the story published in Irish, English and American newspapers of the day, particularly *The Irish Times,* the *Irish Independent* and the *New York Times,* very rewarding in my research.
Magazines consulted included *An Cosantóir* (the Irish Defence Forces Magazine), *Flight* and *The Aeroplane.*

Books:

Alcock, Sir John and Whitten-Brown, Sir Arthur *Our Transatlantic Flight* (London: William Kimber 1969).

Barry, Michael *Great Aviation Stories* (Fermoy: Saturn Books 1993).

Barry, Tom *Guerilla Days in Ireland* (Dublin: Anvil Books 1962).

Brink, Randall *Lost Star* (London: Bloomsbury 1994)

Byrne, Liam *History of Aviation in Ireland* (Dublin: Blackwater 1980).

Chronicle of Aviation (London: Chonicle Communications Ltd).

Colum, Padraic *The Poet's Circuits* (Mountrath, Ireland: The Dolmen Press 1985).

Coogan, Tim Pat *The IRA* (London: Fontana 1971).

Coogan, Tim Pat *De Valera - Long Fellow, Long Shadow* (London: Hutchinson 1993).

Corrigan, Douglas *That's My Story* (London: Robert Hale 1939).

Dangerfield, George *The Damnable Question* (London: Constable 1977).

Denman, Terence *A Lonely Grave* (Dublin: Irish Academic Press 1995)

Dungan, Myles *Irish Voices from the Great War* (Dublin: Irish Academic Press 1995).

Dungan, Myles *Distant Drums* (Belfast: Appletree Press 1993).

Dwyer, T. Ryle *Eamon de Valera* (Dublin: Gill and Macmillan 1980).

Ferro, Marc *The Great War 1914-1918* (London: Routledge and Kegan 1973).

Fitzmaurice Col. J.C. *Bremen Ireland - America 1928* (Dublin: Parkside Press 1953).

Foster, R.F. *Modern Ireland* (London: Penguin Books 1981).

Garrett, Richard *Atlantic Disasters* (London: Buchan and Enright).

Gilbert, Martin *First World War Atlas* (London: Weidenfeld and Nicolson 1989).

Gogarty, Oliver St. John *As I Was Going Down Sackville Street* (Dublin: The O'Brien Press 1994).

Harris, R.G. *The Irish Regiments* (Tunbridge Wells, Kent: The Nutshell Publishing Co Ltd).

Hibberd, Dominic *The First World War - Context and Commentary* (London: Macmillan 1990).

History of Aviation (London: Hamlyn 1996).

Hotson, Fred W. *The Bremen* (Toronto: Canav Books 1988).

Johnson, Air Vice-Marshal J.E. and Lucas, Wing Commander P.D. *Courage In The Skies* (London: Stanley Paul).

Johnstone, Tom *Orange, Green and Khaki* (Dublin: Gill and Macmillan 1992).

Kee, Robert *Ireland - A History* (London: Weidenfeld and Nicolson 1980).

Kee, Robert *The Laurel and the Ivy* (London: Hamish Hamilton 1995).

Kennedy, Ludovic *A Book of Air Journeys* (London: Collins1982).

Kirchberger, Joe H. *The First World War: An Eyewitness History* (Oxford and New York: Facts on File)

Koehl, Fitzmaurice and Von Huenefeld *The Three Musketeers of the Air* (London: Putnams 1928). Unser Ozeanflug (Berlin 1928).

Livesey, Anthony *Great Battles of World War 1* (London: Michael Joseph 1989).

Lyons F.S.L. *Ireland Since the Famine* (London: Fontana 1973)

McIntosh R.H. and Spry Leverton J. *All Weather Mac* (London: MacDonald 1963).

Middlebrook, Martin and Mary *The Somme Battlefields* (London: Viking 1991).

Moody, T.W. and Martin, F.X. *The Course of Irish History* (Dublin: Mercier Press).

Morrow, John H. Jr. *The Great War in the Air - 1909 to 1921* (Shrewsbury: Airlife Publishing Ltd. 1993).

O'Rourke, Madeleine *Air Spectaculars - Air Displays in Ireland* (Dublin: Glendale 1989).

O'Broin, Leon *Michael Collins* (Dublin: Gill and Macmillan 1980).

Quigley, Aidan A. *Green is my Sky* (Dublin: Avoca Publications 1983).

Rosen, Mike *The First Transatlantic Flight* (Hove, East Sussex: Wayland 1989)

Sharte, Bernard *The Flight of the Iolar* (Dublin: Gill and Macmillan 1996).

Sky Riders (London and Glasgow: Collins 1941).

Williamson, Katherine S. *The Golden Age of Aviation* (New York: Todtri 1996).

INDEX

N